LIFE AND MANNERS
IN THE
FRONTIER ARMY

Life and Manners in the

in the

FRONTIER ARMY

by Oliver Knight

UNIVERSITY OF OKLAHOMA PRESS
NORMAN

BOOKS BY OLIVER KNIGHT

Fort Worth: Outpost on the Trinity (Norman, 1953)
*Following the Indian Wars: The Story of the Newspaper Correspon-
   dents Among the Indian Campaigners* (Norman, 1960)
I Protest: Selected Disquisitions of E. W. Scripps (Madison, 1966)
Life and Manners in the Frontier Army (Norman, 1978)

Knight, Oliver.
   Life and mannners in the frontier army.

   Bibliography: p.
   Includes index.
   1. Frontier and pioneer life—The West. 2. King, Charles,
1844-1933—Knowledge—Manners and customs. 3. United
States. Army—Military life. 4. The West—History—1848-
1950. I. Title.
F593.K56   978'.02   77-15457
ISBN 0-8061-1440-1

Preface

A reader moving into this book may be startled to see that it is built largely on the Army novels of Captain Charles King, and possibly will think that using a series of novels as a data base is a crazy way to write history. However, I would not attempt this method unless assured the ground is firm; of this the reader may be confident.

The book is the outgrowth of a short, largely biographical appraisal of King that Harwood P. Hinton asked me to write for *Arizona and the West,* which he edits. At the time, I merely knew of King's classic *Campaigning with Crook,* had once gone through his papers at the Wisconsin State Historical Library, had read some of his short fiction, and knew the outlines of his career, without having been overly impressed by any of it. I thought the short piece for *Arizona and the West* would be the end of it.

To say anything reasonably astute about King and his contribution to the literature and history of the West meant that I had to read all his Western fiction; that is, all that had appeared in book form, because his magazine publications had never been catalogued. In reading his Western novels I recognized many segments that were autobiographical in origin and was satisfied that large portions of the novels grew out of King's own experiences. From those passages in his fiction there emerged a multidimensional image of the people and places of the Old Army and a sense of the atmosphere of those times not to be found in any other factual or official account. In short, King's novels contain invaluable historical commentary which deserves to be put together as social history. Hence this book.

In preparing it I became indebted to many persons: first of all to Mr. Hinton for putting me on the trail, although that was neither his intention nor mine at the start; to Dean Kenneth Beasley of the Graduate School of the University of Texas at El Paso for finding a late-in-the-year grant in the funds of the University Research Institute, which made possible the microfilming of King's papers in Madison; and to Mrs. Margarita Kanavy, Inter-library Loan Librarian at the University of Texas, El Paso, whose expertise was indispensable in locating some of the King books and who found all of them before it was over. In addition, I should like to thank Richard J. Sommers and John J. Slonaker, who made available copies of some documents in the Army Military History Research Collection at Carlisle Barracks, and Alan C. Aimone, Military History Librarian at West Point.

OLIVER KNIGHT

El Paso, Texas

Contents

LIFE AND MANNERS
IN THE
FRONTIER ARMY

1.
Social History
in the Army Novels
of Captain Charles King

The officers and ladies of the Old Army were an
elite if exiled group in the Trans-Mississippi West
during the period of the Indian wars from 1865 to 1890.
They carried into the West the social hierarchies of the
officer class and made themselves aristocrats within
their limited circle. In, but not of, Western communities
—and often far in advance of settlers—they maintained,
often under formidable circumstances, a stylized code
of conduct which gave a unique cast to the life and
manners of frontier posts.

One who had been of their number wrote critically,
but accurately, "The Army is a little domain of its own,
independent and isolated by its peculiar customs and
discipline; an aristocracy by selection and the halo of
tradition. . . ."[1] Although officers' families often lived in
quarters that were no better than the hovels that characterized all frontiers, they held themselves above their
environment and were quite punctilious in their relationships. Yet their isolation—socially, psychologically,
and physically—gave them a sense of unity not easily
to be found elsewhere in the American society of their
time. An officer's wife who had known the pain, joy,
and frustration of that life said in retrospect: "Some-

times I wonder if it was the lack of fuss and pretensions, with everyone knowing the pay of the other fellow, that made the army in general so united, but it was more than that. There was also the solitude of their mutual existence — just a handful of people, so to speak, afloat upon an uncharted sea of desolation . . . and the shared hardships of a bleak climate with its privations, and the daily perils they faced together. These were the factors that brought these Army pioneers closer to each other in some instances than many brothers and sisters."[2]

There was much that was chauvinistic — indeed, Gothic — about the values that governed their way of life and their respective stations. Holding on to what was left of the values of the prewar Army and seeing themselves in a light that was to some extent distorted by their fantasies, the officers and their ladies of any post lived in a miniature Arthurian court where each officer was a medieval knight *sans peur et sans reproche* (one of their favorite expressions, by the way). They carried these assumptions and social forms with them from post to post. Hence, they easily fitted into each new niche of the frontier Army society. Curiously outdated, their standard was nonetheless much higher than the ethical codes prevalent in postwar America. Along with that Romantic view of themselves, they held fast to those values of social conduct learned in Eastern and Southern homes.

Yet it would not do to suggest that the officer caste sought to preserve the metropolitan mores of Eastern "society." On the contrary, the Army lifestyle was as alien to Eastern ways as to those of frontier civilian society. Their formality was balanced by a free camaraderie and a stability in their relationships. At the same time, and inevitably, their lives were corroded by the

4

tensions, animosities, jealousies, and open conflicts that are found in all closely stratified social groups. In their closeness, there was a relationship between unattached officers (bachelor or single) and the wives of married officers that could easily have been misinterpreted by Victorian dowagers, but was perfectly natural in the familial atmosphere of the garrison.

However, generalization is simply eye-burning smog that conceals exceptions. The Army of 1865-90 was a heterogeneous social-institutional grouping that finally brought to an end—for better or for worse—the warfare between Anglo-Americans and Indians that had begun in Virginia in 1622. Many officers of that Army were foreign-born adventurers. Others were former enlisted men and assorted civilians who had remained in the Army after the Civil War. Many of them lacked the first instinct of courtliness, and hence did not fit well into the role of a knight. The wives of such officers— some of whom had been company laundresses before the war—could strain the precise etiquette and social subtleties of the group. Some of the callous self-seeking and political preferment of those years of easy political and business virtue inevitably influenced the Army. In some cases it resulted from the politically expedient commissioning of men whom the professionals would have screened out at first glance had they had the opportunity. But some of the West Pointers, also, pulled every possible string to secure posh jobs in Washington or in the diplomatic service, particularly if they came of influential families. So there were those conflicts, and the jealousies they bred. And the dreary monotony of frontier garrison duty took its toll in alcoholism, excessive gambling, and cruelty to enlisted men on the part of weaker officers. On balance, though, the prevailing

5

code—as ideal, actuality, and expectation—imposed a standard of personal behavior and social comportment that was distinctly high.

Their world, however, involved many more interpersonal relations than those of the restricted officers' circle. The intertwined but ordered military community included the sharply graded caste stratification of officers, their wives and children; the unmarried women relatives living with them or spending a long season with them; and a surprising array of household servants, along with an occasional governess who was quite acceptable as a prospective—and eventual—officer's wife.

At the lower levels, post life was very much enlivened by the enlisted men, whose now shadowed lives and manners are more difficult of generalization. The enlisted stratum included the noncommissioned officers and their red-armed wives who were the post laundresses, and the broods of unkempt urchins who raced around the big black laundry kettles that bubbled over woodfires in the backyards of Suds Row shanties. Coming from all walks of life and all levels of American and European society, they were far more heterogeneous than the officers. A wider spectrum of human behavior —dedication and betrayal, self-control and licentiousness, self-respect and depravity—seems to have been evident in the conduct of the enlisted men than in that of officers. After all, as General William T. Sherman once said to a lady critical of the Regular soldier, "Well, madame, you surely can't expect the possession of all the cardinal virtues for thirteen dollars a month"—the base pay of a private.[3]

In between were the post trader and the veterinary surgeon (always a civilian) who occupied special—and detached—positions in the hierarchy. The in-between group also included hospital stewards (enlisted men of a certain status), hospital matrons at larger posts, the trader's clerks, and a varying assortment of other civilians—teamsters, skilled laborers, hired hands. Adjacent to many frontier posts—like ticks burrowing into a dog's neck—were nearby rum mills and whorehouses, the latter sometimes in wagons.

Taken all together, they were not people who loved the smoke of their own chimneys. Rather, they learned to love, or at least to accept, any hearth and half-decent chimney that a neglectful Congress might happen to provide for the men who were carrying out part of the national purpose. Their contribution to national expansion has been fully treated, and well, in innumerable histories and reminiscences, although a clear and vivid picture of their life and manners is not to be found there. Understandably, most of their habits and everyday activities were left out of such accounts. The writers confined their attentions to major events and more adventurous experiences.

It is therefore to our great benefit that the life and manners can be reconstructed from the Western novels of Captain Charles King, with some of the blanks filled in from the sparse memoirs of others, to give a more consistent picture of everyday life. To be sure, the novel is not a usual source of historical data, nor an altogether respectable one. But King's novels are singular. In the precise details of regulations and tactics (tactics then embracing all the myriad details of Army functions), King was recognized as one of the most knowledgeable men in the Army—active or retired—and was such a stickler for doing things the Army way that he would have been constitutionally incapable of misrepresenting that institution by one iota. Moreover, the main configurations of his pictures of Army life are verifiable through the accounts of numerous contemporaries.

In writing the first series of Western novels that were regarded as serious literature in their day, King filled his books with a profusion of material derived from his own experience and from existing Army attitudes. The literary merit of his books (they had none) is not at issue here. Let it be said in passing, though, that King's Western novels—written between 1882 and 1909—did not endure beyond the age for which they were written, and in which he was one of the most popular authors in America. However, the novels do have an enduring historical value, for he gave them kidney with liberal doses of realism. Not a particularly inventive writer, he relied on literal reports of Army life in creating context and background for contrived Victorian romances. He wrote of the frontier life he had loved and the Western areas he had known intimately. His thirty-eight Western books gave him great scope for including the minute details that were left out of factual accounts. Although his stories degenerated, in time, into a repetitious formula, he never deviated from his faithfulness in describing the Army. The nature of the man—and especially the respect he commanded throughout the Army—allow one to reconstruct, confidently, the life and manners of the frontier Army of the seventies and eighties from his novels.

A strong indication of King's standing among military men came when an unnamed classmate at West Point found what he thought was a slip in a Civil War novel, *Between the Lines*,[4] in which King had referred to "sets of fours" as a military formation. The gentleman gleefully wrote the respected retired captain, thinking to bring him up with a round turn for referring to a formation long out of use by the 1860's. King replied by quoting chapter and verse, including demerits he and that very officer had received at the academy for not being properly aligned in sets of four in the 1860's. Properly put in his place, the officer called the entire matter to the attention of the editor of the *Army and Navy Journal,* who then commented that the officer's faith in "the infallibility of Captain King was completely restored." The editor also referred to King as "that accomplished tactician."[5]

By that time, King's work was so well established that the *Army and Navy Journal* said his novels were "perfect in their portrayals of garrison," adding: "Today he is regarded by many notable critics as the author of the best purely military novels in our language."[6] In 1919, Brigadier General C. B. Devore, who had entered frontier service upon graduation from West Point in 1885, wrote King: "I knew of you long before it was my pleasure to know you personally. Your books . . . told tales in truth, perhaps, more than fiction, of the making of the far west, and the truth plainly told of those interesting days was oftentimes stranger than fiction."[7]

Early in the 1920's, someone in the War Department routinely placed King's name on the list of retired officers no longer available for active duty by reason of age. The matter came to the attention of the Deputy Chief of Staff, Major General James G. Harbord, who promptly ordered that any action affecting King must come directly before the Chief of Staff. Harbord then commented: "I read General King's books before I came into the service. My first commission was in the 5th Cavalry [King's regiment]. General King's name was a household word in that regiment, and his influence was still potent to work up enthusiasm among the youngsters in the regiment. . . . General King has ceased to be an officer, he is an institution."[8]

Perhaps King's ultimate accolade came from Lieutenant Alvin H. Sydenham. Sydenham was graduated from West Point in 1889, the year King served on the Board of Visitors. When the board visited the Academy at graduation, Sydenham said, the cadets took more interest in King than in any other visitor, including General Lew Wallace. "We had a personal fellow feeling for the man who had done so much to make people understand that there is an army, especially we of the graduating class," for the cadets had read his novels regularly as they had appeared in the eighties. "To most of us his army was the army." And then follows the important comment: "When we joined our regiments later at the remote frontier posts, we found there pretty nearly the things he had taught us to expect."[9]

Not only was King the first novelist of the American Army,[10] but even in an age of literary soldiers none was better suited to portray military life through fiction. On his father's side he came from something of a goodly military heritage. His great-great-grandfather had served as a militia officer during the Siege of Louisbourg in 1745. His great-grandfather, Rufus King, served as a major in the Continental Army but became better known as a Federalist leader. His grandfather, the first Charles King, wore the bars of a New York militia captain in the War of 1812, although he heartily opposed the war and managed to sit it out at a desk job in New York.

His father, another Rufus King, who graduated from West Point in 1833 but resigned his commission in 1836, became associate editor of the Albany *Evening Journal* in 1838, beginning a long friendship with

William H. Seward that would prove pivotal to his son's career. Charles King was born in Albany, New York, on October 12, 1844. The next year Rufus King moved his family to Milwaukee, where he became editor and part-owner of the Milwaukee *Sentinel*.

As the son of a journalist who apparently barely made ends meet, Charles King grew up in a small, rented, frame house at the corner of Mason and Van Buren streets in Milwaukee. It became known as King's Corner, and the boys with whom he chummed the "King's-Corner Crowd," whose combativeness in fighting boys of an adjoining neighborhood foreshadowed the future; of the group, King and Arthur MacArthur became generals; two others, rear admirals; and one a United States senator.[11]

During his boyhood, King was inclined toward a military career. He had such a sharp sense of military fitness that, at the age of five, he upbraided General Winfield Scott, commanding general of the United States Army, for wearing civilian clothing at home; Scott's estate adjoined that of Grandfather King in New Jersey; Grandfather King was president of then Columbia College. However, both his mother and grandfather were determined that young King should become a lawyer. With his father's sympathy, he became a marker (guide) for a Milwaukee militia company at the age of twelve. Disregarding his strong preference for a military career, his mother and grandfather had him in what was then Columbia's grammar school by 1858 and in the freshman class of the college in 1861. Only the outbreak of the Civil War diverted him from a law career. When the war started his father became a brigadier general of volunteers, and young King joined him near Washington as mounted orderly—a short and inordinately proud sixteen-year-old. Through the influence of Seward, by then secretary of state, young King received one of President Lincoln's ten appointments-at-large to West Point in 1862.[12] Standing five-feet-four, he barely passed the physical qualifications for the Academy.

At West Point he was in his element, and by his last year he was adjutant of the Corps. One who knew him as a cadet wrote in after years, "He is remembered . . . as one who hated mathematics and devoted only so much of his active brain to the mastering of the exact sciences as was necessary to fulfil [*sic*] the absolute requirements of the institution." He was graduated twenty-second in a class of forty-one in 1866, but was such a master of tactics that he was retained at the Academy as an artillery instructor from June to August, 1866, "a compliment extended to only those subaltern officers who, as cadets, have especially distinguished themselves."[13]

As an artillery officer, later in 1866 he was assigned to command a platoon of Gatling guns—"bullet squirters," in Army slang—of Light Battery K, First Artillery, in New Orleans. During more than a year of Reconstruction duty, he observed attitudes and behavior in the South which he would later use in novels concerning that period.[14] After a few months at regimental headquarters in Fort Hamilton, New York, he was detailed to recruiting duty in Cincinnati from April to July, 1869. That brief tour is memorable for only two reasons: he played with the Red Stockings and had to start wearing glasses.

From Cincinnati he was re-assigned to West Point in September, 1869, as an instructor in cavalry and artillery tactics and horsemanship. His first biographer, Lieutenant Philip Reade, wrote: "This was a rare compliment.

Of the nine hundred and odd other subaltern officers of the army, eligible for such detail—and a large majority desirous of it—the assignment of Lieutenant King for a *second* tour of duty as a military instructor for the corps of cadets is a fact which speaks for itself."[15]

Having transferred to the Fifth Cavalry on January 1, 1871, with the rank of First Lieutenant, King reported to his regiment at Fort McPherson, Nebraska. By that time, Fort McPherson had been rebuilt with the red cedar that grew in the area and which "bore the air of costly furniture" when varnished. But King barely had time to get a glimpse of McPherson and make the acquaintance of the Fifth Cavalry's chief of scouts, Buffalo Bill Cody, before he was on his way back to New Orleans. The regimental commander, Colonel William H. Emory, had been restored to his wartime brevet rank of major general and given command of the Department of the Gulf. He chose the new subaltern as his aide.[16]

During his second tour in New Orleans, King was kept busy as aide and as judge advocate for part of the twenty-six months he spent in the department, but the highlight of the tour came as the result of a horse race. In the spring of 1872, Captain George Rosenlecher of France and Count de Crenneville of Austria challenged any officer to a race on Ladies Day at the Metairie Jockey Club. Emory designated King, a 147-pounder, to ride for the American Army. After a short period of intensive training, he donned a light-weight jockey suit bearing Columbia's colors—blue and white—and a pair of boots that weighed six ounces. In the stands that day a Southern belle was brave enough to wear a Yankee's colors; being with General and Mrs. Emory may have given her the courage. King won the race, received as a prize a gold-mounted whip, and immediately went into the stands where he placed it in the lap of the young lady, Adelaide Lavander Yorke, of Carroll Parish, Louisiana. They were married a few months later, on November 20, 1872. She kept the whip, and in later years sometimes brandished it when admonishing him.[17]

After the birth of the first of the couple's four children, King disengaged himself from staff duty and rejoined his regiment which had, in the meantime, been transferred to Arizona. Reporting to Camp Verde, Arizona, in city clothes and a pince nez, the West Pointer soon learned that a new book of regulations was being developed in the field by Brigadier General George Crook in campaigning against the Apaches. By his own accounting, King "eagerly sought and took the advice of senior sergeants" until sure of himself.[18]

His service at Camp Verde was brief but filled with action. Reporting in May 1874, he first met the Tonto Apaches in battle at Stauffer's Butte (near Diamond Butte) on May 25 and again at Black Mesa (on the Mogollon Rim) on June 3. Belatedly, in 1924, he received the Silver Star for gallantry at Stauffer's Butte.[19]

In October the Tontos swooped down on the Verde Indian Reservation and drove off some cattle. In pursuit, King led a detachment of thirty men, including Second Lieutenant George O. Eaton, recently out of West Point, and Sergeant Bernard Taylor. They tracked the Tontos into Sunset Pass in north central Arizona. Leaving Eaton and most of the command in concealment, he pushed ahead with Taylor and some Apache Yuma scouts, and then had Taylor conceal himself. As he moved deeper into the pass, the scouts faded away, leaving King alone. Suddenly from the silence of the pass, an arrow ripped through the flesh at the corner of his left eye. Then an Apache rifleman planted a bullet in King's right arm just below the shoulder. Unable to fight, all he could do was run. Stumbling, he cut a gash in his forehead and was blinded by the blood. Taylor bounded forward, in defiance of orders, hoisted King onto his back, and retreated, stopping now and again to fire. Eaton and the other men came up on a dead run. So winded that he could barely whisper, Eaton asked anxiously, "Much hurt, old man?" King replied, "Arm's busted—that's all. Pitch in and clean 'em out." The troopers did just that, forcing the Tontos to scatter. Taylor later received the Medal of Honor for rescuing King.[20]

The troops made a mule litter of saplings and a Navajo blanket on which King made a jolting, week-long trip back to Verde. The blanket would later hang in his Milwaukee study where he would write novels based on just such experiences as this one. An Army surgeon recognized that the shoulder wound would ordinarily require amputation but managed to save it by heroic measures—which included making King drink a gallon of whiskey each day.[21] The eye wound healed quickly enough.

The bullet wound took King out of service for most of the following year, and did not heal for eight years. Suffering from an open, suppurative wound and constant exfoliation of the bone, he returned to duty within the year; rode with the Fifth Cavalry when it took the field for the Sioux campaign of 1876; and commanded the advance guard when the Fifth cut off a band of warriors going to re-enforce Crazy Horse and the other Sioux, the fight in which Cody had his celebrated fight with Yellow Hand. He also served as adjutant of the Fifth from 1876 to 1878, and went into the field against both railroad rioters and the Nez Percé in 1877.[22] By 1878, Army surgeons told him he could not possibly pass the required physical for promotion to captain because he could no longer wield a regulation sabre. With the cooperation of the War Department, however, he remained on duty until a captaincy became vacant—a rare and very desirable incident in those years of slow promotion. He was promoted to captain on May 1, 1879, and retired six weeks later, at the age of thirty-four.[23]

Putting aside the uniform he loved, King returned to Milwaukee where he developed twin and concurrent careers as a writer and as a leader in building the Wisconsin National Guard. He taught military science and tactics at the University of Wisconsin from 1880 to 1882, spent the next seven years as inspector and instructor of the Wisconsin Guard, commanded the Fourth Infantry, Wisconsin National Guard, from 1890 to 1892, and was state adjutant general from 1895 to 1897. When the nation mobilized for the war with Spain he returned to active duty as a brigadier general of volunteers, distinguishing himself in the Philippine Insurrection. Coming home in 1899, he became an instructor at St. John's Military Academy. In 1904, the Army assigned him to duty with the Wisconsin National Guard in a position analagous to a modern-day adviser. Holding that post until his retirement in 1931, he was credited with making the Wisconsin Guard a battle-worthy organization by the time the test came in 1917. Too old for field duty in World War I, he was active in training camps. That was enough to give him his fifth campaign badge, making him the only man to wear campaign badges for the Civil War, Indian Wars, Spanish War, Philippine Insurrection and World War I. Two other officers were entitled to wear those badges, but there is no record that either received authorization for all of them.

Concurrent with his militia duty, King became one of the most prolific writers of his time. Between 1880 and 1914 his name appeared on seventy-two books, but the counting of his titles becomes a bit tricky because of some duplication. He wrote fifty-seven full-length fiction and nonfiction works and seven books which contained two novels each. In addition, his name appeared on eight collections of short stories, in seven of which he merely wrote one story each—the publisher counted on his fame to carry the entire book. Of the total, thirty-eight books and story collections deal with the Army in the West. The others are novels concerning the Civil War, Reconstruction, and Philippine Insurrection, along with military history and a biography of U.S. Grant. His Western novels were by far the most popular; twenty-seven of them went to more than one edition, while four of his other works lasted beyond the first edition. In addition, King estimated, he wrote about 250 short stories and articles for *Lippincott's, Century, Harper's Weekly, United Service, Independent, Cosmopolitan, Review of Reviews, Outing,* newspapers, and other magazines.[24] His Western books include twenty-nine full-length novels and one nonfiction work, *Campaigning with Crook,*[25] five books that combined two novels, and three short story collections.

Twelve of his Western books are built around the "—th Cavalry," patently his own Fifth Cavalry, and he worked the same regiment into other books. He set several stories in Fort D. A. Russell, Wyoming, which he had come to know intimately while serving as regimental adjutant there from 1876 to 1878. The "—th Cavalry" books were by far the best. Actually, his novels as a group are so reportorial that one could get tangled in an argument over whether he wrote historical fiction or fictionalized history.

Under the whip of urgent financial need, he began his writing in the most uncomfortable of circumstances. At first an indulgent relative allowed him the use of a garret where he wrote some short pieces for service journals. He also wrote a series of Sunday articles (without remuneration) for the Milwaukee *Sentinel* which were collected into his first book, *Campaigning with Crook.* Later, while on duty at the University of Wisconsin and living with his family in two rented rooms, he wrote other articles for service journals. In 1881 the editors of *United Service* asked him to write a serialized novel of Army life in the West. From month to month he wrote the succeeding chapters, not knowing how the story would turn out (he claimed), for he had to write under such pressure that he didn't have time to plot it out. When it had appeared, Lippincott was so impressed by it that they made it his first published novel, *The Colonel's Daughter.* From that time on, every book was written to order for a publisher. Step by step, the writing income allowed him to move his family from a boarding house to a commodious rented house in Milwaukee. Their own house was bought and furnished with the proceeds from *Marion's Faith,* a sequel to "The Daughter," as he always dubbed it, and a Civil War novel, *Between the Lines.*[26]

Once he had his own study, he decorated it with mementos of his field service. On the wall hung the Navajo blanket which had been his litter, along with campaign maps, photographs of officers, spurs, sabres, field glasses, belts, and the aiguillette and shoulder-knot of an adjutant.[27]

At a flattop desk he scratched out his stories on manila legal cap with a steel pen. He never rewrote and seldom revised. In writing, he said, the "ideas did not flow spontaneously at all, but had to be dragged out by the roots, as it were." That is hard to believe, since he wrote *Marion's Faith* in ten weeks, *The Deserter* in three, and *From the Ranks* in four.[28] On occasion he wrote two novels simultaneously. *Between the Lines* and *Laramie* were written that way in 1886-87; he wrote alternate chapters for each.[29]

But those were the last books he wrote by hand. Although the wound in his right shoulder had finally closed, the constant use of that arm in writing brought its penalty. From the strain of writing for hours at a time, a sharp pain would jangle from elbow to fingertips, "setting my teeth and nerves on edge."[30] It was then that a friend persuaded him to try an Edison dictating machine. As, reputedly, the first author to thus dictate his work, King thereafter plotted his novels by hand, thought them through carefully and spoke them into an Ediphone. His first secretary could not do the job, but by 1890 he had found Miss Lucille Rhoades, who thereafter typed all his work until his death in 1933. After 1893, when he had left his family in Europe for the beginning of a stay of several years, he worked in a dingy office on the third floor of one of Milwaukee's oldest office buildings, the so-called Miller Block. There he marched each day, "erect, active and alert"— with the military step that even West Point drum majors envied. Once his dictation emerged from Miss Rhoades's typewriter, the manuscript was seldom changed to any extent.[31]

The popularity of his first few books brought into publication his first attempt as a novelist. While in the

South he had written a Reconstruction romance, *Kitty's Conquest,* which Harper's had promptly rejected. It had since lain in a trunk until the success of "The Daughter" justified its publication.[32] His description of *Kitty's Conquest* throws in bas relief the reportorial nature of his work. He said he "simply told what I had seen of [carpetbag government and "Senegambia" legislatures] and by no means all."[33] The rapidity with which he wrote his other novels, and the fact that so many of his supporting structures are verifiable, leaves the reader confident that he was in truth a documentary writer. King's works were so close to life that he had to fend off constant assertions that this character or that really was one officer or another. Reade wrote:

> . . . It may be supposed that officers of the Fifth Cavalry suggested some of his characters; but, contrary to general impression, that regiment has furnished very few of them in all his stories combined. There were only two or three in "The Colonel's Daughter" and "Marion's Faith." "Billy Ray" [one of his "heavy" characters], who won so many friends, was never in the Fifth Cavalry in his life. This is a fact, despite the confident assertions of a good many army readers and one or two knowing critics. "I don't know why it is supposed I never knew anybody outside the Fifth Cavalry," said Captain King on receiving a letter which located the entire *dramatis personae* of his novels in that regiment. "One thing seems certain, no one concedes that it is possible for me to create a character,—even such humdrum creatures as these people of my stories happen to be. In point of fact, most of them are as purely imaginary as are all the incidents,—except the Indian-fighting."[34]

There was some flim-flam in that statement. Some of his work is clearly autobiographical. Other portions are based upon his observations and experiences in a setting which he used for a fictional situation. Others seem to be incidents in the history of the Fifth Cavalry which he exaggerated and dramatized for literary effect. On one occasion he flatly told an inquiring reader that "some of the characters are drawn from real life and others are only fictional."[35]

His earliest and best books were written on the basis of diaries and field notebooks which he had kept meticulously while in the West. In 1889 he told a group of graduating cadets at West Point, "By all means keep a diary . . . I kept one almost the entire time I spent on the plains, and it has been worth $20,000 to me. Without it my books could never have been written."[36] The importance of those records can be seen in another way, too. His most solid work was done during the 1880's, with the diaries and notebooks close at hand. After a warehouse fire destroyed them and all his other personal possessions while he and his family were in Europe in 1893,[37] his Western novels became shallow and hackneyed, completely lacking in the rich detail of the earlier work.

With or without the personal records to jog his memory, King knew the Army and its ways thoroughly. As a stickler for accuracy and precision in every aspect of his being, he had a reputation in the 1880's—even as a retired officer—as the "best tactician in the United States Army."[38] Judging from his extensive correspondence with the Adjutant General's Office and the Commandant of Cadets at West Point while he was on duty with the Wisconsin National Guard, King insisted on keeping abreast of the latest changes in the "fine points" of troop movements, military courtesy, posting and duties of sentries, and so forth.[39] In one or two novels, his officers are involved in close argument about such matters. And as adjutant of the Fifth Cavalry he had imposed stern requirements on all troop commanders, much to their resentment, and always had held his ground whenever anyone challenged his orders regarding parade formations or questioned his instructions at weekly "recitation" meetings.[40]

In constructing the incidents that give insight into the life and manners of the frontier Army, King patterned them after his own experiences or those about which he surely had heard. Perhaps it would be more inclusive to say that there were many parallels between his supposedly fictional incidents and actual incidents.

In one, for instance, he elaborated an entire novel upon the consequences that followed after an enlisted man stole a large sum of money from an officer in the field and then deserted.[41] Mrs. Lieutenant-Colonel George A. Custer,* with her habitual way of casting anonymity upon all but her general and family, referred to a parallel incident, saying than an enlisted man stole "a large sum of money from one of the lieutenants" in the field and then disappeared.[42] Several times, King built subplots around noncommissioned officers who stole from the Army in one way or another and then absconded.[43] At a Nevada post, another wife recalled, the quartermaster sergeant stole money from the safe and fled, but was chased down and shot. Her maid had been involved with the sergeant. King likewise involved a maid in a much more elaborate series of post burglaries.[44] He also created a melodramatic gunfight between a young officer and a deserter whom

*Though long outmoded as a form of address, this is the way Old Army wives were known to their contemporaries, and the author has retained it in identifying officers' wives, as King did in his writing.

he had discovered at a rough frontier hotel in Custer City, Dakota Territory.[45] A similar situation had left a young Army wife terrified; she and her husband were stopping in a hotel in Yankton, Dakota Territory, where their room was separated from the next by only a thin board partition. Looking through a knothole, her husband recognized a deserter in a group of gamblers in the next room, one who was wanted for stealing company funds. Pistol in hand, he forced his way into the room and arrested the deserter.[46]

With desertion a major problem in the post-Civil War Army, King had some trenchant observations about deserters and the civilians who either took advantage of them or turned them in for the reward.

> ... among the cowboys, ranchmen, and especially among the "riff-raff" ever hanging about the small towns and settlements, a deserter from the army was apt to be welcomed and protected, if he had money, arms, or a good horse. Once plundered of all he possessed, the luckless fellow might then be turned over to the nearest post and the authorized reward of thirty dollars claimed for his apprehension; but if well-armed and sober, the deserter had little trouble in making his way through the toughest mining camps and settlements.[47]
> ... The civil list of Arizona in 1875 was of peculiar constitution. It stood ready at any time to resolve itself into a modification of the old-day underground railways, and help spirit off soldier criminals, first thoughtfully relieving them of care and responsibility for any surplus funds in their possession.[48]

Casting himself as "Lieutenant Billings," he wove his own experiences into several novels. In some stories, his leading character received the same wounds King had suffered in Sunset Pass—arrow near the eye, bullet in the shoulder.[49] From his experience as ordnance officer at Fort D. A. Russell—an added duty, to that of adjutant—he extracted a scene built around theft of materiel from the post magazine. In the actual incident, thieves had struck during a snowstorm, and he had tracked them into Cheyenne the next day.[50] Easily recognizable, that incident became a key subplot in a novel.[51] He embroidered the fictional incident by including the theft of oats from the cavalry stables, an incident identical to one experienced by Custer at Fort Abraham Lincoln, Dakota Territory. Suspecting who the thieves were, Custer led a detachment into Bismarck and recovered the oats.[52]

Having suffered through Crook's "Horsemeat March" in the Sioux campaign of 1876, King enjoyed the rest in the Black Hills as much as the other "yellow legs" and "doughboys." In one novel he distinctly described himself as the adjutant who was called forward by the regimental commander for instructions:

> . . . the Mexican spurs on the heels of that officer instantly click together as he stands to attention to his chief. A motley garb is that of this same staff official; a dark-blue shirt like that of his senior, a belt supporting revolver and hunting-knife; buckskin breeches, heavily beaded and fringed, thrust into the legs of cavalry boots, the feet whereof have long since worn away and are now replaced by Indian moccasins.[53]

When his steady stream of novels took him to the end of extensive, contemporaneous Indian campaigning, he worked in white criminals as his adversaries. Sending cavalry after horse thieves[54] was quite in accord with the actual theft of Army mounts.[55] He once used a sensation-seeking newspaper reporter as the storm center for a major commotion at a frontier post.[56] Young "live-wire" reporters did cause trouble for post commanders in the West, one of whom wrote humorously of the trouble he had had with reporters poking about his post; the Cheyenne *Leader* said it had received two requests from "Fort Laramie parties" wanting to ventilate their grievances in the press, but the editor referred them back to the fort to obtain justice, saying a newspaper was no place for an Army fight.[57]

King made Army payroll robberies central action devices in three stories,[58] and naturally had several actual incidents on which he could have drawn. In 1884, for example, seven masked men jumped Paymaster C. A. Whipple—a nephew of Bishop Whipple of Minnesota, who was a champion of the Indians— between Glendive, Montana Territory, and Fort Buford, Dakota Territory. The money was saved when a runaway team hauled the paymaster's ambulance out of reach (ambulances were often used to transport personnel). That was the very sort of contrivance King might have used; the sergeant commanding the escort was killed and a private wounded.[59] A few years later, Paymaster D. N. Bash carelessly left his valise, containing $7,500, in the stagecoach at Antelope Springs, Wyoming Territory, where he and the escort had stopped to eat. A cowboy, identified as Charles Parker, dashed up, grabbed the valise, and galloped away; he was not caught.[60]

Feigned robberies, designed to incriminate someone else, appear both in King's novels and in Army records. King wove one of his poorer novels around the shenanigans of "Major Burleigh," a Quartermaster officer who was short several thousand dollars because he had misappropriated government funds and who then went to great lengths, unsuccessfully, to conceal his shortage.[61] Without the addition of fictional complications, that situation was matched by Paymaster James R. Wasson, who had been graduated at the head of the West Point class of 1871 and who had lost $5,500 playing poker with businessmen in Galveston, Texas. He then rigged a situation to make it appear he had been robbed of $24,000 on a train leaving Fort Worth, Texas. Brought to book by the alertness of a superior officer, Wasson was sentenced by a court-martial to eighteen months in prison, although the government recovered all its money.[62]

Many times it appears that King fleshed out his incidents with stock Army stories. For instance, an Army wife remembered a Mrs. Malaprops who said her topaz chain had a "pendulum" and that fresh paint "always did make me nauseous." The poor lady was convinced that Arizona soil had to be "irritated" to produce crops.[63] As a minor not-so-comic relief, King introduced the type—if not, indeed, a caricature of the same lady—in the person of "Mrs. Colonel Whaling" and made her a foil for his most imaginative character, "Gerald Blake," an airy, jesting punster who did bodily harm to Shakespeare and the King's English at large. Under his prodding, the forgetful lady turned the expression into a cavalier *sans peur et sans culotte* and confused bizarre with bazaar.[64] Another that might have been his adaptation of a stock story concerned an absent-minded officer. The most folksy of the lady chroniclers of the Old Army recalled an officer whose absent-mindedness was notorious but reached its height when he planned a rather large dinner party and then sat alone all evening, wondering when his guests would come, until he happened to find the invitations in his desk drawer.[65] King exaggerated such stories in the person of a supporting character who had invited a lady to a dance but was found playing bridge at the general's at 10 P.M., and who, at a christening, forgot himself and wished the mother "many happy returns."[66]

His models extended to the use of famous frontier figures, especially Crook, although he once wrote that of all the Union and Confederate generals he had known, "the man I most revered was [Major General Emory] Upton, to my thinking the finest soldier of his day and generation." King clearly idolized Crook, under whom he had served in Arizona and Wyoming. The idolization is manifest throughout *Campaigning with Crook*, which is perhaps better known to readers of Western history than are King's novels. Crook constantly figured in the novels, always as an infallible father figure righting the scales of justice. By name, by reference (Gray Fox, the Chief), or by description, Crook figured in eleven novels. Although he kept Crook in the background as a Solomon, he did give him brief but telling "speaking parts" in four novels.[67]

In both fiction and nonfiction King gave intimate glimpses of Crook the man (whom he had known in field, in garrison, and in home) that are stronger than the impressions in the combined biography-autobiography and the basic account by Crook's Boswell.[68] Taken eclectically from King's writings, the following passages indicate the extent to which he humanized the Army's greatest Indian fighter and the Indians' most understanding friend.

• Crook never swore, but could "look swear words by the gallon."[69]
• "...the bearded, kindly-faced brigadier" had so won the confidence of Indians that "the wariest redskin will take his faintest promise in preference to any agreement with the great seal of the Indian bureau."[70]

- Crook's beard would "twitch when he was suppressing a smile."[71]
- A cold bath was the only "bracer, tonic and stimulant" that Crook ever was known to use. Where others had coffee for breakfast, he drank hot water.[72] Crook shunned tea, coffee, and tobacco, saying, "They spoiled the nerves."[73] (Nonetheless, Crook died of a heart attack, in 1890.)
- "[He was] least heralded perhaps of any who attained his rank, but best loved beyond all question by those who knew him."[74]
- "Simple as a frontiersman in his dress, he was most at ease in the worn old shooting suit [Crook always wore a canvas hunting suit on campaign]; and in sixteen years of association with him in the field—from the Gila to the Yellowstone, in the garrisons of his various departments, as his guest at his happy fireside; in frequent visits at his headquarters—never did I see him in the uniform of his rank until he lay garbed for the grave."[75]
- "The planets could no more swerve from their course than could George Crook deviate one hair's breadth from the truth."[76]
- Crook "had been through more pitched battles and sharp fights than any general living that day in the wide world . . . .
- "But *luck* was never with Crook. All he ever won in his life he earned by hard, patient and tireless service."[77]
- "Crook knew the Indian as it was given few men to know him, and in his own simple, straight-forward way generally dealt with the Indian direct."[78]

In spite of the adulation he heaped on Crook; King recounted incredible waste and inefficiency in supplying Crook's troops in 1876, a view that is absent from the standard accounts. The gist of it was that King, as acting adjutant of the Fifth Cavalry, was designated ordnance officer the night before the regiment took the field. On orders of Lieutenant Colonel Eugene Carr, an overly adequate amount of new materiel arrived immediately from the depot at Cheyenne—saddles, bridles, other horse equipment, revolvers, rifles, and ammunition— which he had to issue to all the companies as well as the scouts, teamsters, and others. Then it turned out that the ordnance depot refused to take in the worn equipment that company commanders had exchanged for new; King's enlisted assistant (not yet glorified with the grade of ordnance sergeant) left this equipment piled up outside the warehouse. King became liable for $572 worth of "that junk" which then showed as missing on his supply records. Once the regiment reached Crook's base camp at Goose Creek, in northern Wyoming, Colonel Wesley Merritt—by then commanding a brigade of three cavalry regiments—turned over to King hundreds more of the various items with orders to "fit 'em out all you can." Many of the weapons thereupon issued to scouts were never seen again, and King became financially liable for them. When Crook led out his reenforced command on August 5, 1876, King had to leave $40,000 worth of materiel in the wagon train that remained at Goose Creek. The command expected to be out only six days, but it was ten weeks before it came to a halt in the Black Hills.[79]

Eventually, these four or five hundred wagons moved round from the Big Horn by way of [Cantonment] Reno, [Fort] Fetterman, [Fort] Laramie, and Hat Creek to the Hills, where they met us. Meantime, whenever a teamster lost his lariat, or wanted side-lines or a halter, or perchance a blanket or two, as the nights were growing colder, all he had to do was to go and help himself. Everything had been boxed up at the last moment at Goose Creek, but there wasn't an unopened box when they got to the hills.[80]

King could not recover any of the missing articles,

because the original wagonmaster had been fired at Cantonment Reno, and the new wagonboss knew nothing about it. In a final accounting at Fort (then Camp) Robinson, Nebraska, King was still severely short of arms, horse equipments, and other items that were scattered all over the area from the Platte to the Yellowstone. Crook eventually took action that relieved King of some of the debt, but not until long after his retirement was he relieved of financial responsibility for the rest.[81]

Probably more for atmosphere than anything else, but still showing how closely he hewed to actuality, King brought in a number of other frontiersmen — army and civilian — by name. He incorporated passing references to Sherman; Lieutenant General Philip Sheridan; Al Sieber, chief of scouts in Arizona; Portuguee Phillips, whose daring ride had brought relief to Fort Phil Kearny in 1866; "Little Bat" Garnier, a scout on the Northern Plains; Frank Grouard, "Crook's favorite scout"; and Cody, of whom King was to become a champion in the 1920's when a biography of the legendary figure appeared that King thought was distorted.[82]

Writing rapidly, King developed a formula that was a blend of field action and Victorian romance in which good always triumphed. After his first few novels had appeared, he recalled: "Soldiers said it was stirring and realistic. 'You're all right so long as you stick to scouting and fighting,' was the way old comrades put it. But the women wanted love-making, and there wasn't always enough to go around."[83]

The most obtrusive element of his formula was his repetitious use of plot patterns. In almost every novel a love story developed between the noblest of cavaliers and the purest of damsels, with the plot complicated by circumstantial evidence or false accusation. And then, all in a rush, the whole thing was cleared up in the closing pages through fortuitous disclosure of the truth or the steadfast loyalty of a friend who forced the truth from a scoundrel.

Maybe King kept to that formula because it had been so successful, but several events in his military career might have left him with an obsession about circumstantial evidence. In 1865, for example, while he was adjutant of the Corps at West Point, one Orsemus Boyd entered the plebe class in 1864 after having served as a lieutenant in the Civil War. Boyd, who would not accept the indignities heaped upon plebes, immediately became so unpopular that he had to room alone. About that time money began to disappear from the rooms of other cadets. The Commandant of Cadets left the matter in the hands of five ranking cadets with the unfortunate hint that, in his day, the cadets would have taken care of the matter themselves. In train, the ranking cadets arranged a search of Boyd's room, looking for marked, stolen money that had been left for the thief in another cadet's room. One member of the search party, Cadet John Joseph Casey, suddenly suggested they look in a dictionary on the closet shelf. There they found the money. Despite Boyd's violent pleas of innocence, a drumhead court-martial found him guilty. That very evening, the cadets drummed Boyd out of the Corps with the sign "thief" on his back and the band playing "The Rogue's March." With no recourse, Boyd was walking toward the pier where he could take a boat away from the Point when Major General George W. Cullum, Superintendent of the Academy, encountered him. Cullum ordered him back, and, in course, convened a court of inquiry, this one composed of officers rather than cadets. Finding the evidence inconclusive, the court restored Boyd to the Corps. King and three other leaders were court-martialed and sentenced to dismissal; the sentences were remitted, but King was relieved as adjutant.

Boyd finished his education—a complete outcast, since the other cadets held him guilty—and then went to duty with the Eighth Cavalry in 1867. In spite of continued dedication to duty, Boyd was under a cloud until the truth finally emerged in 1871: Casey, who had been ill "with dementia" during his last year at the Academy, had confessed to his roommate, Cadet William John Hamilton, that he was married and had to steal the money to keep his wife from disclosing the marriage, a disclosure which would have caused his expulsion from the Academy. Casey died in 1869, accidentally shot by an enlisted man at Fort Washington, Maryland, but Hamilton kept his comrade's secret until 1871. Himself nearing death from tuberculosis, Lieutenant Hamilton told the story to Lieutenant Richard H. Savage, who then took the necessary steps to clear Boyd's name of another man's crime.[84]

Later in life, King himself became the victim of false reports. In 1879 an insurance company rejected his application for life insurance because two Army doctors—who had barely known him—certified that he was "an habitual soaker of whiskey." He did not get the policy, but was gratified that "I seem to have outlived my detractors and out-thrived the insurance company." Some years later, even when retired, Army auditors deducted a large sum from his retirement pay because he supposedly had been absent without leave while reporting to the Department of the Gulf as Emory's aide in 1871, but he was able to prove that he had been with Emory all the way from Fort McPherson to New Orleans and thus on duty. In 1868 he delivered $500 in commissary funds at Sedgwick Barracks, Louisiana, but in 1870 was accused of having kept the money. At the cost of outraged dignity, he cleared up that one, too.[85]

Tiresome as King's circumstantial-evidence plots become to a modern reader, there were incidents in the Army that could have come right out of his novels (or gone right into them). For example, an attempted burglary of the post trader's store at Fort Fred Steele, Wyoming, was broken up by clerks who slept in the building. One of the burglars, however, had left behind a ratskin (muskrat) cap of the type issued to soldiers as winter uniform. The post commander immediately ordered his three company commanders to assemble their companies—in the dead of night—and inspect uniforms to see if anyone was short a ratskin cap. "As may be imagined, there was some commotion. One poor devil, who had lost his ratskin while on a periodical 'bum' in Rawlins, that wicked place, and who would have had no difficulty in proving that circumstance . . . was loath to be under the necessity of . . . a long conversation with the officers . . . had much difficulty in borrowing a cap, but luckily got it at the last moment. Others . . . were rendered nearly frantic in unavailing search, but, thanks to accommodating comrades who were happy possessors of two or three caps, they turned out in ranks, each arrayed in the all-important article." That case ended with the confident supposition the burglars were tramps.[86]

Even though King is overlooked or glossed over by literary historians, his work was of fundamental importance in the creation of the legends of the West. To some extent, the legendary West may be more important than the historical West, because the "pop" culture of the twentieth century has shaped the popular concept of this aspect of the American heritage more than has the professional historian. King was the first respectable novelist to make the West an important theme in contemporary literature. Through the brisk sales of his novels he had already discovered the significance of the frontier while his young neighbor in Madison, Frederick Jackson Turner, was yet formulating his theory of its significance. While dealing only with the Army, he nonetheless introduced the Army Western a good twenty years before Owen Wister and others placed the cowboy Western in a respectable position in American literature. At the same time, the evanescent quality of his work, as literature, might more properly place him as the connecting link between the low-level dime novel and *Police Gazette* stories and the more enduring Westerns of Wister, Rhodes, and others.

His novels presented to the American people a new view of the events of their time. What are now clichés in formula Westerns—books, movies, and television series—came from his pen when they were fresh, vibrant, and convincing. He wrote descriptions of Indian fighting that are more detailed and realistic than those enacted for the movie camera, and introduced some of the standard elements in soldier-Indian stories: the daring ride that brings relief in the nick of time; the educated Indian who returns to lead an uprising; the character-revealing situation in which the danger of warfare separates the faithful from the cringing; the pursuit of bandits by soldiers; the runaway horse with a beautiful woman's life in danger, headed off by gallant officers. Hackneyed now but new then. And the action was set off by vivid description.

For instance, a short but gripping account of women and troopers caught in a Dakota blizzard ranks him as a master of detail in describing persons, setting, and mood.[87] His report of a court-martial contained as much suspense as the battle scenes, in which he was superb.[88]

From a technical point of view, most of his books were well done. Each was peopled adequately, with sharp characterization and skillfully drawn personality conflicts as subplots. However, he usually wrote over the surface of his subject, never truly penetrating personality, motivation, or situation.

Fortunately for him, he was found in his own day and enjoyed the monetary and other pleasures that went with being one of the most popular novelists of the late nineteenth century. He once asked a publisher how long the next story should be; the publisher replied, "...we have found by experience that the public are satisfied with your work almost without regard to its length."[89] Possibly one factor in his popularity was his repetition of characters from book to book, emphasizing one here and another there, but making the group so many old friends of the reader. Many of his books were interlocked in one way or another. For example, *Marion's Faith, Captain Blake, A Garrison Tangle,* and *The Deserter* all deal with the period 1876-78, which he had spent on the Northern Plains.

Just as the reactions of soldiers indicate how reliable King's books are in depicting the life of the Old Army, the reactions of contemporary reviewers show that he was appreciated as a realistic writer. A publisher's introduction to one book said there had been no stories of the Army in the West until King started writing, but as such stories appeared there then arose a demand for more.[90] Reviewers found his first novel, *The Colonel's Daughter,* nothing short of serendipitous. A reviewer for the *Army and Navy Journal* wrote:

> Capt. King opens a new vein... and one which is instantly seen to reveal fine possibilities. In Army life on the frontier we have combined a caste of society as well-defined and rigid as the English clerical life... and therewith a wildness of surroundings and adventure such as might tempt the imagination of a Dumas or a Mayne Reid to portray.
>
> The fertility of this field of garrison and reservation life has already attracted the attention of several writers. We took up the work of Capt. King with the impression that it might be like some of these, an ephemeral production; we found it, instead, a charming work, worthy of achieving a permanent place in literature. The machinery and scenic effects of the novel are original and have this value, that they furnish a perfect insight into garrison life and Indian warfare....
>
> ... what is newest is the presentation of successive scenes of frontier life.[91]

Set in Camp Verde—which he identified as "Camp Sandy"—and Fort Whipple (after 1879, Whipple Barracks), *The Colonel's Daughter* caught the appreciative eye of Prescott newspapers, too. The *Arizona Miner* said: "Capt. King seems to have carefully noted everything going on around him, and has reproduced a most charming picture of life in Camp Verde, Prescott and Fort Whipple. The characters are finely drawn, some of them with so much cleverness that we are ready to bet we can point out the individuals portrayed." The *Arizona Courier* also said the characters were recognizable.[92]

In subsequent references, the *Army and Navy Journal*

said *The Colonel's Daughter* "was the most graphic word-painting of frontier military life in field, camp, and garrison that has ever been given in print."[93] When *Marion's Faith* appeared as its sequel, the same journal reported: "Captain King's works are valuable contributions to that distinctively national literature . . . for they deal exclusively with scenes, and phases of life, which are as thoroughly American as the aborigines themselves."[94] The consistently high praise of *Army and Navy Journal* reviewers of King's work becomes more impressive as one reads their unhesitating demolition of other books that did not accurately portray the Army.

Other reviewers also remarked upon the realism in King's novels. One wrote that *Under Fire* "deals truthfully and vigorously with army post life in the far West."[95] Another said the characters in *A Trooper Galahad* are "all true types."[96] Not only was King "to be counted as our sole writer of the military romance,"[97] but he gave "minute and accurate descriptions of scene and accoutrement."[98] A critic who would have preferred a bit less perfect goodness in the behavior of King's characters, nevertheless valued King for "giving us frontier life, or, rather, fort life, with the truth and accuracy of an eye-witness and a soldier."[99]

With broader perspective, a critic who knew King's work as a whole assessed him thus: "No writer has pictured more vividly the stirring incidents of frontier army life, the march across the plains, the bivouac, the dash and hurry of Indian fighting, than Captain Charles King; and his breezy, wholesome books are always sure of their public."[100] A decade later, another critic said: "Gen. Charles King has perhaps done more than any other man in this country to acquaint the public with life in the army through the medium of fiction. His long experience as an officer ... added to an uncommon power of observation ... place[s] him at the head of this branch of our literature [by the] faithful representation of military life in which [his books] abound."[101]

King's last Western novel appeared in 1909[102] and his last book, a biography of Grant, in 1914.[103] By the time of his death in Milwaukee in 1933—at the age of eighty-eight, after tripping over a rug and breaking a shoulder —the successive waves of literary fads had passed him by, and his novels were headed for the oblivion in which they rest in many libraries today.

But King's place as a novelist of manners in the frontier army was assured. When he had written an account of his literary career, the editor's note accompanying the article said: "Few, if any, American writers have won a greater or more deserved popularity than General Charles King; and surely none in his chosen field. He has depicted the American soldier, and army life in general, with his pen as faithfully as did the late Frederic Remington with his brush...."[104]

2.
The Ladies
of the Regiment

A woman who married an Army officer led a grueling life that usually shocked her at first and then tested her mettle as surely as ever the pioneer woman was tested. Apparently a majority stuck it out, learning to bend with a life of many vicissitudes and many moves. Some broke under the strain, however, and returned home. For others, the sharp transition from urban life to wilderness meant an early death, usually from childbirth. To a certain percentage—and it may have been a large percentage—marriage into the Army meant a continuation of the only life style they had ever known, for they had been reared in the Army, as had their mothers before them.

Officers' wives were viewed differently according to the status of the observer. One resentful enlisted man said they were "painted dolls" who did not belong in frontier posts because they had no legal status; he thought the only real lady at his post was a laundress; laundresses did have legal status that derived from an act of Congress in 1802. The choleric Duane Merritt Greene, who had been an officer, regarded officers' wives and whiskey as the worst possible influences on any Army post. At the other extreme, an officer's wife recalled the ladies of the regiment as "fitted to grace the most cultured society and drawing rooms of any sphere of life." Another knew, to her own satisfaction, that their very presence had a salutary effect on post life, and that they would go to the ends of the earth just to be with their men. King said there were no other such "heroines as lived in those days in the army."[1]

The various types of women are somewhat blurred in the handful of memoirs left by officers' wives, but appear in rich detail in King's novels. His life-sized descriptions conform to common human experience and are fully in accord with the leaner descriptions in the few available factual accounts. By contrast, the other women of the post—laundresses and wives of enlisted men, usually one and the same—are much more shadowy than are the enlisted men, and the latter are shadowy enough.[2]

The most intriguing substantiation of King's depiction comes from Greene, who maintained that the "lack of discipline is most conspicuous at stations where the number of ladies is greatest," saying that they "monopolize the time of the bachelors as well as their husbands." His substantiation is intriguing, because it is corroboration in reverse; that is, where King pictured their roles in a positive light, Greene did so negatively, and without the details of personality. Wives were the powers behind the throne at regimental headquarters posts where, if there was any latitude, the commanding officer's wife designated the duties to be assigned to her favorites.[3] King's account of just such an officer's wife occurs in the following passage about a regimental commander, "Colonel Riggs," who would approve any lieutenant's application for leave but insisted on having his captains with their companies:

"Confound the man!" growled Captain Greene [the similarity of names here is a happenstance], "here I've been seven years with my troop, saving up for a six months' leave, and the old rip disapproves it! What on earth can a fellow say?"

"You didn't go about it right, Greeney," was the calm rejoinder of a comrade who had been similarly "cut" the year previous. "You should have laid siege to him through Madame a month or so. What she says as to who goes on leave and doesn't is law at head-quarters, and I know it. Now, you watch [Lieutenant Gordon] Noel. That fellow is wiser in his generation than all the rest of us put together. It isn't six months since he got back from his staff detail, and you see how constant he is in his attentions to the old lady. Now, I'll bet you anything you like the next plum that tumbles into the regiment will go to his maw and nobody else's."[4]

And, for the sake of the story, it did—a recruiting detail in Cincinnati—"but everybody said to everybody else that it was all Mrs. Riggs' doing, a fact which the colonel very well knew."[5]

A much more glowing account of the wife's role came from one who happily joined the Third Infantry when it went to Montana by wagon train in 1877.

The officers are singing and whistling, and we can often hear from the distance the boisterous laughter of the men. And the wives! There is an expression of happy content on the face of each one. We know, if the world does not, that the part we are to take on this march is most important. We will see that the tents are made comfortable and cheerful at every camp; that the little dinner after the weary march [she had a cook, by the way], the early breakfast, and the cold luncheon are each and all as dainty as camp cooking will permit. Yes, we are sometimes called "camp followers," but we do not mind—it probably originated with some envious old bachelor officer. We know all about the comfort and cheer that goes with us, and then—we have not been left behind![6]

In a less satisfactory situation the same lady wrote: "But at dreadful places like [Camp Supply, Indian Territory, with its log and mud huts] is where the plucky army wife is most needed. Her very presence has often a refining and restraining influence over the entire garrison, from the commanding officer down to the last recruit."[7]

King agreed that women changed the tone of society in a regiment. After service in Arizona his "—th Cavalry" had been transferred to Fort D. A. Russell where former tiffs and disagreements were subdued through the leadership of women who had not been with the regiment in Arizona. Both men and women remarked that "the —th was a mighty different regiment from what it used to be" in Arizona.[8]

The status of officers' wives was ambiguous at best. Some of them recalled indignantly in their memoirs that the War Department took no notice of them in army regulations, and that their status, legally, was that of camp followers, whereas laundresses and servants (who were also camp followers, at military law) had a legal standing insofar as regulations were concerned. That was not literally true. In military law the wives were camp followers because they were civilians, but regulations at least made oblique references to officers' families, thus recognizing their existence if not fully providing for them. One wife may have captured the essence of that omission when she said that any provision for women to accompany their husbands westward was farthest from the thoughts of officers in

Washington. And yet there was no restriction on officers' marrying as there was in some European armies. Counterbalancing this legal slight is the following observation by Mrs. Custer: "Although Army women have no visible thrones or sceptres, nor any acknowledged rights according to military law, I never knew such queens as they, or saw more willing subjects than they governed." Sometimes a queen could reign without any competition whatsoever, as did Mrs. Dr. M. T. V. McGillicuddy, the only woman with a cavalry detachment in the Black Hills in the spring of 1877. "When the troops are on the march she rides her handsome bay at the head of the column."[9]

As ambiguous as their legal status might have been, officers' wives created rigid caste systems. Greene complained: "There is more caste distinction among the ladies of the Army than among the officers. At Posts where there are many ladies, the garrison is invariably divided into caste and 'affinity' cliques." King depicted that caste system faithfully. At the top sat the commanding officer's wife—known to the Army as the K.O.W., because the literal abbreviation would not do. Taking full cognizance of her important position, King said, "the tone of garrison life depends immeasurably upon its social leader, the wife of the commanding officer. . . ." Again: "There is only one social position harder to fill than that of a minister's wife. The woman who can succeed as 'the lady of the commanding officer' in a bustling garrison could charm the most discordant parish that ever squabbled." But the K.O.W. could also be imperious and alienate everyone, as King's "Mrs. Colonel Pelham" did. In any event, a colonel's wife felt a "confident proprietorship" in a regimental adjutant; as a former adjutant King was in a position to know. The

K.O.W. had so much influence that when a vulnerable post quartermaster defied "Mrs. Pelham" on behalf of a friend, King explained: "It is to be feared that in his zeal for his friend the quartermaster was not strengthening his position, a thing that is of so rare occurrence as to warrant its being made a note of...." Below the K.O.W. various ladies established themselves as leaders in one way or another, King depicting "Mrs. Captain Turner" as the authority on all social questions, for instance. Even as a lieutenant's wife, Mrs. Orsemus Boyd established a certain hegemony at Fort Stanton, New Mexico, in 1870–71 through her baby daughter. She so quickly expressed displeasure if anyone failed to give the requisite attention to "baby" that it became *de rigeur* for post officers, after the morning session with the post commander, to say, "Now we must go see baby, and report her condition."[10]

Referring to the Fifth Cavalry's overland move from Arizona to Kansas in 1875 (but casting it as the "—th Cavalry"), King wrote that the few wives who had been in Arizona and made that march "held themselves (and were held by the men) as having a higher place on the regimental unwritten records than those" who took the easier route by water and rail.[11] What such a regimental march meant to women was detailed by a cavalry officer's wife. When the Eighth Cavalry was ordered from New Mexico to Texas in 1875, it moved in units— collected from the various posts—which made the trip in from eight to sixteen weeks of constant travel. En route, nine babies were born; in each instance, mother and baby resumed the march the day after birth. At each stop along their way to Fort Clark—at Mesilla, Las Cruces, Fort Bliss and Fort Davis—a ball was given in their honor. When encamped for several

44

days near an Army post, the cavalry officer's wife took the opportunity to bake several pies in a dutch oven. Encamped at one of the widely separated streams in the greater Big Bend area, the women did their laundry. On earlier moves in the Southwest, she had "learned instinctively to fall into the regular routine and discipline, and expected no consideration because of my sex." Eating breakfast well before dawn was an unpleasant change at first, but she became accustomed to it, to having the wall tent struck early, and to being bundled into an ambulance for a tiring day of slow travel. By the time they made the move to Texas, she and her husband were experienced Army movers who knew enough to take along a board floor for their tent.[12]

A more idyllic picture of a regimental transfer, complete with dependents, came from a cavalry colonel who wrote:

The baggage wagons jolt along over the rough roads, and the patient mules tug in silence while pulling the heavy freight belonging to the officers, soldiers and their families. Tents are pitched every night, and it is remarkable how soon they are put up by the willing hands of the soldiers. If the evening is cold, stoves are quickly placed [in the tents], and the cooks at once commence preparing the evening meal . . . if a man has a taste for hunting or fishing he readily finds an opportunity of gratifying it. The soldiers leave for the streams as soon as the tents are put up and their horses cared for. . . . The men who do not care to go fishing or hunting smoke in the shade of their tents or converse about the events of the day. . . . The ladies of the party sit by their tents in comfortable arm or camp chairs, and as a general thing are contented and happy. Blood tells here, as in every other condition of life, and those who have been the most carefully reared are usually the most amiable. They take things as they find them, and are cheerful under all circumstances.[13]

While the colonel and the ladies might have thought the enlisted men put up tents and did the camp chores with "willing hands," at least one enlisted man had a decidedly different view of the whole business.

Here [on the march] we meet the greatest bothers that ever appear in a Cavalry camp—women! Two daughters and a son of [Colonel S. D. Sturgis, commander of the Seventh Cavalry] have been riding in an ambulance all day. So they are tired and must have a wall tent put up for their special benefit. A detail is made to do this work, and another detail of soldiers to look after the requirements of the young ladies and the lad out for a frolic.

This compels details to delay the erection of their own shelters, cooking their suppers and giving the proper attention to their horses....The men do the work and the officers get the thanks.[14]

A regimental caravan moving hundreds of, or perhaps a thousand, miles was no glorious outing for anybody. When Colonel Henry B. Carrington led his Eighteenth Infantry out of Fort Kearny, Nebraska, to establish forts on the Bozeman Trail in 1866: "Rocking chairs and sewing machines, churns and washing machines, with a bountiful supply of canned fruits, were duly stored inside or outside of army wagons; while turkeys and chickens, and one brace of swine, added a specially domestic cast to some of the establishments prepared for the journey."[15]

Regimental marches sometimes had tragi-comic aspects. In 1873 part of the Fourth Cavalry made a toilsome march across Texas from Fort Richardson in the

46

north to Fort Clark in the south. Shortly after they reached Fort Clark the officers discovered two things simultaneously: they were to entertain Secretary of War W. W. Belknap and Sheridan at a dance, and their wives each had a colony of head lice, picked up from a visit they had felt compelled to make to some Comanche women in a compound at Fort Concho on the way south. The Negro maid of Mrs. Lieutenant Robert Carter had the immediate cure for the lice: wash the hair in a strong solution of plug tobacco and massage with lard. The treatment got to the lice and almost got to the women. The lard caused tangles that had to be cut away, but Mrs. Carter finally was made ready for the dance. That evening she danced "La Paloma" with Sheridan and promenaded on the arm of Secretary Belknap, neither gentleman knowing how close he had come to having an itching head during the trip back home.[16]

Of the different kinds of women who inhabited officers' row, some were "refined, high-bred, cultured women, some simple-mannered, warm-hearted army girls who knew no home but the regiment, no life but that on the plains," while others were "vapid, frivolous, and would-be fashionable, all full of kindly motive."[17] Although some of the women in King's novels are hackneyed stage props, one nonetheless gets a fairly good delineation of types to be found in any garrison, verified by fleeting references in personal reminiscences.

"Mrs. Pelham," wife of the commanding officer of the "—th Cavalry," is a woman with some social pretensions derived from the status of her family in the East. Before joining her husband at "Camp Sandy," she has made up her mind that her daughter, Grace, should marry an independently wealthy lieutenant of the regiment so as to have "fortune, position, independence, luxury . . . at her feet." To prepare the way she sends a letter to a captain's wife before leaving for Arizona: "Seldom was it that her ladyship saw fit to honor the lesser lights of the regiment with letters written in her august hand." Once at "Camp Sandy," Mrs. Pelham uses a heavy hand in attempting to dominate post and regimental society, and so far alienates both officers and ladies that they contemptuously call her "Lady Pelham." At a dance in honor of her daughter, she is "smiling, portly and majestic, showering confidential salutations upon her intimates and condescension upon the juniors." Her ambitions come to ruin, because her daughter straightaway falls in love with and marries the regimental adjutant.[18]

Frustrated by her daughter's rebellion, "Lady Pelham" proves to be a gross woman given to loud and violent arguments with her husband. behind closed doors. When things become too much for her, she bathes her face in lavender-water as a means of releasing tensions—possibly a rather common tranquilizer of the time. She makes herself so thoroughly disliked that by the time the "—th" has been transferred to Kansas, the other ladies at Fort Hays—which was regimental headquarters for both the Fifth Cavalry and the "—th"— have thrown off her yoke. "Courtesy, civility, and a certain degree of cordiality when in their social gatherings, the ladies were willing to extend to the colonel's wife, but the declaration of independence had been signed and sealed,—they would have no more of her dominion." All are glad to see her leave when the colonel is reassigned.[19]

A more sensible K.O.W. appears in "Mrs. Colonel Atherton" who also is referred to as "her ladyship," but without the same sneer. Nevertheless, she exercises a certain dominion over some of the ladies, causing one of them to comment that she has "under her thumb" some wives who "don't dare call their souls their own." The uncertain sway of such a lady is indicated, however, when she and others are forced to make an unpleasant social call upon a lady outside the garrison as a means of smoothing out and making clear a delicate situation. She lays down the rules for the visit, saying: "[I will] open the subject instantly, and close it in just as few words as I know how. You needn't laugh, Mrs. Freeman, I can be very concise when I try." King said, "when that accomplished lady resolved on a point it was apt to be carried, no matter who opposed."[20]

Depicted as "the most independent woman in the regiment," another of King's characters, "Mrs. Lieutenant Wilkins" is "always at war with every colonel's wife." The buxom lady strives hard to conceal the hint of Irish brogue in her voice, but it sometimes comes through in excitement, anyhow.[21]

[Lieutenant Wilkins] and his sharp-sighted, razor-tongued wife had "joined" together in '67 [when he had accepted a commission in the Regular Army after volunteer service during the Civil War] and long association among ladies of refinement and culture had only slightly dulled the edges of her uncouthness ... except when indulging in a fit of ill temper and consequent explosiveness of language, she kept his home in reasonable comfort. Policy she had, and cared to have, none. She had neither education nor polish, but a faculty of saying just what she thought, and more too, and, to use her husband's rueful admission, "She wasn't afraid of the devil."[22]

Absolutely insolent in braving any woman who seeks to patronize her, she also has cutting words for those she dislikes. When a young officer—who is more social butterfly than soldier—has been reported as painfully but not dangerously wounded, she remarks, "They must have hit him in the head." At the same time, she can be up before dawn to have hot coffee ready for bachelor officers taking the field and is the first to nurse an ill wife who is being ostracized by the others. Her outspokenness is so notorious that, in a socially tense situation, "Mrs. Atherton" says "Jane Wilkins" is sure to say "something horrid." Indeed, her caustic bluntness causes Mrs. Crook (not identified by name) to say she would appoint "a day for prayer and humiliation" if she should find herself in the same regiment with "Mrs. Wilkins."[23]

She wants to see, hear and say everything. So long as the gossip comes from other women, that is. When she hears gossip from her husband, she refuses to believe a word of it, immediately seeking verification from a woman. Nor does she spare her sore-tried husband on other occasions. "With her keen insight she had long since discovered that her husband's associates and intimates in the regiment were not the strong or the good men, and she warned him . . . that whatever he might have against [some of the good men] he had better stamp it out and seek to reestablish himself in their good opinion."[24] Her shrewish ways sometimes drive her husband away from home for an evening of cards with other officers—"the generally accepted signal at Sandy that the wind was in the east at 'Castle Wilkins,' as the subaltern's quarters were dubbed by the 'society' of the post." Abrasive as she is in the earlier years of the regiment, their long service in Arizona and on the Northern Plains places her solidly within the affections of all. By 1879, when the regiment is at Fort D. A.

Russell, her laugh can "be heard half-way down the line . . . a jollier creature never lived, nor one much more thoroughly popular."[25]

"Mrs. Wilkins" is merely the more fully drawn characterization of a type or types who were part of garrison life. As for her concealed brogue, there were others who made no attempt to—or could not—conceal their antecedents. At a dance at a Kansas post there appeared a captain's wife in jewels and finery who not only spoke with a pronounced brogue but was recognized as a former company laundress.[26] Nor was braving a K.O.W. so altogether unusual. Mrs. Custer recorded an instance in which her husband had had an "official difficulty" with a subordinate officer whose wife took revenge by "cutting" Mrs. Custer.[27]

"Mrs. Major Stannard," another of King's fictional women, personifies the likeable, level-headed type who is aware of her station but never presumes upon it. Conceivably, she could have been modeled—if modeled at all—on Mrs. James B. Ricketts, to whom King dedicated *The Colonel's Daughter,* as one "who, whether sharing the lot of a wounded prisoner, or gracing the highest circles of society, has been the devoted wife to one, the faithful friend to many a soldier." The wife of a general stationed in Washington in 1887, she was described as "probably the most beloved of the wives of Army officers." An officer recalled her as "the special patronness of young army and navy officers" in Washington, seeing to it that they met the loveliest young ladies of the season.[28]

"Mrs. Stannard" commands respect among the other wives, a natural leader to whom all show deference. With a quick penetration of character, she is "well-versed in . . . the study of man and womankind." She can, in every situation, shatter the self-serving arguments of other wives, but always with the utmost courtesy. In conversation she invariably turns the topic from gossip to something more pleasant. "Mrs. Stannard's most pronounced characteristic was consummate discretion. She knew whom to trust, and others might labor in vain to extract from her the faintest hint that, repeated carelessly or maliciously, would wound or injure a friend." In her happy, joking relationship with her husband (who complained about gossipy women), she gaily turns the tables on him when he seeks to learn what she has heard from others about a given incident. Their relationship is so stable and considerate that the major, when provoked at home, mutters "dreadful things in Apache," she says, rather than criticize her. With the men, though, he "swore in stalwart Anglo-Saxon. . . ."[29]

The sunshine of Mrs. Stannard's bonny face was something the —th were prone to speak of often, perhaps too often to suit other ladies, whose visages on the domestic side were not infrequently clouded. . . .

Mrs. Stannard's smile was sweetness itself; her eyes smiled quite as much as her mouth, and her very soul seemed to beam through the winsome, winning beauty of her face. All the young officers looked up to her with something akin to worship; all the elders spoke of Mrs. Stannard as the perfection of an army wife; even her closest friends and acquaintances could find no one trait to speak of openly as a fault. It was a smile born of genuine goodness, of charity, of loving-kindness, and of a spiritual grace that made Mrs. Stannard marked among her associates. In all the regiment no woman was so looked up to and loved as she.[30]

An actual Army wife who somewhat fitted the cut of "Mrs. Stannard" was Mrs. Lieutenant Colonel John D.

Wilkins, of the Eighth Infantry, not to be confused with King's "Mrs. Wilkins." On the regiment's march to Fort Whipple, Mrs. Martha Summerhayes came under the influence, observation, and tutelage of Mrs. Wilkins whose two daughters were with her—Caroline Wilkins and Ella, the wife of Lieutenant Charles Bailey of the same regiment. Facing the desert for the first time, Mrs. Summerhayes complained about the unexpected dust, the dirt, and the lack of bath water. Mrs. Wilkins, an old campaigner who obviously saw it her duty to maintain equilibrium among the women (as "Mrs. Stannard" did, in effect), said: "Soon, now, you will not mind it at all. Ella and I are army girls, you know, and we do not mind anything. There's no use in fretting about little things." Mrs. Summerhayes came to conclude that Mrs. Wilkins "represented the best type of the older army woman."[31]

The story of Caroline Wilkins and others coincides with King's fictional creation, in two novels, of the daughters of ranking officers as the belles of their respective regiments. During the same period in which he set *The Colonel's Daughter* in Arizona, Miss Wilkins reigned over the Eighth Infantry at Whipple. Two wives remembered her as the "beautiful and graceful . . . belle of the regiment," who was "accustomed to the devotion of all the officers." She was also a favorite with the women, because "she had too kind a heart to be a coquette."[32] After seven years as the fairy princess, she married Captain Charles Porter of the Eighth Infantry. Another parallel—one undoubtedly could find scores if he wished to search Army records for that sort of thing—was Miss Belle Gilbert, daughter of Colonel C. C. Gilbert, commanding officer of the Seventeenth Infantry. Reporting New Year's receptions at Fort Yates, Dakota Territory, in 1882 a correspondent wrote:

"We don't think officers of the Army or any one else found a more pleasant place to call on the 2d of January than we did at Col. Gilbert's. His daughter Miss Belle, assisted by Miss Falconer, from Ohio, received us. . . . We *all* called there first, and many of us called there last, and enjoyed ourselves for hours." Before the year was out, she—*"la fille du regiment"*—was married to Lieutenant J. C. Gresham of the Seventh Cavalry in the parlor of her father's quarters.[33]

After the necessary complications of a romantic novel, "Grace Pelham" becomes Mrs. Lieutenant "Jack Truscott" in *The Colonel's Daughter;* he shortly becomes a captain. "Mrs. Truscott" appears in later novels as the very model of an Army wife. This is to be expected in more than just the conventional apparatus of the romance, for Truscott was patterned after Lieutenant Eaton, the freshly minted second lieutenant who had been with King in Sunset Pass. "Mrs. Truscott" was always the devoted, loving wife. Once, on a sidewalk talking with other women, she linked her arm in her husband's, and drew close to him—"'publicly cuddling him,' as Mrs. Turner disdainfully expressed it afterwards."[34]

The winning of the other belle—"Lillian Archer," daughter of a post commander—is much less complicated. She herself is much less complicated, an ingenue whose entire life has been spent in the shelter of a simple Army society. King thus is provided an opportunity to characterize the unprincipled officer who dallies with any and all girls and who finally is forced to resign; the good and conscientious officer naturally wins the lady's hand.[35]

The "affinity cliques" to which the highly critical Greene referred appeared in King's novels as a triumvirate composed of "Mrs. Turner," "Mrs. Raymond," and "Mrs. Gregg"—each the wife of a captain in the "—th Cavalry." Constantly together, the three savor every morsel of gossip and make of it a mountain. And they rather well dictate who shall and shall not be accepted as social peers in each garrison. "Mrs. Turner" is a pretty and frivolous woman, much younger than her husband, and with a temper as quick as her tongue. Her husband speaks once too often about the beauty of "Mrs. Stannard's" smile. The fact that they are in the company of other officers and their wives does not keep her from spitting out: "Merciful powers! Captain Turner. Any woman with Mrs. Stannard's teeth could afford to smile from morning till night; but it's all teeth." She, too, has parallels among the female personalities described in memoirs. For instance, Mrs. Frances Roe knew a lieutenant's wife at Fort Lyon whose "sharp tongue and spitfire temper are well-known."

Temperamentally much like her friend, "Mrs. Raymond" is a "fascinating and volatile young matron" whose "absolute inability to keep anything to herself was only too well appreciated throughout the —th." She is a "politic" lady who will do anything to curry favor with a "ruthless old agitator" like "Mrs. Pelham." Personifying another familiar type, "Mrs. Gregg" "...would not have it supposed for an instant she envied any woman her figure. It was a point on which she was easily content. Too easily, said her associates."[36]

Another recognizable type appears in the form—the rather large and portly form—of "Mrs. Colonel Whaling" whose husband commands Fort D. A. Russell while troops are in the field during the 1876 campaign. Garbed in depressing black, she lavishes effusive and

tearful sympathy upon the cavalry wives whose husbands have gone on campaign. She is a Bible-thumper,
which also rather annoys the seasoned women in King's
fictional cavalry regiment, especially since it is her
"exemplary habit . . . to be always found seated at a
little table behind a very big Bible when visitors
called." She constantly refers to her husband as "general," a rank he does not have even by wartime brevet.
She belittles other colonels—who actually are general
officers by brevet—as "merely field officers."[37]

    She admitted the existence of no greater man than "the
general," her husband, and whatever might be the sorrows of
other parents with their children, or housewives with their
servants, Mrs. Whaling pitied,—condoled,—but could not
sympathize. With uplifted eyes she would thank the Giver of
all good that He had blessed her with sons so noble, with
daughters so lovely and so dutiful, with servants so singularly
devoted. In the various garrisons in which the good lady had
flourished, what mattered it that her boys were known to be
graceless young scamps whom cudgelling could not benefit,
or that her daughters squabbled like cats and flew to the
neighbors to spread the tales of their wrongs and mamma's
injustice? What mattered it that her paragons of servants left
her one after another and swore they couldn't stay in a house
where there was so much spying and fault-finding? . . .[38]

    Among the other types of Army women who people
King's garrisons, "Mrs. Captain Freeman" is a devoted
wife and mother who holds aloof from frivolity. She is
strong-willed and strong-minded, with convictions she
does not hesitate to express when pressed. "[Mrs. Truscott and Mrs. Freeman] shared about equally the de-
votions of the entire commissioned force, married and
single, but no two women in the —th cared less for the

distinction." "Mrs. Major Mainwaring" is a sensible woman who seeks to counterbalance her husband's brusqueness with tact and sound advice. "Mrs. Lieutenant Davies" is shown to be an insincere and empty-headed woman — "that pretty little bunch of nerves and nonsense," the surgeon calls her — who can not stand up under the privations of a frontier post and ultimately runs away with a wealthy civilian. "Mrs. Captain Forrest" is an unattractive hypochondriac and overly protective mother who is near distraction while her husband is in the field. "Mrs. Major Miller," devoted to and protective of her husband, stands between him and petty squabbles that would annoy him as post commander at Fort Laramie. "Mrs. Captain Belknap" is a dark-eyed coquette who knows how to use her heavy eyelashes so well that her husband is constantly uneasy. "Mrs. Major Granger" enters as a *femme fatale* who has little use for her much older husband and great use for his independent fortune and the attentions of younger men. "Mrs. Captain Blake" is a retiring and shy young matron whose father had been a small ranchman near Fort D. A. Russell.[39]

King made it clear that Army women were not well informed.[40] Generally, it appears from his portrayal that both officers and their wives were shallow and neither were at all well read. That depiction gains strength whem compared with the memoirs of both men and women, for both sets of accounts emphasize action and movement, not contemplation. To say they were shallow is not intended to be invidious. They can be taken as people of character, honor, and persistence who were adequate to their place and the calls made upon them. Their environment was limited and certainly did not call forth the responses appropriate to a metropolitan setting.

An example of the lack of knowledge on the part of Army wives comes from Mrs. Summerhayes' recollections. After only a few months in Arizona in 1886 (a second tour there), the Eighth Infantry received orders —late at night—to move to Fort Niobrara, Nebraska. "We looked, appalled, in each other's faces, the evening the telegram came, for we did not even know where Fort Niobrara was." They all rushed to Major Thomas Wilhelm's quarters, "for he always knew everything," and rousted him out of bed. He replied, "Why, girls, it's a hell of a freezing cold place, away up north in Nebraska."[41]

As an elitist and apparently something of an intellectual snob, King could be expected to look down on the general intellectual level of his comrades and their wives. But there certainly were a number of women with outside interests who attempted to keep up with the world from which they were so isolated. A doctor's wife at Fort Lapwai, Idaho, wrote to her mother, "I find lots of comfort and entertainment in my books and papers at this lonely post."[42] A number kept diaries, including Mrs. Margaret Carrington at Fort Phil Kearny and Mrs. Elizabeth Reynolds Burt.[43] At Camp Halleck, Nevada, Lieutenant and Mrs. Boyd, "unwilling to become rusty . . . read with avidity all printed matter that reached us." What reached them was not always what they wanted, for some of the magazines addressed to them were pilfered from mail sacks along the way.[44] But even in the larger and older posts reading matter was scant. While Crook's field headquarters were at Fort Laramie in the Spring of 1877, his aide, Lieutenant John G. Bourke, read everything he could find in the company libraries, but had to concede, "Living on the frontier, an Army Officer's chances of literary treasures are so slight that he must cheerfully embrace whatever opportunities come within his reach without waiting for a selection."[45] Needlework occupied the time of some women, and others dabbled at painting, while one was believed to be the author of "The Cattle upon a Thousand Hills," which detailed the Arizona cattle business in the *Overland Monthly* of March, 1887.[46] Overall, however, memoirs and other accounts substantiate King's generalization about the limited intellectual horizons of the officer caste. His numerous references to the Chicago *Times* would indicate that that newspaper was about the only one read at posts on the Northern Plains.

Limited their interests may have been, but they were an intensely loyal lot of women. They were part of a regiment and proud of it. For that reason, a troop commander's wife would refer to "our troop" and to the regiment as "Ours."[47] The presence of that proprietary feeling is apparent in Mrs. Custer's writings.[48] But Mrs. Lydia Lane, who had known the prewar Army, noticed that usage in 1868 with a trace of asperity which implied that she thought it presumptuous or possibly faddish for wives to speak of "*our* regiment" or "*our* troop." The dating of her remark suggests that the term may have become fashionable in the wake of the success of Thomas William Robertson's play, "Ours," which was first produced in 1866 and became popular with Army people.

"Mrs. Captain Cranston" always follows her husband wherever he goes, shares the privations of a remote cantonment at the (thinly veiled) Red Cloud Agency in Nebraska, and soothes his worries. She is a woman of spirit who can judge quickly whether another woman has the backbone to be the wife of a frontier officer. She resembles Mrs. Burt, who began her frontier career in 1865 and was proud to say later, "My husband never changed permanent station thereafter that I and the children did not go along." She would have had good cause to go back to Ohio after the birth of their second child in a tumbledown shack at Fort Sanders, Wyoming, in 1867, as he wanted her to do, but she insisted on accompanying him to Fort C. F. Smith, Montana, when he was detailed to that dangerous and exposed post on the Bozeman Trail. In 1876, the wife of Dr. Jenkins A. FitzGerald wrote that her husband thought they would be home by 1879 and urged her to go home and wait for him. "I won't go home until he does," Mrs. FitzGerald wrote. "It would be dreadful to be home with him out here." In a passing remark, King wrote, "I have known many and many a couple who have risen together through every grade in the line, loved, loving and lovers to the end."[49]

Regimental pride meant that all the wives were proud of all the officers and vice versa. One Seventh Cavalry officer claimed that the women of the Seventh sang, played, painted, and rode better than any other women anywhere, and Mrs. Custer responded with the remark: "If our officers were not all handsome, one was deceived into thinking they were, for the brilliant eyes, the glow of health, the proud carriage of the head, which is a soldier's characteristic, and, above all, the symmetry of their well-developed figures, gave one the impression that there was little to be desired in the general make-up of the men."[50]

The loyalty and sense of oneness extended beyond the regiment. When unescorted Army wives happened to be aboard a train, any officers aboard "always send their cards by the porter the moment they find army ladies on the train." It was, King added, "the commonest civility" for an officer "always" to introduce himself to a woman who was known to be an Army wife.[51]

At any moment, though, that close relationship might be shattered, for frontier Army people lived close to death. Warfare took a comparatively light toll—932 killed between 1865 and 1890 for an average of thirty-seven per year in the entire West. But disease, accident, exposure, and childbirth took many lives. The Army had its own way of conducting funeral services, which King vivified with the burial of an officer.

. . . to the wailing notes of the band, the solemn *cortege* formed around the new-made grave among the foot-hills west of the post. There stood Canker's company, dismounted, and in full-dress uniform, the escort of the soldier-dead; there stood the gray-haired chaplain, whose tremulous voice rose and fell in mournful cadence on the still evening air; there, leaning on their sabres, were grouped the officers of the garrison, the general commanding and his aides, all with reverently uncovered head, many with tear-dimmed eyes; there stood a mourning, weeping group of ladies, the wives of brother officers, and among them many a heart faltered in the dread that any day it might be their lot to stand there and see that same flag lifted from the form of him who was all in all, as this had been all in all to her who lay sore-stricken in the desolation of her home. All around were grouped the soldiers of the post . . . the solemn tones of the old chaplain gave thanks "for the good example of all those Thy servants who, having finished their course in faith, do now rest from their labors." The heavy clods had fallen . . . and then the sombre throng fell back from the grave, the bright-plumed helmets of the escort ranged up in line, the muffled word of command was given, the carbines flashed their parting volleys . . . , the notes of the trumpets floated away with the smoke of the discharge, "Taps" . . . died away in distant echoes across the valley, and all was over. Ay,

61

put out your light, old fellow.... But now, *allons! Le roi est mort, vive* the next man! Lieutenant Stafford becomes captain *vice* the deceased. It's an ill wind that blows nobody good. Our turn may come next. Who knows? It's all in the business. Soldiers cannot stop to mourn. Life is too short, anyway. So strike up your liveliest music, trumpeters. "Fours right," gentlemen of the escort. "Left front into line, double-time," go the platoons as they clear the enclosure, and the band bursts into the ringing, lively, rollicking quickstep from *La Fille de Madame Argot,* and with elastic steps we march away from the grave.[52]

The happy music at the end of an Army funeral shocked Mrs. Summerhayes when she heard it for the first time. For explanation she turned to her husband, Lieutenant John Summerhayes, who said: "You see, it would not do for the soldiers to be sad when one of them dies. Why, it would demoralize the whole command. So they play these gay things to cheer them up."[53]

Eastern-bred ladies had to become accustomed to many other things on the frontier, too. "Mrs. Turner" bemoans the effect on her complexion of the "dazzling suns and blasting gales" of Wyoming, while critically observing "the havoc played with the cuticles of the other ladies." Trouble with complexion was truly a source of worry. After a summer on the Plains, Mrs. Custer said, the women had to "try to get our complexions into condition again." And their hair as well, for "the sun fades and streaks the glossiest locks out there, and the wind breaks and dries the silkiest mane." During one of their several crossings of the Plains, Major William B. Lane told his wife that the hot winds of Kansas had turned her face the color of a new saddle, whereupon she followed someone's suggestion that she cover her face with a chamois mask. It may have protected her face, but it so terrified her baby that she could not continue using it. The ladies always exchanged tips on how to deal with the West, one of the more successful being the use of a champagne basket as a cradle during a long wagon trip.[54]

Important as their complexion was to some of the women, other responses were more fundamental. When Katherine Garrett went to Fort Lincoln in 1874, her sister, Mrs. McIntosh, met her at Columbia, Dakota, for a stage ride to another rail connection at Grand Rapids. Without a male escort, Mrs. McIntosh was armed and, by treating everyone in a hard, fearless manner, let it be known she could take care of both of them. "Mollie's sensitive, musical nerves used to go jittery at a discord struck on a piano or guitar. This country had certainly changed her."[55] Pistol-packing Army women were exceptions, however.

The more general response to the frontier may have been more like that of Mrs. Roe and Mrs. Boyd, who had a love affair with the "gray loveliness of the West." Keen horsewomen both, they gloried in the beauty and atmosphere and freedom of the West. Before joining her husband in Nevada in 1869, Mrs. Boyd had thought New York the only habitable place on the globe. After tours in Nevada, Arizona, New Mexico, and Texas, she found in two trips to New York that no homesickness had ever equaled what she felt for the West. "I missed the quiet and freedom from that mad rush which seems an inevitable part of life in a great city." The West had so changed her that she could "never become reconciled to localities where the eye cannot look for miles and miles beyond the spot where one stands, and where the density of the atmosphere circumscribes the view." Mrs. Roe, who loved hunting as much as riding, recoiled at the prospect of the transfer of her husband, Lieutenant Fayette Roe, to the headquarters of the Department of the Platte in Omaha. "I am almost heart-broken over it, as it will be a wretched life for me—cooped up in a noisy city."[56]

Negative responses to the frontier are equally revealing. After a year of doing her own laundry at Camp Halleck, the wealthy wife of a second lieutenant persuaded her husband to resign and move to New York. Nor could all the Army-bred girls tolerate the shock of frontier living. One example was Mrs. Captain Washington L. Elliott, the daughter of Major George Blaney. Three years in the Southwest were enough for her; she went home for a visit and never returned; her husband joined her in Carlisle, Pennsylvania, some time later.[57]

Despite the racial prejudices in the West, Mrs. Boyd and Mrs. Summerhayes longed to live like the Mexican women (the term Mexican-American was several decades in the future) they saw in Arizona and New Mexico. "How I envied the Mexicans," Mrs. Boyd wrote, adding: "When living among them one feels the necessity of absorbing some of their traits, which are indeed needed in a country where progress is unknown, and where the customs of centuries past still remain, not as traditions but as facts. They were always kind and gentle, and...[made] most admirable nurses for the children, except for their over indulgence." Isolated in the lonely sweat-box of Ehrenberg, Arizona, where her husband was in reality a forwarding agent for Army freight, Mrs. Summerhayes wanted desperately to wear the cool, short-sleeved, loose *camisas* of the Mexican women. Her husband would not hear of it. For her it had to be what other Anglo women wore in cooler climes—high-necked, long-sleeved dresses throughout the summer. Going as far as she could, she learned to smoke cigarettes and sleep all afternoon, at least. During a long visit in the welcome coolness of San Francisco, she told an unbelieving and highly prejudiced New England aunt that the Mexicans "are the only people who understand the philosophy of living."[58]

The response to the frontier brought to light many fears which Army women understandably lived with in the West. All were deathly afraid of Indians when traveling by wagon. Next to her fear of Indians, Mrs. Lane—who crossed the Plains six times with Army caravans—feared river crossings more than anything else.

Some of the fords were reached by a steep and dangerous road, leading from the top of a bank, to the water's edge, down which the cautious driver guided his sure-footed team. Sometimes there was a drop of a foot or two from the bank into the swift-running stream. Then I clasped my hands and shut my eyes tight, but never a sound escaped me. With shouts and yells the mules were rushed through the water, men on horseback riding beside them to keep them in the track; the air was blue with the profanity thought necessary when driving mules.

The last agony was in the effort made to reach the top of the wet and slippery straight-up-and-down bank on the other side, and this feat was accomplished with even more noise than before, the shouts and cracking of whips making an appalling din. . . .

When the ambulance stopped at the top of the opposite bank, which the mules, panting and half drowned, managed at last to reach, I opened my eyes with a feeling of gratitude that one stream, at least, had been safely crossed.[59]

Taking wagons across Western rivers and streams was always dangerous, but Mrs. Boyd had an unusually

close—and freakish—crossing of the Rio Grande near
Las Cruces in 1875. The only way to cross the full and
deep river was on a raft manipulated by pulleys and
ropes. The raft had neither side-rails nor guard-chains.
After the raft had left the bank, bearing a heavily
loaded ambulance with her and her children in it, they
discovered that a favorite dog had been left behind.
Encouraging the dog to swim the river, someone
thoughtlessly made the same sound that ordinarily
started the mules. At once, the mules started forward
blindly, and the leaders' forefeet had reached the edge
of the raft before a man caught them by their heads.

Mrs. Boyd's reaction to that incident is indicative
of what happened to the women who proved up to the
demands of the frontier. "If people should dwell continually on the perils of Western life they would be
wretched.... That journey embraced every element of
danger, and yet I actually became callous." Her ad-
justment also left her indifferent to the violence in
Lincoln County, New Mexico, where she had reveled
in the sharp air of Fort Stanton. "Army officers' wives
hear of bloodshed with much the same feeling as is
experienced by women living in cities when they learn
of frightful accidents which involve ... none who are
near and dear to them." She also so overcame her fear
of rattlesnakes, scorpions, and tarantulas that she could
say, "I have met many army ladies who live in constant
terror of snakes, tarantulas, and scorpions; though no
longer sharing their fears, I always sympathize with
them." Reptiles and venomous insects bothered many,
but one wife particularly detested the bats that clung
to her bed clothing at night in a New Mexico post.[60]

The women had no monopoly on a fear of rattlesnakes, though. Troopers surrounded sleeping places
with horsehair lariats, as did cowhands. One uneasy

infantry lieutenant borrowed a camp cot from a cavalry officer, who shared the same tent, because he was afraid of them; the young cavalry officer said, with a touch of bravado perhaps, "Some have been killed here but I do not fear them."[61]

Other women expressed the same fears without giving as clear evidence of having accommodated themselves to them. Forced to cross the Missouri River at Bismarck with the river full of ice, Mrs. Custer dropped to the bottom of the boat "and hid my eyes, and no amount of reference to dangers I had encountered before induced me to look up." Similarly, Mrs. Frances Grummond crossed the whimsical Platte in 1866, knowing that a line of poles indicated quicksand where others had perished. "This was not a comforting assurance to the lone woman in the ambulance, with every nerve on tension."[62]

What those selected experiences prove, if anything, is that the ladies of the regiment were intensely human, and became heroines only to the extent that they stood up to the demands of an alien land nobly.

Imperfectly as officers' wives emerge from the sources, their profile is sharp and fine-grained compared with what is revealed of laundresses. Laundresses became a fixture in the Army when Congress authorized four per company in 1802, allowing them to be carried on company rosters and authorizing quarters and rations for them.

Living in shanties or log houses some distance from the main part of the post, they come forth in King's novels as a brawling and uncouth lot. One is a coquette who marries a sturdy sergeant whom she turns into a problem soldier, running him into debt and turning the heads of other men. "Garrison life and girls spoil many a good cavalryman," observes the sergeant's troop commander. Conceding that officers owe a lot to their wives, the troop commander asks: "But what chance has the average trooper? What manner of woman has he to mate with, if he mate at all?" In only one novel did King really emphasize a laundress, for it suited his purposes to make her an accomplice in crime. As "Mrs. Sergeant Clancy," she has in days gone by been the beauty at soldiers' dances, but by the time of the story is a "tall, angular woman" who has become a virago and bully. "The artificiality of her charms could not stand the test of frontier life. No longer sought as the belle of the soldiers' ball-rooms, she aspired to leadership among their wives and families, and was accorded that preeminence rather than the fierce battle which was sure to follow any revolt." She drives "Clancy" to drink and theft. In another account, a laundress's daughter is willing to knife anybody who tries to do her lover harm. Brawling or not, they got their pay for washing clothes, because "one of the unwritten laws of the rank and file in the good old days [was] to square with the laundress if you didn't square with anybody else." Regulations stipulated that enlisted men were to pay the laundresses at the pay table; the men were to be paid quarterly.[63]

King's characterization of the laundresses is in keeping with first-hand accounts left by autobiographers. They were industrious, red-armed women who maintained their rights "with acrimonious volubility ... and they were ever ready for a fight." Many were "pugilists," but threw stove wood and anything else at hand when fighting each other. One threatened to kill a lieutenant who had punished her husband by having him hung by his thumbs for having been drunk on duty. Fighting their own kind might have suited their Irish tempers—and most appear to have been

68

Irish—but the nearness of Indians was something else
again. Rumors that the Nez Percé intended to attack
Fort Lapwai drove all the women and children into
one house in 1877 (when most of the men were in the
field). Three officers' wives "wore ourselves out in
trying to quiet the excited laundresses."[64] King characterized one laundress in this cameo: "A little, old Irish
camp-woman. . . . She had much true Irish wit, and her
small, withered face was full of fun. A thick, close-fitting
white muslin cap with a deep ruffle hanging from it
added to her comical expression.[65]

Laundresses could be pretty damned independent,
too. Army regulations specified that they were "to do
the washing for the company officers and their families"
as well as enlisted men (at a fixed price of seventy cents
per month for soldiers and one dollar per dozen for
officers). That meant nothing, as far as officers' families
were concerned. A laundress at Camp Halleck refused
to wash for officers' wives, causing one gently bred
Eastern girl to redden her knuckles at a scrub-board.
Another time, a weary caravan pulled into Fort Stock-
ton, Texas, for a one-day stop. The women needed
clean clothes for their families, but the post laundresses
refused to labor on the Sabbath. "[It] might speak well
for their piety; but I am inclined to think they had
something more entertaining on hand for the day, and,
having worked hard all week, did not care to put themselves out to accommodate us."[66]

By an act of Congress, laundresses were phased out
of the Army between 1878 and 1883, but only to the
extent that they no longer had a place on company
rolls entitling them to quarters and rations. Generally,
the laundresses were terminated as of 1878, with the
proviso that the laundress-wife of an enlisted man
could remain on the roster until her husband had

finished his current enlistment. A "hitch" being for five years, some laundresses thus remained on the roster until 1883.[67] Actually, laundresses remained a part of the garrison in spite of the law. As wives of enlisted men, they lived as before in two-room cabins of log, or plank, and canvas "in sheltered nooks" at the back of the post, and continued to scrub the garrison's dirty clothes. They were recognized as "acceptable adjuncts to a garrison in post, and are of no little service outside the strict letter of the law."[68]

Although officers' and enlisted men's wives could never fraternize, there was, naturally, curiosity in both groups. Through various novels King shows that officers' wives knew who the laundresses were and were acquainted with the traits of each. The soldier who thought officers' wives were "painted dolls" told of watching an officer's wife and a laundress pass each other on a post sidewalk, each dressed in her best. They passed without speaking, but assuredly surveyed each other's costume. The laundress did not look back for a more complete appraisal, but the officer's wife did, and stumbled over a wheelbarrow.[69]

More than any other one factor, the women gave frontier forts a distinct, self-sufficient character. Each served, predominantly, the function of woman in the nineteenth century—child-bearer and keeper of the lodge fire for a liege lord. The courage, hardships, privations, dangers, and adventures are not to be denied—nor their influence upon their husbands' decisions—but life in the Old Army could hardly have been "glittering misery"—the European cliche which Mrs. Summerhayes fastened upon it so long ago[70]— or the desertion rate would have been higher among women than among enlisted men.

3.
Cavaliers
and Blackguards

T he officers of the Old Army were a more mixed lot than in any other peacetime period except the years after World War II. West Pointers predominated in the company ranks, but a large proportion of the field ranks were held mostly by men who had served during the Civil War and were adjudged good enough to keep when the Regular Army was reorganized after the war. However, the nonprofessionals as a group shared in the ideals and the code that distinguished the career Army officer.

Someone signing himself "Soldier" wrote: "The majority of soldiers are forced into the Army by those genial, wholesouled qualities incompatible with the selfish ideas prevalent in civil life; and, far from being dishonorably inclined, they frequently have notions of honor approaching the absurd."[1] Major General J. M. Schofield, commanding the Military Division of the Pacific, alluded to that ideal—and the concept of honor itself—when he said in an annual report: "It is not necessary even to refer to the generally recognized high standard of honor among military men.... The Army officer holds his commission for life, or during good behavior. It embodies all he has or hopes for ... a court-martial is always ready to inflict disgrace and imprisonment for any breach of honor."[2] The carryover of the knightly ideal can be seen in the statement that "it is ... the pride of the true soldier that a brave man is generous, manly, and unselfish, devoted to works of chivalry."[3]

On the other hand, Greene, scorning "the airs of nobility" which many officers assumed, wrote:

[The Army is not] the Dorado of morality, honor and chivalry that many believe; the heart of a Sidney does not invariably beat under the Army "blue." Grand men, whom no age nor country has surpassed, are to be found on its roll ... but manly virtues and high moral worth are no oftener found in the Army than in civil life.

It is worthy of remark that the chivalrous spirit which had attained its full perfection in the Army before the Great Rebellion of 1861 is nearly extinct. . . . If a mighty change could take place in the quarter where it is most needed, the Army, although forming a body virtually cut off from the rest of the world, would constitute a society of the higher order. The present organization lacks that ambition—that *esprit de corps*—which characterized the Army prior to the war. . . . Degeneracy has been increased by the appointment of men who have not received a military education. . . . The homogeneity that should characterize the military establishment has been destroyed by the mingling of incongruous elements. The contact of the truly meritorious professionals with nonprofessionals has given rise to arrogance, and has almost annihilated the spirit of chivalry.[4]

Greene's indictment appears to have been more severe than the facts warranted, for the officers of the Old Army truly seem to have been inspired by a strict code of honor and gentlemanly conduct. Colonel James B. Fry said officers lived under both the general code

of American society and "an exacting special code."
They took care of their own delinquents, trying them
in public courts-martial, which was not true of delinquents in other professions. Higher authorities were
resented if they set aside the punishments a court-
martial had imposed. President Hayes was particularly
criticized for mitigating forty-one out of sixty court-
martial sentences of officers who had been found guilty
of drunkenness on duty, misuse of public property,
selling pay accounts to different individuals, conduct
unbecoming an officer and gentleman ("too gross,
vulgar and profane for republication"), of cruelty to
enlisted men, and other gross offenses.[5]

Beyond the concepts of honor and duty and their
ramifications—which any gentleman presumably would
understand intuitively—the code was not specified.
But it appears throughout King's novels in nuances. A
woman in one of his books declares: ". . . the rules that
held good for ordinary sinners were not applicable to
an officer of the army. *He* must be a man above suspi-
cion, incapable of wrong or fraud, and once stained he
was forever ineligible as a gentleman."[6]

The tenets of the code explain why such shock was
felt when two highly respected officers violated the code
in 1883. Lieutenant Colonel Guido Ilges, who had acquired a reputation as an Indian-fighting infantryman
against the Northern Cheyennes, was court-martialed
for having sold duplicates of his draft on the War Department for his pay account to different banks. He
was dismissed from the service. His case caused the
Army and Navy Journal to comment, "There has been a
tradition, which many accepted, that dishonor in money
matters has not been known in the service."[7] The
second scandal, involving Major Azor H. Nickerson,

who had become known as one of Crook's aides, caused a real uproar after he retired in 1882. He put his wife and child on a ship bound for Europe, with all outward display of affection. While she was gone, he obtained a divorce in Philadelphia on grounds of desertion, without informing her. She returned to find he had immediately married the daughter of his boardinghouse keeper in Washington. Thereupon she started court action in the District of Columbia to invalidate the Philadelphia divorce, obtain a genuine divorce, and acquire almost all his property. Until the court case could be resolved, the adjutant general ordered Nickerson to remain in Washington and stopped his retirement pay in the meantime. Instead of remaining in Washington, Nickerson fled to Canada. It was fully expected that he would be court-martialed, but he was allowed to resign his commission in November, 1883. When the New York *Times* asked what view the Army took of such behavior, the *Army and Navy Journal* replied:

[The Army view] is the one which must be taken by all honorable men, only that the Army feels more keenly and more nearly his disgrace because it is that of an officer high in rank and of gallant service. . . . Conduct like his can often go legally unpunished in civil life . . . but it surely brings upon an officer of the Army loss of his commission, and makes him an outcast from military society. The higher the standard of honor expected of an officer of the military service the better pleased are all honorable men who hold commissions. They want to be tested by the highest only, and they want no military associates who will not bear the test.[8]

Through the behavior of his officers and his judgment or treatment of that behavior King described several aspects of the unwritten code. For example, an officer would go to any length to protect a lady's name, even if silence should damn him.[9] It was considered a point of honor for an officer on leave to cut it short voluntarily when his regiment was ordered to the field,[10] and an officer who remained on "fancy duty" in Washington or elsewhere could not be "of the right sort" if he did not join his regiment immediately on Indian campaigns.[11] For example, the *Army and Navy Journal* reported that, "the prospects of active service in the Far West has caused Captain W. C. Rawolle, 2d Cavalry, lately on duty at Jefferson Barracks [Missouri], to relinquish this service, and he starts at once to join his troop in General [Alfred] Terry's command."[12] Honor was still so tender that officers resorted to the code duello even in the postwar era: ". . . in those benighted days of magnificent distances from the centres of civilization and the exploring grounds of reporters of the press [c. 1870-71], many a stirring row was settled without it ever being heard of beyond the limits of the garrison in which it occurred."[13] Another element of the code limited an officer's personal affairs to the concern of his regiment alone; it was bad manners for the officers of another regiment to even ask questions.[14]

But when an officer had placed himself in a bad light in garrison, he could overcome it by distinguishing himself in the field. "Nothing so quickly demolishes prejudice in garrison as prowess in the field. Not infrequently has an officer gone forth under a cloud and returned under a crown. It is so much easier to be a hero in a single fight than a model soldier through an entire season—at least it was so in the old days."[15]

Officers were expected to order their lives within the strict confines of honor and duty. Colonel George A. Forsyth said that both West Point cadets and recruits were drilled in two things above all others, honor of the service and duty.[16] Mrs. Boyd grudgingly admired that sense of duty:

> Though a sufferer all my life from army discipline, which has continually controlled my movements, yet, when chafing most against its restraints, I have admired the grand soldierly spirit which made nearly every officer uncomplainingly forego all personal comfort for the sake of duty. No one outside the army can realize what the true soldier relinquishes when he foresakes home and family for the noble cause.
>
> Every one has heard of the mad courage displayed in times of war . . . but tame submission to petty and altogether unnecessary hardships, because in the line of duty and part of a soldier's fate, is, in my opinion, far more praiseworthy.[17]

The adherence to such a strict unwritten code certainly did not derive from any aristocratic class affiliation, for officers came from predominantly middle class and rural backgrounds. A study of the 3,792 cadets admitted to West Point between 1842 and 1886 showed that 827 were sons of farmers and planters; 495, merchants; 455, lawyers and judges; 271, physicians; 263, mechanics; 246, army officers; 179, no occupation listed; 102, clergymen. The others, ranging from one to ninety-three each, were spread over sixty-two other occupations.[18] The small number of officers' sòns does not indicate the lack of an army tradition at all. On the contrary, an officer virtually lost citizenship when he put on the uniform. Unable to vote in territorial elections and lacking influence with congressmen from his home state (most officers, anyhow), he did not have a base from which his son could obtain an appointment to West Point. Some sons got to West Point through the President's appointments-at-large. Others had to take the circuitous route of enlisting, qualifying as a noncommissioned officer, and then taking one of the annual examinations for promotion from the ranks. Or he could qualify for direct commissioning from civilian life if there were vacancies to which he could be "gazetted," as the term was.

Within that group of officers—averaging slightly better than 2,000 per year for the entire Army—there were those who lived by and up to the neo-feudal standards of chivalry as well as those who were governed by a self-serving sense of personal value. Both ends of the spectrum appeared in King's characterization of officers. Again and again, he used "knightly" and "young athlete" to describe what he considered to be the better type of officer. Naturally, he used the non-chivalrous officer as the villain or as a trivial person. In between, he portrayed many different types of officers. His lack of inventiveness suggests strongly that he was forced to use as prototypes men he had known or heard of (or perhaps a composite of observed traits). Each he measured against the code which was, at base, a soldier's conception of manliness. He wrote admiringly of the officers who came up to the expectations of chivalry and contemptuously of those who did not. His Indian-fighting officers are often more believable and conceivable as human beings than the almost always competent and dedicated officers who appear in most military reminiscenses. The reason may be obvious enough; namely, that those who wrote memoirs did not see fit to mention incompetent or dishonorable officers, or to risk libel suits resulting from such candor.

Since King was not making a sociological study he did not attempt a catalog of types, but in depicting Army officers in garrison and field he made them conform exactly to a wife's recollection that officers "off duty ...

relax with the abandon of boys out of school, but, on
duty, they snap into grim-visaged, purposeful men."[19]
Picturing infantrymen around a campfire, King wrote:

> There were many types of soldier there,—men who had
> led brigades through the great war and gone back to humble
> bars of the line officer at its close; men who had led fierce
> charges against swarming Indians in the rough old days of
> the first prairie railways; men who had won distinction and
> honorable mention in hard and trying frontier service; men
> who had their faults and foibles and weaknesses like other
> men; and were aggressive or compliant, strong-willed or
> yielding, overbearing or meek as are their brethren in other
> walks of life; men who were simple of heart, single in purpose
> and ambition, diverse in characteristics, but unanimous in
> one trait—no meanness could live among them.[20]

As a cavalryman, King was much more detailed in
his vignettes of officers of horse, as in the following
selection describing "Major Stannard" and "Lieutenant
Ray":

> Typical cavalrymen are those two, who, chatting quietly
> together, are riding somewhat in advance of the returning
> companies [from drill]. The major is a man a trifle over forty,
> short, stout, with massive shoulders, chest, and thighs, a neck
> like a bull, a well-shaped head covered with straight, close-
> cropped brown hair, innocent of kink or curl; a florid face,
> bronzed and tanned by years of life in sun and wind and
> storm; clean-shaven but for the drooping brown moustache
> that conceals the rugged lines of his mouth, and twinkling
> blue-gray eyes that peer out with searching gaze from under
> their shaggy brows. Firmness, strength, self-reliance, even
> sternness, can be read in every line; but around the gathering
> crowsfeet at the corner of his eyes, and lurking under the
> shadow of the grim moustache, are little curves or dimples or
> something, that betray to the initiated the presence of a

humorous vein that softens the asperity of the soldier. Some who best know him can detect there a symptom of tenderness and a possibility of sentiment, whose existence the major would indignantly deny. The erect carriage of the head, the square set of the shoulders, the firm yet easy seat in the saddle, speak of the experienced soldier, while in the first word that falls from his lips one hears the tone of the man far more at home in camp than court. There is something utterly blunt and abrupt in his manner, a scathing contrast to the affected drawl brought into the regiment by recent importations from the East, and assiduously copied by a professed Anglomaniac among the captains. Rude indeed may he sometimes be in his speech, "and little versed in the set phrase of peace," but through it all is the ring of sturdy honesty and independence. He uses the same tone to general and private soldier alike, extending the same degree of courtesy to each. No one ever heard of "old Stannard's" fawning upon a superior or bullying an inferior; to all soldiers he is one and the same—short, blunt, quick, and to the point. Literally he obeys the orders of his chiefs, and literally and promptly he expects his own to be obeyed. He has his faults, like the best of men: he will growl at times; he is prone to pick flaws, and to say sharp and cutting things, for which he is often ashamed and sorry; he can see little good in the works or words of the men he dislikes; he absolutely cannot praise, and he is overquick to blame; but after all he is true as steel, as unswerving as the needle, and no man, no woman could need a stancher friend than the new major of the —th, "old Stannard."

As for Ray, no officer in the regiment is better known or more talked about. Ten years of his life he has spent under the standard of the —th, barring a very short but eventful detail at "the Point." Nebraska, Kansas, and Arizona he knows as well as the savannas of his native blue-grass country. He has been in more skirmishes with the regiment and more scrapes of his own than any fellow of his age in service, but he has the faculty of "lighting on his feet every time," as he himself would express it, and to-day he rides along as buoyantly and recklessly as he did ten years ago, and the saddle is Ray's home. Ephemeral pleasure he finds in the hop-room, for he dances well; perennial attraction, his detractors say, he finds at the card-table, but Ray is never quite himself until he throws his leg over the horse he loves. He is *facile princeps* the light rider of the regiment, and to this claim there are none to say him nay. A tip-top soldier too is Ray. Keen on the scout, tireless on the trail, and daring to a fault in action, and either preternaturally cool or enthusiastically excited when under fire. He is a man the rank and file swear by and love. "You never hear Loot'nant Ray saying 'Go in there, fellers.' 'Tis always, 'Come on, boys.' That's why I like him," is the way Sergeant Moriarty puts it. Among his comrades, his brother officers that is to say, opinions are divided. Ray has trusty friends and he has bitter enemies, though the latter, when charged with the fact, are prone to say that no one is so much Ray's enemy as Ray himself—an assertion which cannot be altogether denied. But as his own worst enemy Ray is thoroughly open and above-board; he has not a hidden fault; his sins are many and they are public property for all he cares; whereas the men who dislike Ray in the regiment are of the opposite stamp...Ray tolerates no slander, and let him once get wind of the fact that some man has maligned him, there is a row in the camp.[21]

However, "Ray" develops through several novels into one of King's ideal types—true cavaliers in the tradition of the Round Table—and becomes a captain, which represented the very pinnacle for a good many officers of the period. "Ray" comes onto the scene a rake, a hard drinker and gambler, but marriage changes him into a solid, dependable citizen of quiet habits. Always eager for field duty, he is "a lithe, deep-chested, square-shouldered young fellow, with nerve and spring in every motion," a picture of "elastic health and vigor."[22]

King's first example of the romanticized, ideal type

is "Jack Truscott." As a sternly military adjutant of the
"—th Cavalry," "Truscott" draws the respect if not the
affection of every other officer. He has about him a
"certain uncompromising 'hit-or-miss' way of doing
his duty." Through several novels he embodies the
spirit and nobility of the cavalier, always ready to
answer the call of duty, with an acute sense of honor
that places him above pettiness, a dignity that will
not let him defend himself against false charges, and an
absolute refusal to drag a lady's name into any unpleasant situation.[23] He also has acquired a modest
fortune through wise investments in Western mining
activities—always a nice touch in Victorian novels,
but often quite true in the West. Officers began investing in mines at least as early as the 1860's when a good
mine was known as a "Shanghai" rather than a bonanza,
a term that came into usage later.[24] In the early 1870's,
officers at Camp Verde prospected, located, and
registered mines in nearby Copper Canyon, but lost
track of them after leaving Arizona. Others, such as
Captain Frederick Eugene Trotter, Fourteenth Infantry, who had mining interests in Utah and Idaho,
were more fortunate. The great cattle boom provided
a windfall for some officers, including Lieutenant J. H.
Waters, Twentieth Infantry, who made $7,500 in one
year by investing in Texas cattle while stationed at Fort
Reno, Indian Territory.[25] Lieutenant John L. Bullis,
Twenty-fourth Infantry, acquired more than 60,000
acres in Texas, including mineral lands in the Chenati
Mountains in the Big Bend area.[26]

Among King's "favorable" characters, the naive
and young "Lieutenant Hollis" can "no more cherish
ill will or malice than Ray could save money." He
finally proves himself in combat, but deviates from the
model of the good officer: "He was brimful of life ...

a fair rider, a jolly good-natured companion, a most accomplished dancer, and leader in all social entertainments; but life to him seemed vested with no higher objects than those involved in [dances and parties]. Military duty was a necessary evil, grudgingly performed and more frequently slighted that social duties might have his utmost time."[27]

"Lieutenant Ned Perry" symbolizes something of the average. "A fairer type of the American cavalry officer, when once he got in saddle and settled down to business, one would hardly ask to find. Tall, athletic, slender of build, with frank, laughing blue eyes, curly, close-cropped, light-brown hair, and a twirling mustache that was a source of inexpressible delight to its owner and of some envy to his brother subalterns, Mr. Perry...was full to the brim of health, energy, animal spirits, and fun."[28] That same expression—brimful of energy, animal spirits, and so forth—is used to describe many of King's younger officers. Later in character-revealing action, Perry emerges as a true-blue cavalier.[29] Without obtrusive emphasis, the importance of the lush, curling "cavalry" mustache of the period is demonstrated over and over in character descriptions. "Lieutenant Brewster" also is "the very picture of stalwart, soldierly, brave-eyed manhood."[30] Such passages are too much for twentieth-century sensibilities, but the sentiments undoubtedly were those of the soldiers themselves—not just of the novelist.

"Lieutenant Hearn" possesses "that faculty, in which so many are lacking, of inspiring the men with enthusiasm and interest."[31] In these incidental remarks one perceives the problems of the Old Army in developing what the Army has come to call personal leadership. "Lieutenant Leonard," adjutant of another cavalry regiment, is a man of knowledge, erudite in his profession and strong in character. He is especially assiduous in seeing that justice be done evenhandedly.[32]

In addition to "Major Stannard," King profiled several other squadron commanders. One is "Major Mainwaring" who on occasion "burst" into the adjutant's office: "There is no other way of describing the major's method of entering a room. It has been said that he was blunt both in speech and action. A soldier for years of his life, no amount of domestic polish had ever succeeded in smoothing off the rough edges of the camp. Mainwaring prided himself on being direct in everything he said and did." There is kindness under his rugged exterior, but people who for the first time hear him speak "declared him a brute." He never says anything behind a man's back that he will not say to his face, "and the Lord only knows what he hadn't said to people's faces." He reads doggedly in an effort at self-improvement without fully understanding the novels he reads. "There were few topics that could be discussed, outside of horse-shoeing, grooming, and company kitchens, in which Mainwaring could be considered an authority, but in one and all was he disputatious, challenging the speaker to prove the words, even, as sometimes happened, when the challenged party was a woman and entitled to assert no stronger reason than 'Because.' "[33]

With others as with "Mainwaring," gallantry goes by the boards when an officer feels called upon to "put down" a woman, more definitely than the gruff major's challenge at the dinner table. Mrs. Summerhayes had two such unpleasant experiences. While stationed at Camp (later Fort) McDowell, Arizona, about 1876, she was desperate for a cook at a time when enlisted men could work for officers; when she heard that some recruits were arriving, she immediately asked if there

were any good cooks among them. Her husband's
company commander "smiled a grim smile" and asked:
"What do you think the United States Government en-
lists men for? Do you think I want my company to be
made up of dishwashers?" On another occasion, when
they had first arrived in Arizona in 1874, Mrs. Crook
told her at Fort Whipple that she was just the sort of
woman the general liked. But when she finally met him
several years later, and went out of her way to please,
Crook treated her with only "indifferent courtesy."[34]

Nor did gallantry allow officers to overlook slips
in which an uninitiated young woman might offend
their dignity. Mrs. Roe discovered that in her initial
confusion of actual and brevet rank. An act of Congress
permitted officers to be addressed by the title of the
highest rank held by them during the Civil War. When
she and her husband reported to Fort Lyon in 1871, she
as a bride and new to the Army, she learned that the
captain commanding her husband's company was called
general and the first lieutenant, major. At dinner one
evening she got so mixed up that she addressed the
"general" as mister—the form of address reserved for
lieutenants. He straightened back in his chair, and the
reactions of the others made her want to run from the
room.[35] She at least escaped the treatment described
by Greene:

> This class of officers often have the extremely bad taste
> to carry their *hauteur* into the social circle. If a lady, through
> ignorance or mistake, addresses one of them with a title below
> his rank, or gives the full rank instead of the brevet, he swells
> with emotion, and, with insolent brevity, corrects her.[36]

As a squadron commander, "Major Chrome" is "so
horribly slow that his own comrades chafed under his

command," and the regimental commander really
wants him to retire and make way for "a live man."[37]
"Lieutenant Colonel 'Black Bill' Briggs" knows "about
as much of Indian strategy as he did of Sanscrit, and
Briggs was a man that couldn't be taught."[38]

King's "unfavorable" characters are described more
precisely than his *beaux sabreurs*; it is the presence of
such a variety of types that gives his novels their realism. One such type is "Captain Canker," a "harsh and
arbitrary" troop commander who is "a martinet in his
way, and a man whom a little brief authority would
transform into a nuisance." He is "one of those peculiar
company commanders (and there are many who in this
respect strongly resemble him) by whom the subalterns
attached to his troop are regarded as a species of personal property." He never gets along with any of his
lieutenants, is disliked by almost everybody in the
regiment, and is always a faultfinder. A former infantry
officer, he thinks the transfer to the cavalry has made
him an authority on horses and horsemanship. "Profound discretion in the selection of his 'mounts' had
enabled him thus far to escape the ignominy of a 'throw,'
but he never rode or could ride a horse twenty-five
miles without laying that horse up chafed and sore for
days afterward, yet he was incessantly punishing his
men for faulty horsemanship." But when faced with a
call to action, "Canker" becomes a man of decision, a
leader with "a soldierly ring in every word" and a
"bearing that commanded the respect" of officers and
troopers alike.[39]

During the troop drill of the morning Mr. Ray, dismounting his men for a five minutes' rest after a half-hour of
sharp exercise, was occupying himself in a comparison of the
different company commanders. Well over to the west of the

plain Captain Turner's chestnut sorrels and Tanner's bright bays were having an enlivening, though impromptu competitive drill. It was pretty generally conceded that these two troops were very evenly matched, and, except among the partisans of other companies, it was as generally agreed that they were much ahead of the rest of the regiment in point of snap and style in drill. Both captains were fine instructors and individually liked and respected by their men; whereas Canker, who really had enjoyed finer opportunities for keeping his men up to a moderate degree of proficiency, never could succeed in making anything out of them. He studied hard, he worked faithfully, he even furtively watched the methods of such officers as Tanner and Truscott, and strove to profit by what he learned in this way; but the cavalry officer is born, not made; and, handicapped as he was with the disadvantages of a bad seat, a bad hand, and a very bad temper, Canker found it all up-hill work. He had fine material in his company, but was desperately unpopular among them, so much so that none would re-enlist with him on the expiration of their terms of service, but would 'take on,' as they expressed it, with other troops, notably Tanner's and Turner's. Ray's, too, was a favorite command since he had been placed in charge; but its captain, now on recruiting service, had been very inefficient, and since his departure much of its time had been spent in mountain-scouting, where drills were unknown and discipline lax. It was Canker's habit, when betrayed into speaking of the matter at all, to say that 'the secret of the superiority of Tanner's company was that he got his best men from me;' but in the depths of his heart he knew that statement to be absurd. It did not help him much to hear, as he did hear, in the inexplicable way in which such things are brought to our ears... that his men said that all they needed to make them the best-drilled troop in the —th was to have a captain who was capable of teaching them something. Altogether, drill-time was a sort of purgatory to both officers and men in Canker's troop.[40]

An officer of different stripe, "Captain Cranston"

appears to have been the middling sort of professional officer. But as a man he is unafraid to put his head on the block to obtain justice for another. "Cranston" walks with a stiff gait which is the result of a Civil War wound but which the uninformed mistake for "military hauteur." Another common officer is "Captain Curran," mentioned in passing as an "easy-going old dragoon, and for years before his retirement it was an open secret that his first sergeant 'ran the troop' to suit himself and that the captain never permitted his subalterns to interfere."[41]

Also in this middling group is "Captain Rolfe," about thirty-five years old, with a "thick, heavy, and curling" mustache sweeping from his upper lip.[42] He has about him an imperious air that causes the regimental adjutant to say: "I respect his ability, but damn his egotism. Rolfe in this regiment is just like the one juror who said they could long ago have agreed on conviction but for the eleven blooming idiots who held out for acquittal."[43] As a "stern, self-willed commander," he has a touch of the arrogant.

It chafed [Lieutenant Brewster], however, to note that Rolfe, in that calmly superior way of his, was pressing on into [Brewster's quarters], as much as to say, 'It is my will that you give up what you have in view and attend at once to my behest,' just as though Brewster were still his second lieutenant, instead of First Lieutenant Brewster commanding the 'Black Horse' troop. It must be confessed that there was about Rolfe an intangible something that ever seemed to give that impression to the juniors. It was one of the things that set their teeth on edge . . . and set them against him.[44]

Abrasive and dishonorable officers appear in King's books. One is "Captain Devers" who seems to have been based on a cavalry officer whom King described in his nonfiction book *Campaigning with Crook.* During the 1876 campaign, Lieutenant Colonel W. B. Royall ordered the unnamed officer to put his troops in camp on the other side of a river, facing east.

A prominent and well-known characteristic of the subordinate officer referred to was a tendency to split hairs, discuss orders, and, in fine, to make trouble where there was a ghost of a chance of so doing unpunished. Presently the Colonel saw that his instructions were not being carried out, and, not being in a mood for indirect action, he put spurs to his horse, dashed through the stream, and reined up alongside the victim with, "Didn't I order you, sir, to put your battalion in camp along the river—facing east?"

"Yes, sir; but this ain't a river. It's only a creek."

"Creek be d——d, sir! It's a river—a river from this time forth, *by order,* sir. Now do as I tell you."[45]

Such wrongheadedness, endowed upon "Devers," became the basis of an entire novel, *Under Fire.* "Devers" is so contrary that superior officers warn each other that he is the "trickiest" of subordinates, with the result that he is usually assigned to one- and two-company posts. That suits him exactly, although he could have been one of the most valuable officers in service "if he devoted to obeying an order one-tenth the energy he throws into finding a way to avoid it."[46]

One of Devers's idiosyncrasies was a hatred of doing things as anybody else did them. This in a service where absolute uniformity was expected was prolific of no end of chaffing. In every garrison where his troop was stationed he had become notorious. If the other companies turned out in white gloves at retreat, Devers's would come in gauntlets. When dress parade, dismounted, was ordered ... one mild November evening, he marched his men out in arctics and fur caps, and claimed that to be the proper full dress for the season.[47]

King's own spleen may have been vented in making so much of "Devers" as a dissenter, for he had had abundant and irritating experiences with company commanders who preferred to go their own way. That was particularly true in the winter of 1876-77 when the Fifth was headquartered at Fort D. A. Russell, he as adjutant and the regiment being whipped back into disciplined form after long months of field service and separation in different posts. Writing autobiographically and referring to himself as "Mr. X.," King described the difficulty of obtaining uniformity:

> ...the adjutant was as intent on the "setting up" of the six companies on duty at headquarters as was the colonel himself, and thought [delinquent paperwork for the long summer campaign of 1876] a somewhat secondary consideration to getting the men (and officers) up to a thorough tactical proficiency.
>
> It was gall and wormwood to his soul to mark the slouchy carriage of the men, their clumsy salute, and the utter lack of steadiness in their ranks. It was exasperating to see the blunders of the non-commissioned officers for the first week of guard-mounting, and with all his might he started in to straighten things out. His theory was, that in order to get the men up to the standard the non-commissioned officers must be thoroughly instructed, but the colonel held the captains responsible for this, and, as bad luck would have it, every captain had individual ideas of his own to instil into the minds of his sergeants, as a consequence of which six totally different systems prevailed; each captain thought his the best, and was fiercely jealous of anything that savored of interference.
>
> The colonel required weekly reports from his company

commanders of the proficiency of their non-commissioned officers, and established a system of marks by which he could judge of their relative merit. This seemed all right to the one West Pointer among the captains, was looked upon as a nuisance by some of the others, and absolutely denounced by one of the very best company commanders in the regiment, on the ground that "it reflected on the intelligence and faithfulness of the captain to require a report from him." It was simply marvelous to see into how many meanings the simple language of the tactics [which corresponded to modern *Field Manuals*] could be distorted, and how obstinately the adherent of each particular interpretation maintained the correctness of his theory. The recitations of the officers to the colonel had developed the fact that, as a rule, the higher the rank the less the knowledge of the subject; but then, as Captain Canker remarked, "These West Pointers retain their school-boy habits, while we men who were educated in the school of war itself are not accustomed to this sort of nursery talk."[48]

The presence of a Captain Canker in both fiction and autobiography speaks for itself, but the important insight afforded by King's work is that of an Old Army in which the wide dispersal of troops resulted in various and independent ways of doing things. Seldom were all troops or companies of a given regiment at the same post or on the same campaign. The officers had a job to do and each did it as he saw fit. King had an interesting explanation for that when he addressed officers of the Wisconsin National Guard in 1883. He said Guard officers knew the fine points of tactics better than did Regulars because an officer on the frontier had to devote his full time to making his company steady, soldierly, united on parade, good at skirmishing, and precise in company movements. Hence, they paid "little or no attention . . . to 'points.'"[49] Their duty was getting a professional job done, not looking good in minor parade-ground maneuvers.

Manipulating "Devers" as a fictional character, King illuminates a bit more of the officers' code. With a simulation of the "Horsemeat March" as the background, "Devers" willfully misinterprets an order in such a way that he sends a lieutenant with a small detachment into an ambush in which "Devers" can not support him. The lieutenant is wounded and his men killed. Unknown to the fevered lieutenant, "Devers" slips out of responsibility by writing a report which lays the blame on the younger officer. Months later, an investigation shows "Devers" to have been at fault. All along he demands a quick trial, once he is arrested and ordered before a General Court-Martial, thinking that a trial can not be held for months. When it comes quickly, he slips away, resigns under fire, and has the resignation accepted in Washington through political influence. His regiment is infuriated. Returning to the East, "Devers" becomes a colonel on a governor's staff. Some years later, he finagles his congressman into introducing a bill that will restore him to the Army — a not frequent but not unheard of maneuver at the time. The officers of the regiment immediately send a remonstrance to the House military affairs committee, and the bill is dropped. At that point a young officer adds a verse to a popular ditty in which the last line is "the accent is on" a syllable in the preceding line. He and the other officers sing it thus:

> We had a cap in our corps
> Who left us years ago,
> Who never said a manly word
> Nor struck a manly blow.

He never faced when he could dodge,
He only spoke to slur
And now he is a colonel
But the accent's on the cur.[50]

"Captain Buxton" may typify many officers of the
Old Army. "A good soldier in some respects, Captain
Buxton bore the reputation of having an almost un-
governable temper at times, of being at times brutally
violent in his language and conduct towards his men,
and, worse yet, of bearing ill-concealed malice, and
'nursing his wrath to keep it warm' against such of his
enlisted men as had ever ventured to appeal for
justice." His prejudice against one man causes him to
punish the man—who is guilty of nothing—by making
him walk and lead his horse in the rear of a column
moving across the Arizona desert. "Buxton" is always
harsh in his treatment of all inferiors. Never losing "a
chance to make an ass of himself" in any situation, he
has a marked idiosyncrasy—talking about European
wars when his scant education makes it impossible for
him to get century, general, and place right.[51]
    "Buxton" would seem to fit Greene's descriptions of
officers who treated enlisted men as dirt, or as machines.
"Officers of this class," Greene wrote, "are invariably
deficient in soldierly instincts. They never assume responsibility for the mistakes in which a lack of military
knowledge constantly involves them, but audaciously
charge it to their subalterns, or their men."[52]
    King's blackguards, however, are not cast as op-
pressors of enlisted men. Rather, they reveal themselves
in dishonest and contemptible behavior. Dissolute officers, for instance, are always treated with contempt in
his works, and then passed over. His most consummate
blackguard is the gray-bearded "Lieutenant Gleason"

who proves to be a coward, who both fawns upon and attempts to browbeat the wives of other officers, and tries to frame an officer for his own embezzling as a member of a horse board, a detail of officers who bought cavalry remounts. "Gleason" devotes entire nights to poker, but the officers of his regiment will not play with him. As a general theme, though, the real blackguards, novel after novel, appear among enlisted men who were fit only for treason, stratagems, and spoils.[53]

The seriousness of alcoholism among officers came into King's books, but was not overly emphasized. He pinpointed a common problem through a passing reference to a captain who was a perennial drunkard and always did something "disreputable" when drunk. It happens once too often, and he is to be court-martialed, with the sentence a foregone conclusion this time. Somewhat sadly, King describes him as a man who rose from the ranks of the prewar Regular Army to command his regiment during the Civil War.

Many officers were, in truth, court-martialed for drunkenness, some being cashiered and others punished by fine or suspension from rank for varying periods. Greene complained, however, that the "impunity of alcoholism in the Army" caused a number of them to go scot-free through a remission of the court-martial sentence by higher authority. One poor devil caught it coming and going. A senior captain at Fort McKinney, Wyoming, he was charged with conduct unbecoming an officer and gentleman for beating his wife while drunk; for good measure, his commander also charged him with conduct unbecoming an officer for having lived with such a woman anyhow, but the department commander struck out the latter charge.[54]

Above the company and battalion levels, King dealt with some of the junior officers' resentment in his depictions of regimental and post commanders. That is, the sound and praiseworthy officer is revealed through a series of actions, whereas the "unfavorable" types were succinctly identified as such. He wrote that "the unbiased testimony of the subalterns and even the troop commanders of every cavalry regiment in service would go far towards establishing the fact that all colonels of cavalry [have] some peculiarities of temperament and disposition."[55] Beyond that, however, his cavalry colonels were always men of wisdom, common sense, dash, self-sacrifice, devotion to the good of the regiment, and justice, such as "Colonel Atherton."[56]

Conversely, his infantry colonels are often types of officers he obviously disliked. One is "Colonel Whaling," commanding officer of Fort D. A. Russell in 1876, whom he tags an "office soldier."

> His theory of success was founded on common sense; take care of your health, avoid dissipation, shun any and all danger, volunteer for nothing, do only what you are compelled to do, shift all possible work on somebody else's shoulders, preserve a purely negative record, and—you are bound to rise to the highest grades in the Army.[57]

A similar type is "Colonel 'Pegleg' Stone" who "was essentially a 'red-tape' soldier,—one who knew the regulations and recognized nothing else, [and who] made in busier times his own life and those of his officers something of a burden."[58]

As an ingrained field soldier himself, King understandably bathed the "carpet knight" with abuse. Whether designated as carpet knight, ballroom soldier or wire-puller, this type of officer—either unfit for field service or using family and political influence to obtain easy assignments in Washington or other Eastern

94

cities—especially irked King. Once there, they could display gold braid and brass buttons to awed young ladies. During the years immediately after the Civil War, "friends at court had more to do with a fellow's sphere of duty—very much more—than had the regimental commander or even the adjutant-general." And once in Washington a soldier learned that "an ounce of influence is worth a pound of pure record."[59] King made a major character of only one carpet knight, "Lieutenant Gordon Noel," whom he paints in bright yellow. Throughout the book, "Noel" proves to be a social parasite, an outright phony, and an officer who exaggerates physical complaints and uses family political influence to escape combat duty. A well-dressed officer certainly was not necessarily a carpet knight, but one who paid attention to his dress and/or the caparisoning of his horse was a "Dandy Jack" or a "swell" to soldiers.[60]

An unwitting self-portrait of a carpet knight can be found in the memoirs of Lieutenant Colonel O. L. Hein which would have been better titled "The Many Parties I Attended and the Prominent Society People I Knew." He was a wire-puller. In 1880, for instance, he wanted to be detailed to recruiting duty in St. Louis. Having come from an influential family in Georgetown, he used an old friend, Miss Margaret Edes, to obtain an invitation to the home of Secretary of War Robert Lincoln. That got him the St. Louis detail. Later, he wangled diplomatic posts.[61]

The injustice of influence in an institution which should have treated all officers evenhandedly was excoriated by the editor of the San Francisco *Report* who wrote, "Maybe politics and money have the say in England; they certainly have here."[62] As much as the tart Mrs. Summerhayes hated Arizona and wanted out, she could say, "But then, while I half-envied the wives of the wire-pullers, I took a sort of pride in the blind obedience shown by my own particular soldier to the orders he received."[63] It was the tanned, grizzled Indian campaigner, obeying the orders he received and living the soldier's life as the fates might dictate, who dominated King's heroic picture of the Army.

However, King was contemptuous of former infantry officers who "were saddled upon the cavalry and artillery" when the Army was reorganized in 1871, and thus probably reflected the basic attitudes of cavalrymen who, traditionally, held themselves above other fighting men. Indeed, it was the cavalry's historic role as an aristocratic branch that kept Congress from creating cavalry regiments as such before the 1850's. In reflecting their attitudes, King has a cavalry major express it thus: "those infantry fellows showed profound discrimination in getting rid of their chaff, but they had no mercy on us. When a man ain't good enough for a doughboy officer, he ain't fit for anything."[64] Explaining the significance of the consolidation of 1871, King said, "several score of semi-invalided and semi-mustered-out footmen, dozens of whom had never straddled a horse in their lives (and to this day are objects of wonderment to their men when they 'get into the saddle'), became full-fledged cavalry officers"[65]

The only mercy King shows those awkward misfits is in his description of "Lieutenant Bucketts," regimental quartermaster of the "—th Cavalry," who faces up to the cavalry rule that an officer must pay forfeit with a basket of champagne the first time he is thrown,[66] and immediately wins friends because of his honesty. "Bucketts" has been a colonel during the war, and has then accepted a commission in the infantry. With the consolidation, he has come to the "—th" as an aging and rheumatic second lieutenant. When he joins the regiment in Nebraska, his baggage consists of one trunk and three baskets of champagne. "'Gentlemen,' said he, 'I understand that a cavalry officer who is thrown has to set up the wine for the crowd. The law of the land has made me a cavalryman, but all the Congressmen from the Capitol to John Chamberlin's couldn't make me a horseman. There's my credentials [the champagne]: pitch in, and let up on me hereafter!' Bucketts was a popular man from that day."[67] As a superb horseman himself, King could be expected to look down on converted footmen and sneer at their efforts to ride, but Mrs. Custer thought—and indicated the entire Seventh thought—it hilarious when the new cavalry officers tried to learn how to stay on a horse, and that all concerned took it in good humor.[68]

The ideal horseman appears as "Lieutenant Ray": "The erect carriage, the perfect seat, the ease and grace with which his lithe form swayed with every motion of his steed, all present could see at a glance."[69] A character who is of any importance whatsoever comes in for a critical appraisal of his horsemanship. For instance, King refers to "Lieutenant Dana's...graceful, easy seat" and "Major Mainwaring's" good "if bulky horsemanship."[70] To proclaim a cavalry officer a good horseman was among the highest accolades King could bestow. He observed in passing, however, that it was more difficult for most men to acquire a light, gentle hand on the rein than to acquire a good seat.[71] A more explicit description of the cavalry seat came from Mrs. Roe who had learned to ride in the East but who was re-educated by cavalry officers at Fort Lyon. "I ride the army way,

97

tight in the saddle, which is more difficult to learn. Any attempt to 'rise' when on a trot is ridiculed at once here, and it does look absurd after seeing the splendid and graceful riding of the officers."[72]

King's general description of Army officers as trim, athletic, and filled with energy and good health is supported by an actuarial study. At the request of an insurance company in 1886, the *Army and Navy Journal* made the study which showed a surprisingly low mortality rate among officers—.017 per year for the period 1865-86.[73]

Their professional ability drew praise from a French author who accompanied Carl Schurz on a tour of the Far West. He found American officers superior to the ordinary run of European officers in manners and general information. "Discipline is very severe," he reported.[74]

Good, bad, and indifferent, the officers of the Old Army had that camaraderie which marks any group of healthy men with common purpose. The scene below is set in the Black Hills at the end of Crook's "Horsemeat March," where the "—th Cavalry" is in camp awaiting orders. "Lieutenant Ray" is en route with 400 recruits and over 400 horses to the cavalry command that has been forced to eat many of its horses on the tiring march from the Little Missouri. Word of his approach is carried to camp by "Lieutenant Blake," whose jesting nonsense both delights and baffles his comrades.

And it is an old friend who, laughing, joyous and jovial, is greeting man after man with hearty handshake and jubilant hail. He has the voice of a stentor, has Blake, and the legs of a spider; . . . A dozen yards away are two trim orderlies, dismounted and holding their own horses and those of [Blake and a young officer who has accompanied him]; and it is the sight of these fat, sleek, beautifully-groomed sorrels, such marvellous contrast to the hundreds of gaunt, famished steeds herded along the valley, that bring these born cavalry-men in admiring throngs about them.

"Got any more sorrels like these, Blake?" shouts Gregg in his resounding barytone. "Just what I want for my troop!"

"Ay, marry, that we have! and bays for Freeman and chestnuts for Turner. Ray's been parcelling out their paces all the way up, and every mother's son of them steps like a four-year-old and shines like satin."

"What ho, bully rook!" he shouts, . . . as he steps quickly forward . . . to greet Captain Wayne, who, with Wilkins trailing behind, comes panting up the slope. "What are these, so withered, and so wild in their attire?"

"Did you bring plenty of bays, Legs? I want to say right here that if I don't get first choice there'll be a row."

"Thou Mars of malcontents! Listen to him now," laughs Blake. "Not so much as a 'how do you do?' for me, and nothing but anxiety for horseflesh. You old hippophagist! you've been living on it long enough this summer to need a change."

"I never ate a mouthful of it," protests Wayne, wrathfully. "I'd sooner eat my boots."

"Well, what did you live on? Have you been sucking your paws like a hibernating bear?"

"I've lived on the hope of seeing my troop mounted on new horses, nothing else," says Wayne, throwing himself down on the turf. "Legs, you look too swell for one of us. I don't mean your legs, man; when I say legs, I mean you."

"Thou dost belie me, Wayne! 'Tis but the combined effect of living in such high latitudes and on such low diet. A summer in Cheyenne, with such companionship as ours, would physic a Falstaff. Wait till we're back in Kansas this winter, and I'll show you a pair of legs Adonis might sigh for."

Just at sunset on the following day, and in a valley deeper, narrower, more romantic than that in which the command was camped at dawn, two long columns of horse have halted and are busily unsaddling and pitching their tents for the night. The column from the south is the big detachment of recruits led by Lieutenant Ray, and around him the officers of the regiment gather for hours, and many a rough-looking trooper, too, has hovered about until he could catch the lieutenant's eye, and then, encouraged by the kindly gleam of recognition, has come forward to salute the young soldier whose name is on every cavalryman's lips this night [for having distinguished himself in battle earlier in the summer], and to be rewarded by a cordial shake of the hand. It is late in the cool, star-lit evening before most of the party seek their blankets, and Stannard and Jack Truscott, though they have been with Ray since the previous afternoon,—having ridden forth to meet him at the Gap,—are among the last to go. Blake's voice is heard declaiming a general good-night to the —th over among the tents, and his elocution just now is of that spasmodic and uncertain character which must be expected of a man who is compelled to dodge the boots and repel the insinuations hurled at him from every tent-door within range. It is true that the —th has had to eat some of its horses to keep alive, but the regiment is sensitive upon the subject, and Blake's effusion is conceded to be even worse in taste than the scanty breakfasts of September. But he rants on:

> "Good-night, I have to say good-night
> To such a host of howling swells.
> Good-night unto this famished band,
> All scrawny with—

"Confound you, Wayne! Take your spurs off your boots before you sling them at me again.

> "Good-night to Freeman's beauteous bays,
> Good-night to chestnut sorrels dear,
> Good-night unto those luscious steaks
> And all the feeders nestled here.
> This jovial band detains me? then
> I'll have to say good-night again."

Groans and objurgations come from every side; but he persists:

"Sleep well, comrades mine; may dreams of horse-flesh, breed no night-mares. Wilkins, get thee to bed. If thou venturest forth in stocking feet again, thou'lt catch thy death o' cold. Thou art more than half hoarse, now. Thou'lt be a living chevaux-de-frise. Nay, it boots not what you sling," he laughs, as he stoops and picks up the nearest foot-gear and hurls it at the advancing Wilkins. "A thousand more mischances than this one have learned me how to brook this patiently. List, list, oh, list!" he declaims, as he backs cautiously away.

But here a dash from half a dozen tents and volley of boots and billingsgate drives the disturber of the peace from camp, and, pursued until out of range by missiles of every imaginable kind, he comes laughing and leaping in wildest spirits to the camp-fire where Truscott, Ray, and Stannard are still chatting, and throws himself panting upon the buffalo robe.

"Upon my soul, Blake, you're more a ranter every day of your life," says the major.[75]

A duplicate in miniature of King's description is to be found in Mrs. Gibson's recollection of the Seventh Cavalry in camp near Fort Lincoln in 1874. The good-natured kidding and grumbling by officers at bedtime exactly matches the descriptions of Blake's antics and raillery (but without the contrived play on words). The same kind of banter marked her first night at her sister's home in Fort Lincoln. Immediately after taps, Lieutenant Benjamin Hodgson entered, and Mollie McIntosh chided, "Good heavens, Benny, can't you keep out of this house?" Hodgson claimed he wanted to be the first to welcome her sister, but Mrs. McIntosh insisted all he really wanted was some of her maid's cooking.[76]

Along with camaraderie went intragroup tensions that derived from rank stratifications, personality conflicts, jealousies, and contempt. Forms of address indicated a man's standing. Customarily, frontier comrades greeted one another with slaps on the back and "old fellow." Formally, a lieutenant—of whatever age or time in service—was addressed as "Mister." But the use or absence of that title told a great deal about his place. A superior officer might use the officer's last name, or his first name, but when he addressed the subaltern as Mister, it was a "well-understood barrier to all army intimacy." By the same token, when a subaltern "is 'mistered' by his comrades [of the same rank], it simply means that he is not one of them," and that they have gotten "his equation down fine," Army slang for taking a man's measure. When an officer proved impossible as a man, he was referred to as "that man Gleason," for example.[77]

Cliques also formed, with "Canker, Crane, Wilkins and others of that ilk" forming the sorehead group through several novels. On campaign, lieutenants "Crane" and "Wilkins" consort more with "Canker" than with the other captains, "and then there is the jolly element that ever clusters around Blake, whose spirits defy adversity, and whose merry quips and jests and boundless distortions of fact or fancy are the joy of the regiment. With Blake one always finds Merrill and Freeman and some of the jovial junior captains, and, of course, the boys,—Hunter, Dana, Briggs."[78]

Other manifestations of group tensions appear, such as the remark that the second in command of a regiment "is rarely, if ever, thoroughly *en rapport* with the colonel."[79] Such a schism is entirely understandable in an Army where promotion was so slow that officers coldly calculated their chances of promotion in terms of the death of their best friends. One officer, who had been ill for some time, was astounded when he saw his name crossed off a roster in which a friend was estimating his own chances of promotion.[80] It was not unusual for a man to wear a lieutenant's shoulder strap for twenty years or more, growing gray as a file-closer (one who marched in the rear to keep troops closed up). That was the case with Mrs. Summerhayes' husband who spent twenty-two years as a lieutenant because promotion in the Eighth Infantry "had been at a standstill for years" until President Cleveland opened it up a bit, in this case by promoting Summerhayes to captain and transferring him to the Quartermaster's Department.[81] Jealousy over promotion may have accounted for what King shows as resentment, by mediocre officers, of young lieutenants who read—"boning up to be a general," they called it.[82] That long time in rank could become wearing in other ways. King has a veteran captain explain to a lieutenant that there are officers "who find it very easy to make their juniors' lives a burden to them, and without overstepping a regulation."[83] Transfer was one way out of such a situation, which young Lieutenant Roe took at Camp Supply in 1873 because of unspecified difficulties with his company commander.[84]

Regimental politics also produced conflicts. The following autobiographical selection, from a novel, reveals the tensions surrounding King's appointment as adjutant of the Fifth Cavalry. For literary purposes, he compressed time and modified circumstances. That is, King (Billings, below) became adjutant officially on October 5, 1876, after having served as acting adjutant since the previous July, whereas Lieutenant Walter S. Schuyler (Stryker, below) was detached from the Fifth to serve as Crook's aide in June of that year. He also changed the setting; he became adjutant at Fort D. A. Russell, but here places the scene at a Kansas post where the lieutenant colonel has just assumed command of the regiment. Even if it is not fully autobiographical, the selection can be read as illustrative of post tensions.

A new era had dawned on the —th; the staff sent in their resignations, and were promptly and pleasantly notified by the new commander that he hoped they would not deprive him of services that had been so valuable to his predecessor; whereat they resumed duty with lighter hearts. It was all well enough where Bucketts was concerned; he had been quartermaster for years and no one expected anything else, but there were those in the regiment who hoped there might be a change in the adjutancy. The office was held by one of the senior lieutenants, to be sure, and one who possessed many qualifications which were conceded, but his appointment had been something of an accident.

He, too, had come into the —th by transfer in '71 for the avowed purpose of seeking service on the Western frontier with the cavalry. As it was the artillery which he abandoned for that purpose, the —th admitted that here was a fellow who might be worth having, but, to the scandal of the entire regiment, no sooner was the order issued which doomed them to a five years' exile in Arizona—then overrun with hostile Apaches—than the newly transferred gentleman accepted a detail as aide-de-camp on the staff of a general officer, and the —th went across to the Pacific and presently were lost to recollection in the then inaccessible wilds of that marvellous Territory. Here they spent four long years of hard scouting, hard fighting, and no little suffering, while the aide in question was presumably enjoying himself in unlimited ball and opera in a gay Southern capital. Suddenly he turned up in their midst just in time to take part in the closing campaign which left the Apaches for several years a disarmed and subjugated race; he happened to get command of a well-seasoned and thoroughly experienced "troop," and through no particular personal merit, but rather by the faculty he had of seeking the advice of the veteran sergeants in the company, he had won two or three lively little fights with wandering bands of hostiles, and had finally been quite enviably wounded. It was all a piece of his confounded luck, said some of the —th not unnaturally. Many a gallant fellow had been killed and buried, many another wounded and not especially mentioned, and all of them had done months of hard work where Billings had put in only so many days, but here he came at the eleventh hour, and they, who had borne the heat and burden of the campaign and received every man his penny, couldn't help a few good-natured slings at the fact that Billings' penny was just as big and round as theirs. The department commander had been close at hand every time that fortunate youth came in from a scout, and even Ray, who was incessantly seeking the roughest and most dangerous service, could not repress a wistful expression of his views when he heard of the final scrimmage far up towards Chevelon's Fork. "Here we fellows have been bucking against this game for nigh onto four years now, and if ever we raked in a pile it's all been ante'd up since, and now Billings comes in fresh—never draws but he gets a full hand—and he scoops the deck. He has too much luck for a white man." The remark was one that, said by Ray himself in his whimsical and downright manner, was destitute of any hidden meaning, and Billings, who had not seen Ray for years, would never have misunderstood it, but when he first heard it six months afterwards, and while Ray and himself had yet to meet, it was told semi-confidentially, told as Ray never said it, told in fact—by Gleason; and Billings, who was of a nervous, sensitive disposition, as outspoken in a way as Ray was in his, was hurt more than a little. He had known Ray a dozen years before when both were wearing the gray as cadets at the Point, but they were in different classes and by no means intimate. Each, however, had cordially liked the other, and Billings would have been slow to believe the statement as told him for a single instant except for two things,—one was that Gleason was a new acquaintance of whom up to that time he knew nothing really discreditable; the other was that just before the regiment came East from Arizona the adjutancy became vacant. . . . Billings was brought in wounded and sent off by sea to San Francisco as soon as he could travel . . . and when, some months later, he rejoined the regiment in Kansas, it was with much mental perturbation that he received from "Old Catnip" [nickname for Colonel Pelham] the offer of the still vacant adjutancy.

Most of the senior lieutenants were on detached service when they came in from Arizona. Everybody thought Stryker would get the detail as soon as he returned from abroad, whither he had gone on leave after making, as mountain scout leader, the best four years' record in the regiment; but Stryker came just as Billings did, and to Billings, not Stryker, was the adjutancy tendered. What made the regiment indignant was, that so far from being in the least put out about it, Stryker placidly remarked that Billings was the very man for the place. "He isn't entitled to it," said the —th; "in ten years' service he hasn't spent ten months with us." But Stryker did not see fit to tell them what he knew and the colonel knew,—that he had been tendered and had accepted the position of aide-de-camp to his old Arizona chief, and was daily awaiting orders to join; and Ray was off scouting with his troop when Billings reached headquarters, and had to face, as he supposed, an opposition . . . Pelham and Stannard knew that it *had* to be Billings or a second lieutenant, but Billings had at first no such intimation. Possibly his strong sense of self-esteem might have stood in the way of acceptance had he supposed that he was merely a last resort. . . .[85]

The officers of the Old Army stand out in great detail but the enlisted men rest in shadow. The fact that enlisted men serve only as a backdrop in most of King's writing can be taken as an indication of their lowly status and lack of individual worth in the eyes of officers, or it might simply be that the conventions of the day did not tolerate a romance of fineness and delicacy among the *hoi polloi*. Irish and German immigrants predominate among his troopers, introduced through rather weak efforts to portray their accents.[86]

As a type rather than as personalities, the non-commissioned officers are treated with more respect. "Old sergeants gave the tone to younger soldiers in all the customs of the service." During the Arizona campaigns, sergeants held almost despotic powers over their men but seldom abused them. Stern, rude of speech, they were respected by both officer and trooper. Sometimes the "old war-worn sergeants would be a trifle supercilious with green subalterns."[87]

The type of non-commissioned officer most familiar to the rank and file as well as to their superiors was the old-fashioned "plains-raised," "discipplin furst and rayson aftherwards" ... Brave to rashness and faithful to the very death, they had reason to look for respect and appreciation. They were men whose only education was that picked up in the camps and campaigns of the famous old regiments to which, when mere recruits, they had been assigned. They were invaluable in the army, and would have been utterly misjudged out of their element anywhere else.[88]

When a man enlisted, he "took the blanket"—an American variation of the English phrase, "taking the shilling." After a very brief period in recruit depots where he received little if any training, the recruit was dispatched to regiments where he was known as a "Johnny Raw." There, the "new men must take a great deal of bullying from the elders,... it was purposely done to try their temper and test their sense of subordination."[89] Throughout, though, King shows the enlisted man as being crisp and soldierly in adhering to military courtesy. A mounted trooper throws his carbine over his shoulder and dismounts before addressing an officer, and, if King is to be believed, the use of the nautical "ay, ay, sir," was common in the Old Army.[90] The men addressed each other as "fellers." With the common American assumption of superiority, King called them the best skirmishers in the world, although he had never observed foreign armies.[91] Otherwise, not much could be expected from a man who was willing to labor for thirteen dollars a month. Enlisted men —living a life of penury and deprivation—caused much trouble at payday. "Runagates"—those who did not come back from town after being on pass—had to be hunted down by a detail that searched for them in "groggeries, gambling hells and brothels ... being abused and insulted by slatternly women and bar-room loafers."[92]

When a man left the service he received a discharge without the gradations known in today's Army. But there was what amounted to a dishonorable discharge, too. At the bottom of the discharge paper, space was provided for the company commander to comment on the man's character. He had either to make a comment or cut off that part of the discharge paper, causing a man without a character endorsement to be known as a "bobtail."[93]

Understandably, noncommissioned officers were distrustful of men they suspected of having been "bobtails" or deserters. For many men enlisted more than once under assumed names. King was certain there were many false names in the 400 recruits who reenforced the cavalry column at Fort Robinson at the end of the 1876 campaign.[94] He may have been right. One of the champions of re-enlistment and desertion under an assumed name was one who enlisted as John Lamb in the Fifth Cavalry in 1876 and deserted in

1877; enlisted as John L. Potter in the Fifteenth Infantry in 1878 and deserted in 1880; enlisted as Steven
K. Fletcher in the Third Artillery in 1883 and deserted in 1884; enlisted as John A. Lamb in the Eighth
Cavalry in 1884, deserted in April 1886, was apprehended two days later, escaped two weeks later, and was
again apprehended within two days.[95]

King accurately portrayed one of the more insidious
traits of enlisted life when he wrote that a sergeant
would lend a soldier three dollars and expect five
dollars in repayment.[96] During the intense self-search-
ing that swept through the Army in the mid-1880's a
writer who signed himself "N. O. 'Shylock,'" then
stationed at Fort Concho, said first sergeants loaned
money at twenty-five and even fifty per cent interest.
"The men who borrow are the 1st sergeant's pets, and
when they commit themselves, instead of being tried
as others are, they are let off by his influence, for
should their pay be stopped by a G.C.M. he would be
the loser."[97]

If an enlisted man distinguished himself, or prepared for it, he could look toward a commission. Regulations provided that a noncommissioned officer could
be commissioned after passing a series of examinations, with the final one being held at a stated time for
all applicants each year.[98] King was within the bounds
of realism when he had his enlisted men commissioned
for gallantry.

In summary, the men of the Old Army were the
varied mixture that is to be expected in any organization with a nondifferentiated population. But only in
the reportorial passages of King's novels do both warts
and halos show.

4.
The Garrison as Family

In the isolation and monotony of frontier service, it was expected that the garrison of any post be "like a big family." This ideal clearly was put forth with only officers and their families in mind. The necessary gulf between officer and enlisted man prevented its ever being attained as stated. Even within the officers' circle alone, the ideal was never attained universally. Whether a family spirit did come to exist in a given post seems to have depended on the size of the post as well as the personalities. That is to say, the family spirit seems to have been the product of interaction within a group large enough to sustain it as desirable and without undue strain, but not so large as to impose constraints nor so small as to create barriers when the members of the group were incompatible. The optimum size may have been a medium-sized post of four to eight companies, particularly if the companies were all of the same regiment.

At one- and two-company posts the social atmosphere could vary from one extreme to another, chiefly depending on personalities. A family atmosphere held together the skeleton force at Fort Bridger, Wyoming, in the early 1870's, and a member of one of the officers'

families at Fort Lapwai in 1877 wrote that "all know
ever so much of each other's affairs, and we talk them
over like family matters." At the other extreme, the
four officers' wives at Fort Selden, New Mexico, in
1868 were not even friendly toward one another, while
the three officers' wives at Fort Rice, Dakota Territory,
in 1873 did not speak to each other. The heat and
desolation of Camp McDowell, Arizona, so grated on
the nerves that "many" of the officers were not on speaking terms in 1871. The large posts could vary, too.
There is suggestive evidence that Fort Leavenworth,
Kansas, in the early 1880's took on the constrained but
familiar atmosphere that marks a small town, whereas
an even larger post—Fort Clark, where twenty-five
companies were massed in 1877—produced conditions
that made the women at least feel "more like one large
family than like strangers." In that instance, it was the
almost constant opportunity for wives and children to
be outdoors that engendered the family sense; the
converse is markedly implied—that the post was so
large there would not have been a family atmosphere
had the families been cooped up most of the time.[1]

One officer with wide frontier experience said
nostalgically: "Social intercourse, on account of their
isolation and peculiar experiences, was without formality; companionship begot friendship and affection. To
have lived a season together in a frontier post weaves
a bond that is never loosened. . . . Oh, the tales those
old abandoned forts could tell . . . —tales of love, tales
of war, tales of the hunt, of red men and white men,
tales of danger and of death, of peace and of life!
They have known them all. Romance, chivalry, and
heroism once lived within the walls that are now
shapeless mounds."[2] Another officer wrote: "Whatever

may be the cause, there is, no doubt, a charm about life at a frontier post which it would be difficult to explain. There is a freedom from restraint, a sort of good-fellowship on all hands, and a desire to please your neighbors in all reasonable things."[3] The same writer acknowledged that the frontier forts "are not remarkable for their beauty usually," but people "can live in them, and sometimes these people enjoy themselves as well as others who are more favorably situated."[4]

Their flexibility allowed frontier Army people to rise above their circumstances, for they lived in quarters as varied as the environments of the West and without regard to anything the regulation writers in Washington had contemplated. Army regulations clearly specified the number of rooms allowed an officer of each rank, and the frontier Army as clearly ignored them. Throughout the period, regulations allotted one room to a lieutenant, two to a captain or chaplain, three to a lieutenant colonel or major, and four to a colonel, as well as a kitchen in each case. Regulations also specified the standard room in officers' quarters should be 225 square feet north of 38° and 270 square feet south of that parallel, but in all cases that the room should be at least fifteen feet wide.[5]

The regulations did not obtain uniformly throughout Western posts. When Lieutenant Roe reported to Fort Lyon immediately after graduation from West Point in 1871, he and his bride had a two-story house with three rooms downstairs and two up. The disparity in quarters, however, probably resulted from the manner in which posts were built. When higher authority decided to place a post at a given spot, a command was sent forward to build it with soldier labor. Not waiting for Congressional authorization or appropriation, the Army thereby scattered small forts all over the West.[6]

Initially, the troops built with what was at hand. Sometimes it meant officers and troops lived in dugouts. Or it meant cabins made of green logs that would soon shrink and leave gaping holes where the chinking had been slapped on perfunctorily. Or adobe. Or just tents. Or a combination of all.

As a post matured and was enlarged here and improved there, the tendency to build beyond regulations occurred. As usual, Greene blamed that on the women. Using Fort Hays as an example, he said: "Large sums of money are expended for constructing and altering buildings to make them conform to the ideas of affectedly-fastidious ladies.... It sometimes comprises the changing of plans and specifications for new buildings after they have been approved by the Secretary of War." The extent to which quarters assigned exceeded the allowance was indicated in a dispatch from Fort Douglas, Utah, which said the abandonment of other posts, and the consequent concentration of those troops at Fort Douglas, would begin "to crowd the officers down to their allowances, in some cases, probably." Overcrowding also was indicated at Fort Concho whence an officer delightedly wrote in 1883: "Those of us who lived in that overcrowded, dilapidated old hulk of a post, one year ago, are rejoicing in the improvements [being made]. The Juniors have made their last bow to the attic ceilings, kitchen odors have been brought down to their proper level, and the sonorous breathing of our sleeping neighbor, across the narrow hall above, is heard no more."[7]

The quality varied just as wildly as did the types of quarters. In 1887 the *Army and Navy Journal* endorsed the comment of a correspondent who wrote that buildings at Army posts were monuments to "the general stupidity" of post commanders and quartermasters who did not have sense enough to realize that their competence as soldiers did not give them competence as architects and builders.[8]

At Fort Sedgwick, Colorado, officers and troops lived in dugouts in 1866 which Sherman said were such hovels that they would not have been used for slave quarters in the prewar South. Many more lived in tents. At Fort Richardson in 1871-72 field and staff officers lived in frame houses, but the company officers and their families lived in tents. Lieutenant Robert G. Carter built what came to be dubbed "Carter's Village," consisting of a hospital tent and two wall tents, joined together, framed and floored, with another wall tent serving as kitchen a short distance away. His wife gave birth to a daughter there during a norther so severe that troops had to hold down the guy ropes while she was in labor. She was lucky, compared with the young wife who gave birth in a tent elsewhere on the Texas plains. With no other woman anywhere nearby to help her, the baby died and she became permanently blind from the glare of the sun on the white canvas of the tent. Experienced Army folk learned to line the inside of the tent with green cambric. Lieutenant Boyd and his wife lived an entire year in tents at Camp Halleck—two tents divided by a calico curtain—and suffered both from snow in winter and intense heat that sunburned his wife under the canvas in summer.[9]

In the desert, officers' wives endured winter and summer in adobe shacks whose thick walls provided a degree of comfort that was offset oftentimes by uncovered windows, and which had brush roofs from which snakes sometimes fell to the floor and from which mud invariably drenched their belongings during a hard rain. In the course of one prolonged period of rain, the bedridden wife of Colonel Andrew Porter was protected at Fort Craig, New Mexico, by a tent fly over her bed and an umbrella over her head. At Fort C. F. Smith the Burt family of five lived in a two-room cabin in which the dirt floor was covered by gunny sacks; they made their beds on the floor of the front room by night, taking them up and piling them in the back room by day. The intense cold of northern Wyoming forced Lieutenant Grummond and his bride to tack blankets around the bed space for warmth at Fort Phil Kearny in 1866 and to cover the kitchen windows with old newspapers. After the spaciousness of a two-story house at Fort Lyon, the Roes found themselves at Camp Supply in a hut built of vertical logs, plastered with mud, and having a roof of poles and mud. In Arizona, Mrs. Boyd moved into the first house of her married life—a long adobe at Camp Date Creek, divided into two rooms by canvas curtains; there was a rough, wooden floor with cracks two inches wide between the boards. Officers lived in considerably more comfort at Fort Stanton where the stone houses had two rooms each, with a detached kitchen and dining room about fifteen feet in the rear.[10]

But even in larger and more important posts the quarters often were barely tolerable. Usually the post commander had a house to himself. For the other officers, Army practice was to place at least two families under the same roof, their apartments separated by a common hallway or by a thin, wooden partition. Occupation of duplex—or larger—quarters was "often productive of strained relationships between the occupants." That enforced intimacy caused one couple always to go out on the parade ground, late at night, where they could have their arguments in private.

That at least saved them from the experience of the Custers whose nightly "romp" caused neighbors at Fort Riley, Kansas, to spread the rumor that Custer beat his wife. The Custers could not have had much room in which to romp, because quarters usually had "tiny parlors" and small dining rooms. A dining room large enough to accommodate twelve persons "was in those days a decided rarity." Two or more families living in the same building also were subjected to the nerve abrasions coming from other peoples' noise, for few doors could be made to close without a slam. Ordinarily, too, the kitchens were detached from the main quarters, as were the dining areas in some cases. All had outdoor privies.[11]

At Fort Whipple the quarters were all alike, "low, broad houses with hall in the center, and two rooms about sixteen feet square on each side; pantry and kitchen back, also an attic above. I often looked through the cracks in my house to the light outside." The Fort Laramie quadrangle was surrounded "by quarters and houses of every conceivable pattern except that which was modern and ornamental." But at Fort Meade, Dakota Territory, officers' quarters had mansard roofs and large plate glass windows.[12]

Fort D. A. Russell, built in 1867 near Cheyenne as a major post, was constructed "at fabulous expense of the cheapest possible materials," with some buildings having been prefabricated in Chicago. As of the mid-70's captains and majors — two families to a house — lived in brown clapboard cottages which contained a parlor and dining room downstairs and two sleeping rooms upstairs. The two bedrooms opened on a narrow landing at the top of the stairs. Lighted by a dormer window, each was under a sharply sloping roof. From the rear window the occupants looked upon a dreary waste. The bare and brown backyard, in which nothing would grow, was cluttered with outbuildings used as kitchen, coalshed, woodshed, trunkshed, boxshed and servants' quarters. The yard ended at a high, rickety, unpainted, warped, and weatherbeaten wooden fence.[13] King, who knew those quarters well, gave an intimate picture of life within a captain's quarters at Russell:

Mrs. Freeman was seated in her cosey parlor, a work-basket at one side and a cutting table on the other. That there should be anything incongruous in the use of the state apartment of the little army home for such purposes never troubled her bonny head a particle. There were only two sleeping-rooms aloft, the children's and her own. There were only two rooms on the ground floor in the house proper,—the parlor and the dining-room. The kitchen was in an annex to the cottage. The servants' room in an annex to the kitchen. . . . In the days when most of the commissioned force were bachelors . . . it made little difference that four lieutenants were sometimes crammed into quarters intended for only one; but when wives and children began to come, it made a good deal. Then the limited appropriation vouchsafed by an omniscient Congress was strained to the uttermost farthing . . . and makeshifts of every buildable description were tacked on the rear elevations of the brown cottages: "linters" [lean-tos] on the flanks of those intended for officers of higher rank; "linters" to the kitchen annexes, and ramshackle sheds, of every possible shape but shapely, to the sheds already spiked to the main establishment,—nails would not have held against the Cheyenne zephyr. Like those interminable structures children sometimes build with cards, there really was a substantial framework to one portion, the original nucleus of the pile, but all the rest was shanty. Man after man the successive

117

commanding officers had striven to effect some degree of improvement and uniformity in the back yards of the garrison, but found that there was a sight even more pitiable to be encountered first, and that was the bill of particulars of the appropriations for repairs of quarters at Fort Russell. Man after man the successive post quartermasters had yielded to the importunities of the occupants and furnished plank and scantling, spikes and nails; and year after year had this pennywise patchwork been going on, until the result was a veritable architectural crazy quilt minus all that makes the quilt attractive, — its bright variety of color. Nothing on earth was ever much more unpicturesque than a rear view of the fort.

And yet people were happy in those quaint old rookeries, now fast vanishing from the face of the earth; were even more comfortable so long as the short summer lasted; but when the wintry gales began, threatening to lift the flimsy structures from their iron anchorage, no amount of fuel would keep them warm. All around their bases they were banked with earth, hard rammed and sodded, though the sod refused to sprout. Every knot-hole was plugged. Extra sheets of tar-paper were tacked together throughout the interior,[14] and ten thicknesses of the Chicago *Times* were laid beneath the carpets, — the only instance wherein the editorials of that enterprising sheet were ever known to stand between the army and the blasts of adversity.[15] Yet even tar-paper and the *Times* could not prevail against the Wyoming gales, and despite these vaunted barricades the wind still blew where it listed and we heard the sound thereof many a time and oft to the utter exclusion of all bugle calls, and there was nothing but the still small voice of conscience to warn the martial occupants that reveille and stables were due, and 'twas time to be up and doing.

Now, Mrs. Freeman's bright little parlor was as warm and cosey and cheery as any in the post, yet she sat with her dainty, slippered feet close to the big coal stove that cumbered the room, and a thick Indian shawl was thrown over her shoulders. Within a radius of six or eight feet of the stove all was warm enough. Beyond that limit the biting wind that forced its way through imperceptible cracks and crannies triumphed over the glowing base burner and the carpet was bulged up in the middle like a segment of some big balloon. The children, delving at their lessons in the dining-room beyond, could not resist the temptation of slipping from their chairs and darting in from time to time and jumping on the huge puff of "Body Brussels" in hopes of hearing an explosion similar to that produced when smashing an inflated paper bag; but the maternal mandate to return instantly to their seats was the only audible result.

A sweet homelike picture she made, this dainty bit of wife and motherhood, as she sat there busy with her needle-work, yet keeping watchful eye upon the reluctant students of the other room. The red gold of her wealth of hair was tinged with the fierce glow from the anthracite; the soft bloom of her rounded cheek was deepened by the intense heat of the burning mass. She had a pretty, birdlike way of poising her head on one side and surveying her work at each new turn, and her parted lips—soft and crimson—would close with an air of womanly decision and her bright head nod sagely as she communed with herself upon the probable effect of the garment she was designing. Once in a while she would glance at the clock, as though impatient for some one's coming. Her husband [would come] at noon, when he usually overhauled the children's slates.[16]

Virtually identical conditions existed at Fort Laramie. Quarters were poorly constructed, but they at least had good stoves. "We could keep comfortable in our living room at least. At night it was impossible to make the dining room and kitchen warm. Milk was found frozen solid in the pans in the morning. . . . The precious sack of potatoes was covered with a buffalo robe and placed near the stove in the living room each night."[17]

In sharp contrast, Army families dragged themselves through the long hot months of the Arizona desert.

Windows were closed and blanketed by day against the blazing sun and torrid heat, but, soon after nightfall, every door and window was usually opened wide and often kept so all the night long, in order that the cooler air, settling down from *mesa* and mountain, might drift through every room and hallway, licking up the starting dew upon the smooth, rounded surface of the huge *ollas* . . . and wafting comfort to the heated brows of the lightly covered sleepers within. Pyjamas [*sic*] were then unknown in army circles [early 1870's], else even the single sheet that covered the drowsing soldier might have been dispensed with.[18]

Some families in Arizona slept on the porches—protected by a *ramada* or a lattice of interwoven boughs. Some even slept on the parade ground where Mrs. Summerhayes once awakened to find a bull looking down at her.[19]

Generally, officers' quarters were furnished with crude but practical furniture. Although there were exceptions among officers' wives who brought out treasured pieces, including pianos, the home of Lieutenant McIntosh at Fort Lincoln probably was typical. Old canvas tenting had been stretched over the walls to make the rooms warmer; a stove stood in the middle of the living room; campstools and unpainted wooden chairs provided seating; the dining table was made of three planks resting on sawhorses, and also served as a bed for a guest, an ironing board and a bench. Mrs. McIntosh had been brought up in Washington, amid mahogany and rosewood antiques, but she took the Spartan furnishings of the West philosophically, saying, "It's no use buying anything worth while until we settle

down." The bedroom floors were carpeted by gray
army blankets stitched together, the bedrooms furnished with soldiers' cots (many homes used hospital
cots), campstool, and table. The dressing table was a
set of shelves nailed into a packing box. Elsewhere in
Fort Lincoln, window coverings were made of un-
bleached muslin dyed in beet juice.[20]

Post quartermasters were authorized to make furniture at posts supplied only by wagon train, but in
reality were expected to make do with dismantled crates
and scrap lumber. From that they made bedsteads,
tables, benches, and wardrobes. Officers could buy the
same material at cost to use in making their own furniture. Most of the furniture in the comparatively commodious quarters of Fort Lyon in 1871 had been made
by post carpenters. The drawers of frontier furniture
were apt to come out "grudgingly and with much jar
and friction." [21] Arizona presented some special problems because of aridity:

Furniture, even such as [the post commander] had bought
in San Francisco, and would live to a green old age along the
Pacific, came speedily to pieces in the hot, dry atmosphere of
Arizona. Little enough there was of cabinetware, to be sure,
because of the cost of transportation; but such as there was,
unless rivetted in every seam and joint, fell apart at most
inopportune moments. Bureaus and washstands, tables, sofas
and chairs, were forever shedding some more or less important section, and the only reliable table was that built by
the post carpenter, the quartermaster.

And so these pioneers of our civilization, the men and
women of the army, had no little experience in cabinet-
making and upholstering ... soldier folk turned clothing
boxes into couches, soap boxes into cradles, and pork barrels
into *fauteuils*. Chintz and calico, like charity, covered a multi-

tude of sins, as declared in unsightly cracks and knot holes. . . .
The best dining-room set . . . was sawed out from sugar
barrels.[22]

In other words, officers and wives in quarters really
lived without any more comfort than the Carters knew
in a tent at Fort Concho. "We hung our gray blankets
at the sides of the well ventilated tent to keep out the
wind; made a dressing table out of a barrel, covering it
with gaudy chintz, bound with red; covered a rude,
wooden 'bunk' with a chintz valance all about it in
order to hide the butter keg, the commissary box, and
the boards stowed away for furniture, etc. On a shelf
over our heads at the head of our bed was our box of
groceries."[23]

In a bachelor's quarters one might find, as a writing
desk, "a big, old-fashioned rectangular box, brass-
bound, and with compartments for stationery and valuable letters, and the conventional secret drawer
opened by pulling up a brass pin in the edge of the
lower half of the box,—about as unreliable a secret-
keeper as one's feminine relations."[24] Or in another's
quarters the visitor might see the mantel decorated
with photographs of friends and family, or "a plain
wooden table with a pigeon-holed desk upon it, the lid
of which, turned down, made the writing shelf. In the
pigeon-holes were numerous folded papers, well-filled
envelopes, packages of tobacco, a briar-root pipe, a
pair of old shoulder-straps, several pairs of gloves,
some fishing tackle, some *carte-de-visite*-sized photographs, a damaged sabre knot, and the inevitable ac-
cumulations of odds and ends with which a subaltern's
field-desk is apt to be littered."[25]

Regardless of the uniform discomfort of the quarters, a senior officer reporting to a post could turn a junior out of a house he chose on the basis of what his rank entitled him to have; he could do that only once, however, unless someone senior to him forced him to move. When the turn-out happened, the whole officers' row "would go tumbling like a row of bricks until the lowest and last was reached."[26] Appropriately, ranking-out was known colloquially as "falling bricks." Mrs. Summerhayes, new to the Army in 1874, was stricken at the thought of turning out Lieutenant and Mrs. Edward Lynch at Fort D. A. Russell, but they were stiffened to it by Lieutenant and Mrs. Thomas Wilhelm—old Army hands with the brevet rank of major—who insisted they must do it in keeping with Army custom. "They'll hate you for doing it, but if you don't do it they'll not respect you. After you've been turned out once yourself, you will not mind turning others out."[27] Even for a miserable log shanty at Camp Supply the Roes were given exactly two hours to vacate in favor of a newly reported captain. Before it was over six or more captains and first lieutenants also had to move, and the department's inspector general—who happened to be present—ordered the quartermaster to double two sets of quarters. On another occasion, the Boyds had a comfortable house at Fort Clark in 1876— double parlors downstairs and two bedrooms upstairs, cramped but adequate for their family of five. With an influx of additional companies, a captain claimed their quarters but at least had the decency to wait for a few days since Mrs. Boyd had just given birth to a child. Because Boyd was still a lieutenant, his entire family was then forced into one room, plus kitchen. During their six years at Fort Clark, there were perhaps fifty cases of bricks falling, involving at least ten families each time. Ranking-out reached the ultimate in absurdity in the case of a second lieutenant and his bride who were forced to live in a hall between two other families; when he was ranked out even of that he resigned in disgust.[28]

As the man who assigned quarters and was responsible for their upkeep, the post quartermaster drew the resentment of many officers' wives. At Camp Halleck a bachelor lieutenant was both quartermaster and commissary officer. Since he thus controlled all supplies — for officers bought food from the commissary — he was in a position "to make us either comfortable or the reverse, as he chose." When the Roes found themselves in a log hut at Camp Supply, they "had almost to get down on their knees to the quartermaster" before he would issue the canvas they wanted as a room divider. When the department inspector general ordered the doubling of two sets of quarters, one set was the quartermaster's own. But he foiled it by dividing off two rooms so small that no one could possibly occupy them, thus retaining the space for himself and family. Mrs. Roe was maliciously delighted that that particular quartermaster had received the order, which meant the construction of quarters for the Roes. "One can imagine how he must have fumed over the issuing of so much canvas, boards, and even the nails for the quarters of only a second lieutenant."[29]

Notwithstanding the quartermaster's subordination to the post commander, the latter's wife sometimes had cause for complaint, as did Mrs. Custer at Fort Lincoln. "The quartermaster's own house was something to turn us all green with envy, for he had all the workmen at his disposal. It was painted, had closets, with little shelves here and there [almost without exception, lady memoirists complained about the lack of shelves and closets], that women dote on, and many trifles that seemed to us the sum and substance of domestic elegance." The ladies of Fort Lincoln merely envied his wife, saying, "I don't blame *her*; but I would like to read him a lesson on equal distribution." In turn, some wives came down hard on quartermasters. One, who had begun her Army life during the Mexican War, was by the 1870's "fearless in stating her opinions, and was dreaded by the quartermaster because of the determined manner in which she went at him when it was necessary to have her house repaired or painted." Another complained that "the quartermasters were always using up scraps of paint; no two rooms were alike and each one uglier than the other."

On behalf of the sisterhood, King's "Mrs. Captain Turner" condemns the corps with unanswerable finality when she denounces "Captain Buxton" as one whose finer sensibilities have been "blunted by a lifetime in the quartermaster's department" before he has been transferred to the cavalry.[30]

Actually, the ladies may have expected and demanded too much from the harried quartermaster.

There is never a time on the frontier when the dames of the garrison, from the lady of the commanding officer down to the widow of the late Private Moriarty (who still hangs on to her husband's old company for sustenance), are not besieging the post quartermaster with some plea or other,—a partition to be put up here, a chimney repaired, glass put in, a new coat of paint in the parlor, a storm-door like the colonel's, a new stove like the one you gave Mrs. Major, or a wash-biler an' findher like Mrs. Mulligan's. They are always pestering him for something. The great depot at Jeffersonville does not contain the volume of stores that could be asked for by the women of a four-company post in one winter; there is never enough of any one item to go round, and always more applicants than there are coal scuttles; somebody has to be refused and frequently fifteen or twenty somebodies, and then nothing under heaven can save that quartermaster's reputation. The patience of Job (without his boils), the meekness of Moses, and the resources of Rothschild might help that functionary in his desperately hopeless task of satisfying a whole garrison, but they couldn't do it long. The more you give women the more they demand, and the annual appropriation for the purchase of army stores and supplies could readily be distributed among the laundresses of any one regiment ... without satisfying their cravings for more. It isn't always that they really need the article demanded, they simply want something that some other woman hasn't, so that she may want and cannot get it, and the rule is general, being by no means confined to the sturdy wives of the rank and file, but applicable to the ladies whose garments they weekly washed and mutilated at New York prices. God help the nervous, sensitive, or irritable man who has to take these duties on his shoulders; not one in a hundred could long maintain a mental balance, let alone the financial ditto.[31]

Tried and handicapped by flimsy, drafty, and inadequate quarters, the officers' wives still had to be homemakers. Along with the enforced expedients in furniture and window dressing, they had to make do with what the frontier offered in food, clothing, and entertainment. "Army women have a gift of making even a burrow look cheery and attractive, though they do accumulate an amount of truck that becomes embarrassing in the inevitable event of a move."[32]

The garrison family spirit showed itself in the making of clothing, to which officers' wives—not to mention the laundresses—had to resort. Some clothing, cloth, and accessories were ordered through agents who would buy at department stores in New York or Philadelphia, and later through mail order catalogs. By and large, though, the women appear to have been practical, and to have engaged in what one called "impromptu sewing bees." They also exchanged patterns, books, and recipes.[33] In sewing circles, as well as other ways, Army wives trained brides much as a recruit or new officer had to be trained. One device they all learned—and it probably was general throughout the population—was to place camphor in clothing that was packed for storage.[34]

In managing their houses, officers' wives seem to have been singularly helpless. Their surprising dependence upon servants—sometimes a whole complement—implies that most of them had come from homes of some comfort. The retinue of servants also indicates that they lived extravagantly on the officers' comparatively low salaries. Those who left memoirs confessed they had not learned to cook before marriage, and most had no inclination to learn. Servants, however, were always scarce on the frontier. Officer after officer retained maids in innumerable sequence, only to lose them to enlisted men who married the domestics almost immediately. The expedient of choosing the oldest-looking, ugliest, and most repugnant of women was no safeguard against losing her to matrimony. One officer's wife brought many governesses out to the West, always losing them to officers. As a consequence, servants are treated with indignation and scorn by King as unreliable persons who "fled the house, as frontier servants will" when scarlet fever struck the family, or as independent beings who had to have an evening out, "for even on the far frontier did our domestic tyrants hold their employers to the weekly allowance of social freedom." At posts near cities a woman could be hired temporarily to assist a mother immediately after the birth of a child, bringing into the home "that awesome potentate in petticoats ... the monthly nurse." Not only were servants scarce but all households had a continuing train of troubles with them. The burden had to be borne, because the officer's home was dependent on them.[35]

Only strikers and Chinese made satisfactory servants, as a general thing. A striker was an enlisted man who worked for an officer until 1881 when Army regulations—citing an unenforced law of 1870—prohibited officers from employing soldiers in private service. Before that, many enlisted men were happy to work for the extra five dollars a month paid by an officer, to live in private quarters, to eat better than in company messes, and to be excused from guard duty, drills, and roll calls. For a few years thereafter the rule against soldiers as servants was enforced, but the striker never did disappear entirely. Almost always King depicted the striker as a devoted factotum, and several wives expressed their preference for strikers, especially as cooks. All strikers, however, were not happy in their work. One was court-martialed for attempting to poison the family, but the sentence was disapproved on the grounds that he had been denied the right to present testimony that would have impeached the witnesses.[36]

"One schooled Chinaman," King wrote, "easily and efficiently did all the housework of a lieutenant's humble quarters and was generally employed in that capacity in almost every garrison of the Far West." The women who had Chinese servants swore by them. Having lost her Chinese cook, Mrs. Roe said: "I shall miss the pretty silk coats about the house, and his swift, almost noiseless going around. That Chinamen are not more generally employed I cannot understand, for they make such exceptional servants. They are wonderfully economical, and can easily do the work of two maids."[37]

The wives shared recipes and everything else they had. In most posts officers' families had to eat Army food bought from the commissary, but in some posts—such as Fort D. A. Russell—a wagon made a daily trip into Cheyenne with market baskets and order slips for the various households along the row. Buying groceries from the commissary officer—on credit—frequently meant that young ladies who had led sheltered lives in the East were forced to live on soldiers' rations—bacon, flour, beans, Santos coffee, tea, rice, sugar, condiments, and maybe dried apples. From the commissary they could obtain only yellow soap. Sometimes they could supplement the ration with high-priced articles from the post trader's store, such as old and hard-packed butter (but in Arizona the butter usually had to be poured), and dried vegetables. On innumerable occasions officers—as well as troops—would go for months at a time without tasting even a lowly potato. When ranchmen or farmers would come to isolated posts with produce and vegetables the prices sometimes would be so high that junior officers could not afford them.[38]

The family spirit of the garrison came to the rescue of the hungry Roes at Camp Supply in 1872. With the commissary open only on Saturday mornings for officers, they had laid in a week's supply of food. One morning they discovered it had been stolen from a cellar in their yard. "As soon as word got abroad of our starving condition, true army hospitality and generosity manifested itself. We were invited out to luncheon, and to dinner, and to breakfast the next morning. You can see how like one big family a garrison can be, and how in times of trouble we go to each other's assistance."[39]

To offset the monotony of Army rations, some wives —city-bred— acquired milch cows and chickens which they took from post to post. But King told one yarn about a costly substitute used by officers at Fort D. A. Russell. Officers borrowed cows for the winter from a ranchman who had been a captain during the Civil War. In return for the milk, the officers fed and cared for the cows during the winter, and assumed responsibility for them. When spring came, however, gates strangely would become open and the cows gone. The ranchman and his hands would make a pretense of searching the range to no avail, and the luckless officers would have to pay twenty-five or thirty dollars, as well as the costs of search, for each cow, certain all the while that the cows were grazing with the rest of the herd. "'Don't let Bryan lend you a cow,' was the advice tendered each new arrival among the married officers.[40] Maybe it was only a yarn, but it is of a piece with the many connivances to which others fell victim in the West.

As trying as the closeness and overcrowding could be, it also carried with it a sense of security so complete that quarters were never locked. Indeed, in the heat of Arizona doors were not even closed.[41] "Opportunities for theft in garrison are or were illimitable. People never thought of bolting their doors by day, and, as to money, silverware, jewelry and the like, women who possessed such property rarely placed it under lock and key."[42] Consequently, King exaggerated some complications of plot involving theft or illegal entry.[43] But theft did occur, as at Fort D. A. Russell where an enlisted man was arrested for burglary of officers' quarters as well as of barracks.[44] Army people even slept with doors unlocked, nor did they bother to lock trunks or closets. One wife said that in her many years on the frontier she "almost forgot the use of keys." With the doors left open, "one's home became a social thoroughfare, more or less, according to one's popularity."[45]

Thus running in and out of each other's homes "as though it were one big family," Army folk treated each other "with a hospitality and warmth that one never sees outside the army." Always they opened their doors and their larders to others of their kind passing through. When newlyweds reported to a post before their quarters were ready, they were taken into the home of another officer and shared meals with various families.[46]

As intimate as they were on a daily if not hourly basis, officers and their wives created a social milieu that seemed both rigidly formal and casually informal. The informality was marked by a sense of familiarity that caused both men and women to think nothing of any officer calling at any door to ask either matron or maiden to come out and see something, or go for a ride, or go driving.[47] The isolation in which they lived—an aristocratic caste cut apart from other army personnel and only sometimes consorting with frontier civilians— forced the people of officers' row to be dependent upon each other for companionship "day after day, month after month." Army society greatly benefited from the free time that officers were given while in garrison. "The officers, instead of being immersed in business cares, were ever ready to be amazed or amused, as the case might be, with the results of our industry, and absolute delight was manifested over the most trifling plan for social enjoyment, which doubled the pleasure."[48] Having to depend upon one another fostered a spirit—"when gentlemen *are* gentlemen and ladies *are* ladies"—that united them socially.[49] It was somewhat odd, however, that people who knew the most intimate details about one another could assume the most formal of airs at formally arranged entertainments, especially dances, for which even in the small posts invitations were sometimes issued. Both the ladies' recollections and routine news reports show how important dancing was in the life of a frontier post. King explained it by saying that only social gaiety could take frontier soldiers' minds from their cares and hardships which might, otherwise, have left both body and mind to collapse.[50]

To have their dances, officers and their wives had to make use of whatever building could be converted to that purpose, for Army regulations made no provision for a dance hall on any post. The ladies of Fort Hays were so determined to have a dance hall that one of them contrived the perfect solution: the post had a chaplain but no chapel; there was a chapel at the abandoned Fort Harker. Therefore, ask Washington for authority to move the chapel from Harker to very active Hays; Washington would be certain to approve such a noble plan. Washington did. Once at Hays, however, the structure was rebuilt with one end barely designed to meet the needs of worship and the remainder fitted up for dances and other entertainments; that is, the rectangular building was more in the form of a barracks than a chapel to begin with.[51] Many such dance hall-church combinations served the social needs of frontier posts. Hays was such a dancing post that, early in the summer of 1876 before the Fifth Cavalry knew it would have to take the field to re-enforce Crook, officers and ladies would drop their croquet mallets and waltz on the grass when the band marched forth playing a German air.[52] At a regimental headquarters post there was never a problem with music, for the regimental bands served nobly and frequently as dance orchestras. The smaller posts made do with any kind of music-makers. Dances and hops might close early in the evening, but what the Army people loved most were "germans," cotillions to German and Austrian waltz melodies that often lasted until three or four o'clock in the morning.

Because dances were so important, they come to life in King's novels with great detail and verve. Here he describes a ball at Fort Whipple which had a reputation as a gay post.[53]

The well-waxed floor, on which the post quartermaster had lavished his finest boarding, and enthusiastic bachelor officers hours of individual supervision and personal effort, shone like satin. . . . Around the walls, draped with flag and guidon, and glittering with sabre and scroll-work, were interspersed dozens of lamps with polished reflectors. Candles and kerosene furnished all the illumination. . . . Crude and warlike as may have been the decorations, never did the "swellest" German at Delmonico's present much better music or any better dancing than was to be found at the large garrisons of the frontier, and certainly for genuine enjoyment an army ball yields the palm to no other. An army lady never becomes a wall-flower. She has this one compensation for marrying in the service. After two or three seasons in the great cities of the East even the prettiest girl becomes to society people *passée,* and, once married, only when exceptionally attractive and brilliant does she continue to be sought as a partner;[54] but, owing probably to the dearth of young and unmarried ladies, the army wife retains all the hold she ever had upon bellehood, even increases it in many instances, and the bright and witty and dancing woman, though her children be tall as herself, never lacks for "attention." As for the army girl, with any vivacity, with any pretensions to beauty or grace, she lives and moves as a queen.

And so the ball-room was filled with dancers; the sombre uniforms of the staff and infantry, the gayer trappings of the cavalry, the aiguillettes of the aides-de-camp mingling with many an exquisite toilet that would have shone resplendent in the distant East. It was long after midnight, supper had been served, even the musicians, in detachments, had been fed and otherwise comforted, some few elders had slipped away and gone homeward, but the ringing music of "Le Roi Carotte" sent ten full "sets" through the figures of the Lancers, and compelled many a staid spectator to beat time with his feet. Many a group of lookers-on watched the spirited movement of the dance from corner and doorway. . . .

Waltz, lancers, quadrille, and galop succeeded one another in rapid succession as the night wore on, and still even matrons and "chaperons" danced untiringly; still some new sweet strain from Paolo's orchestra would call the half-wearied ones again to the glassy floor. There was marked diminution among the spectators at the windows where, earlier in the evening, dozens of the soldiers and soldiers' wives had gathered to feast their eyes upon the scene within. . . .

It must have been late in the morning, past three o'clock, when, after a genuine romp through the merry figures of the army quadrille, the dancers hurried out in couples to the club-rooms for a breath of fresh air and a sip of punch or lemonade.[55]

On that occasion King had the gathering enlarged by a group of officers and their wives who had come from "Camp Sandy" for the ball, which was not an infrequent practice. Such groups regularly went from Whipple to Camp Verde for dinners and dances. For a masked ball at Fort Lyon in 1873 guests came from forts

Leavenworth, Riley, Dodge and Wallace.[56] The practice was so common that Greene charged that officers
would come from a distance to attend a party or dance,
"ostensibly on official business, so that their transportation and hotel bills, *both ways,* should be paid by the
United States."[57] A ball identical to that described by
King welcomed Crook back to Arizona in 1882, the
dancing lasting until 3 A.M.[58]

At Whipple the dancers could glide over a waxed
wooden floor, but it was also usual in other posts to
cover a rough floor with canvas and wax the canvas.[59]

The complete Indian fighter thus had to be a good
dancer, too, and it was an honor for an officer to be
asked to lead a german.[60] For a highly organized german at Fort D. A. Russell, the assembly hall was
decorated much as that at Whipple. Two sergeants in
full dress guarded the entrance to the dance hall as
well as the entrance to the ladies' dressing room to one
side. (In another part of the building the nondancing
men could enjoy themselves in the card room; in some
regiments women were allowed in the card room, in
others not.) As the couples entered the dance hall, they
either presented themselves to the couple designated
to receive or, if none had been designated, to the wife
of the commanding officer. The ladies then took their
seats in camp chairs around the dance floor, each attended by an officer; if her husband preferred cards,
another stood by her. The leader of the german used
a small silver whistle to signal dancers to or from their
seats.[61]

At this instant the music began. All promenaders on the
floor, with the strict sense of discipline that pervades a military cotillion, at once sought their places . . . a long rectangle
of glistening white canvas shown under the swarm of Chinese

lanterns pendent from the flag-draped roof. Both long sides of the room were taken up by the dancers; the ladies, in their dainty toilets and with fluttering fans, seated, each with her attendant cavalier in full uniform, or the conventional black and white, as he happened to be military or civil, by profession. Behind the row of chairs, sacred to the use of the thirty couples in the dances, was a row of seats for lookers-on. Right in front of the stage were the pretty tables, on which were heaped the favors.... Down at the lower end of the long room a number of officers and visitors stood looking on, while a dozen ladies not dancing were seated in a semicircle, leaving only the clear space that led to the ladies' dressing-rooms,—that flag-draped archway guarded by those two splendid-looking [sergeants].[62]

Before taking her partner's arm to be escorted to the floor, a lady pinned her fan beside the corps badge on his chest. But as exciting as it was to dance with a fully uniformed officer—and the lady chroniclers confessed to being in love with brass buttons—there was a penalty. During the movements of the waltz or the intricate figures of the cotillion, a lady could snag her dress of medal, badge, or aiguillette, or scratch her nose or chin on his epaulets or shoulder-knots. It was even worse in tender moments when an officer embraced his lady. "How horribly those big epaulets got in the way, and service medals and sautache braid scratch at such times!"[63]

The enlisted men also had their dances, at which the laundresses were the honored guests. Post and regimental custom varied, but at least some of the post officers and their wives attended each company dance. Sometimes the post commander and his lady attended. In some posts it was customary for the dance to open with the commanding officer dancing with the wife of the ranking noncommissioned officer who in turn danced with the C.O.'s wife. At Fort Stanton, about 1870, there were not enough officers' wives present for them to have balls of their own, "but we always opened those of the soldiers."[64]

With the informality of a family and the formality of social usage, Army people managed a rather complete, and sometimes elaborate, protocol within the garrison. In addition to the informality with which they flitted in and out of each other's homes, the ladies also paid formal calls daily. When two of them went calling together, they were—in King's phrase—"hunting in couples." Singly or in groups, the ladies regularly made a round of calls upon each other, and almost always addressed one another formally, as Mrs. Jones. Quite informally a group would gather on this front porch or that for a morning chat and again for an afternoon visit. Officers going about the garrison on duty would often stop to speak briefly with such groups.[65]

Dinner parties—though small because of the smallness of Army dining rooms—kept people from growing altogether stale. "Garrison dinner 'bids' must be answered as promptly as those in city life." It was customary for officers to wear full dress uniform when dining out, which meant they had to wear the "wobbly" shoulder-knots (commonly referred to as epaulets, although in strict usage of the time only generals wore epaulets, which had a gold fringe, while officers of lower grade were authorized to wear shoulder-knots which did not have the fringe) and the red silk sash (worn by all arms) "that few men wore properly."[66]

Diversity was provided by parties of all sorts. At Fort Keogh, Montana, "The Social Fifth," as that infantry regiment dubbed itself, did not believe in monotony; it scheduled Friday evening hops and a regular round of dinners and parties. At other times garrison people—as at Fort Laramie—packed off for a day-long picnic or buggy ride, or gathered for lemonade on the veranda in the afternoon, and played charades in the evening. Army life was "peculiarly gay and light-hearted," with officers and wives taking advantage of every occasion for fun. Going-away parties for an officer or a couple could become boisterous, including one in which everybody got so drunk that men and women alike joined in a "war dance." The drunken hostess berated a guest who did not finish his drink; "her language and manner would have intimidated a man of less nerve."[67]

Especially in larger posts the social circle was enlarged and enlivened by young ladies spending a season with relatives or friends, and usually husband-hunting.[68] A regimental commander explained:

A few young ladies coming from civilization have a wonderful effect on brightening up everything, and, no matter whether they are from the east, south or west, they are always a valuable acquisition, their bright faces and graceful ways being so different from that of the officers and men. There is a certain stiffness about a military man in spite of himself, and it is all his female relatives can do to make things appear easy and pleasant; and under such circumstances it is no wonder that charming young people are so highly prized in frontier garrisons.[69]

Unmarried ladies immediately attracted suitors—a swarm of them in larger posts. King and his wife had such a guest at Fort D. A. Russell during the winter of 1877-78 which he described thus:

We had a charming girl visiting us that winter. All the bachelors at the post were paying her devoted attention. There was not an hour from guard-mounting to midnight that some of them were not infesting the premises, and Mrs. X not infrequently had to order the laughing crowd out of the house when midnight came, declaring that her friend and guest must be allowed a few hours between visits.[70]

Flirtations and romances immediately sprang up among the bachelors and the young ladies. This led to the game known as "catching the weasel"; if a swain found the girl asleep, he could kiss her; if she found him asleep, he had to buy her a pair of gloves. "Many a forfeit, both lip and glove, had there been claimed and allowed in army days whereof we write."[71]

When the young people did not recognize that they were meant for each other, the ubiquitous matchmaker(s) appeared. The matchmaker went to work in earnest in several of King's novels, but he does not provide any particular insight into the psychology or modus operandi of the woman who seems unable to stand the sight or thought of an unmarried man. He made a matchmaker of a character obviously modeled on Mrs. Crook and of "Mrs. Major Waldron." Although he also made matchmaking a muted characteristic of "Mrs. Stannard," who was always right and wise, he could hardly have exaggerated had he chosen to emphasize that trait in any of his characters, for it abounded in the Old Army, especially since that was an age in which it was both economically and socially desirable for dependent young ladies to be hustled under the protecting roof of someone else. In the Army, for example, Mrs. Lieutenant Colonel W. L. Elliott was "an indefatigable matchmaker" at Benicia Barracks, California, in 1871, always looking out for the interests of the officers of the First Cavalry, or perhaps for the "several very charming young damsels" to whom she introduced them.[72]

When Katherine Garrett went to Fort Lincoln to visit her sister, Mrs. McIntosh, in 1874, it developed that her sister, the Custers, and others had already matched her with Lieutenant Frank Gibson of the Seventh Cavalry. The two targets cooperated beyond anyone's fondest hopes, meeting, falling in love, and becoming engaged in a matter of days just before the departure of Custer's expedition to the Black Hills. When Miss Garrett announced the engagement to her sister, Mrs. McIntosh said bluntly, "I'm not surprised, because I planned all this before you came out." Small wonder that in a land chronically short of women a correspondent at Fort Davis promised "Eastern mammas" that if they would send their daughters to Davis instead of fashionable Eastern resorts "none of them will languish for the addresses of chivalrous young men."[73] If a girl turned down a suitor she "gave him the mitten," while the rejected man "carried a willow" instead of a torch.

"Only to a few has it happened that the love of their lives has been found in garrison," but that was a purely relative comparison, for many matches were made at Army posts. There was, however, at least one strong superstitition among Army people: it was unlucky to announce engagements on Friday evenings.[74]

Of those matches many were consecrated in garrison by chaplains or by civil magistrates. A few examples, perhaps representative, will suffice. Wearing a gown made by the ladies of the post, Miss Garrett was married to Lieutenant Gibson in the McIntosh quarters at Fort Lincoln; as the bride came down the stairs she saw "gaily gowned women" and officers in full dress packing the small quarters; canvas covered the rough floors of living and dining rooms. Gibson had ordered flowers from St. Paul, Minnesota, which had not arrived, but the bride substituted long stalks of soap-weed wrapped in satin below the huge, white, odorless blossoms; after the vows, bride and groom walked through an arch of crossed sabres into the dining room where she cut the cake with her husband's sabre.

Another wedding involved Lieutenant Sydenham who, just six months out of West Point, received a letter at Fort Keogh from his fiancee terminating their engagement in January, 1890; by May he was married to the sister of Lieutenant Joseph A. Gaston of the same post. At Fort Stanton the marriage of Assistant Surgeon R. C. Newton and a Mrs. Kirkwood of Philadelphia "made quite a stir at that post, where weddings, like angels' visits, are few and far between." Isolation and deprivation of many things did not prevent some garrison weddings from being somewhat sumptuous. When Miss Gilbert was married to Lieutenant Gresham at Fort Yates in 1883, the chaplain entered her father's parlor first; Mrs. Gilbert then entered on the arm of the groom, and the bride on the arm of her father. The bride wore white moire and satin, with veil and orange-bud diamond ornaments.[75]

Miss Gilbert's wedding brings up the matter of the dress of officers' wives on the frontier. While spending many years far removed from metropolitan centers, their clothing became "ridiculously old-fashioned," and a number of women recalled the sharpness of their chagrin at realizing their clothing was out of fashion when they returned to the East on visits. But on the frontier they wore their best, which obviously had been pretty good when purchased. The jaundiced Greene observed: "To wear clothes wisely and well seems to be the chief aim in life of many. No sacrifice is too great for them, even to the extent of involving their husbands in debt beyond the reach of their salaries." Some wore riding habits fashioned after the uniform of the husbands' arm, and many wore forage caps while riding.

Too preoccupied with action sequences and plot complications to describe ladies' gowns in detail, King was nonetheless writing realistically when he repeatedly referred to the beautiful "toilets" of the women. Out of date perhaps, but even at scrubby posts like Fort Concho the ladies could appear in formidable array. At a New Year's reception one wore a black velvet dress with train, diamonds, and Valenciennes lace; another, a black lace dress over "an exquisite shade of cherry adornments"; a lieutenant's wife, cream satin and tulle; another, black satin, with train; a young lady visitor, blush pink with opening buds in cream and white; a doctor's wife, white lace dress with a mistletoe cluster; a captain's wife, a "stylish suit of corduroy." A man wrote that dispatch — presumably — but either his wife was a careful society reporter or he possessed powers of observation beyond those of an ordinary man.[76]

Flirtation was not confined to unmarried persons, for an important part of garrison regimen involved flirtations between married women and bachelor officers, although they were within a particular and rigid code. The men seem to have been governed by the idealism of the Round Table, making the flirtations alternations of gallantry and queenly response rather than clandestine love affairs. Those flirtations surface in reminiscences just enough to show their existence and importance. Greene made much of them:

There is a freedom of manners among the ladies of the Army that does not obtain in the best civilian society. This may be attributed to their exclusive mode of life, and to the common belief that the officers are all Chevalier Bayards. This is, in some respects, a pleasant feature of Army life. Married ladies may accept costly presents and receive little attentions and visits from agreeable bachelors without provoking the jealousy of their husbands or offending the general sense of propriety. It is a recognized privilege of an Army lady to call upon any officer for a favor in the absence of her husband.

Perversion of manners from their wonted simplicity stamps Army society with a peculiarity seldom found among people who assume to have reached the acme of social attainment.[77]

In consequence, bachelor officers had to study the art of flirtation if they expected to get along. Greene was especially critical of the number of women who had married officers much older than themselves, insinuating that that was part of the reason for flirtations with younger officers. One time he saw the wife of the post commander and a young lieutenant holding hands, and swinging their hands as they walked across the parade as though they were newlyweds. "[The women's] thoughts do not range beyond the shores of to-day, nor do they manifest a desire for anything but 'brass buttons,' costly dresses, fine dinners, and flirtations with bachelors." Moreover, he recorded another aspect, of which he haughtily disapproved: "A lady of fine social qualities, whose husband may be an irredeemable drunkard, a disgrace to the Army, and a fraud on mankind, insures his commission by the adroit manipulation of her admirers."[78]

Of the ladies only Mrs. Roe came right out and said flirtation. She confessed to having "commenced a rare flirtation in cozy corners and out-of-the-way places" with a senior officer at a masked ball in Helena, Montana. Of another occasion in 1873, when a new hospital at Fort Lyon was used for a dance before being put to its intended use, she wrote that "the new hospital was simply perfect . . . the corridors were charming for promenading, and, yes, flirting."[79] An equally candid statement came from a Fort Concho correspondent who wrote that the social life of the Army enabled "belles of beauty . . . to practice unconsciously, as if from habit, those bewitching arts of flirtation and the social graces which caused many gallant sons of Mars to capitulate long ago, and indeed does not now want appreciation from the younger soldiers." Indirectly, other ladies confirmed the prevalence of flirtation. Mrs. Gibson attested to flirtation when she described her sister as being "in her element" in "entertaining a couple of men at once" in camp near Fort Lincoln.[80] More obliquely, Mrs. Custer wrote:

I think it would have been very hard for me to have kept a level head with all the attention and delightful flattery which the ordinary manners of officers convey, if I had not remembered how we ladies were always in the minority.[81]

Officers all watch and guard the women who share their hardships. Even the young, unmarried men—the bachelor officers, as they are called—patterning after their elders, soon fall into a sort of fatherly fashion of looking out for the comfort and safety of the women they are with, whether old or young, pretty or ugly. It often happens that a comrade, going on a scout, gives his wife into their charge.[82]

As an example of some of the pleasantries exchanged, O. L. Hein—at the time a socially inclined lieutenant of the First Cavalry—received the following note just as he was about to be rotated from Camp Verde to another station:

Whipple Highlands [Fort Whipple] May 1 [1873]

Lieut. O. L. Hein

DEAR SIR:

A young girl sent to me these flowers at Easter—and told me to give them to the handsomest and bravest man that came in from the Indian Campaign. I send them to you. Your beauty of face and form—is the gift of Heaven. Your bravery is unquestioned, and your own merit. I send you these books desiring to alleviate in any way that offers the hard lot of a tour of duty in Arizona,—perhaps they are not the kind of reading you care for—but you will see that I desired in some way to entertain you—do you care for cake? I propose to send you and Colonel [Captain J. J.] Coppinger some loaves of cake.... Would you like to come up here on detached service? provided the General commanding, approved of General Dana's wish to have you with him, to give him help in making drawings for quarters. No one has authorized, or knows that I have asked you the question but I know Gen. Dana often finds himself pressed for time and would be greatly helped by your competent assistance.

With kind regards, your friend,

HESTER DANA
Wife of Gen. J. J. Dana, U.S.A.[83]

As a novelist of manners, King made full use of such flirtations, thereby preserving the quality and nature of them beyond the sketchy, objective recollections of memoirs. Time and again he referred to "innocent

145

flirtations" on the part of officers' wives who exacted "homage" from a bachelor officer. "It is a fact well understood in army circles that few officers are too old to tender such attentions, and no woman too old to receive them." There was also another side to it: "Younger officers almost always, as a rule, had chosen some one of the married ladies of the regiment as a repositary [*sic*] of their cares and anxieties, their hopes and fears."[84]

"Mrs. Captain Turner" becomes the personification of flirtations between married women and bachelors. Eighteen years younger than her husband, she is about thirty, pretty, and frivolous. The other ladies say she "dances and dresses as though she were not twenty, and that no one else in the regiment can match her in the art of 'making up.'" It comes to be accepted in the "—th Cavalry" that every young man reporting to the post has to put in an "apprenticeship" of adoration of "Mrs. Turner," calling for and escorting her to the weekly hops and being always at her beck and call. When "Lieutenant Hollis" reports, he becomes the latest victim, "dancing around the limited circle of which her apron-string was the radius." After having served his term, the young man becomes one of her "graduates," giving place—sometimes with a sigh of relief—to the next victim.[85] But the handsome, heavily mustached "Lieutenant Ned Perry" will not come within her circle or anyone else's.

"I do wish," said Mrs. Turner, "that Mr. Perry would settle on somebody, because just so long as he doesn't, it is rather hard to tell whom he belongs to." And, as Mrs. Turner had long been a reigning belle among the married women of the —th, and one to whom the young officers were always expected to show much attention, her whimsical way of describing the situation was readily understood.[86]

Her expectation that each will be at her feet for about a year is denied her when "Lieutenant Maynard" suddenly shifts his devotion from her to "Miss Nathalie Baird," the companion of the invalid "Mrs. Major Barry":

> Then Mrs. Barry was becoming interested in Maynard's devotions. When she first arrived at the post, and knew him and heard him referred to as "Mrs. Turner's latest," she was not disposed to like him. She had heard of Mrs. Turner, but never before had been stationed at the same post with her. She forgot at first that every young fellow on reporting for duty at regimental headquarters was immediately "annexed" by this fair, volatile, and would-be youthful matron. She forgot, until laughingly reminded by Mrs. Stannard, that Hunter, Dana, Hollis—almost all the boys in fact—had served their apprenticeship. Blake, the regimental jester, said that plebehood in the regiment had its infallibly visible signs just as it had at West Point. In the —th the most prominent symptom was dancing attendance on Mrs. Turner. But Maynard had barely been well settled down into the traces—had served much less than half the twelve-month—when the Barrys came to the post, and with them [Miss Baird], and Mrs. Turner's sway became uncertain. She still assumed airs of proprietorship—Maynard still had to call for and escort her to the weekly hops, and only the night before, seeing him making for the outer air in the midst of the dance, although she was leaning on the arm of a partner at the moment, she called after her "orderly," as Blake designated her successive victims, and languidly spoke: "Oh, Mr. Maynard, would you mind bringing me a glass of water," and then when he obediently turned and presently appeared with a brimming goblet, she sipped a ripple or two from the surface and, ig-

noring her partner for the moment, murmured, "Where were you going?"

"Over home a few minutes. I have no dances now, you know, until after supper [which usually was served at midnight]."

"You won't find a soul up at the Barrys, unless you've made an appointment. Have you?"

"None whatever, Mrs. Turner," answered Maynard, flushing with annoyance and embarrassment. "Nor did I think of going there."

"I think you are very mean to want to leave me the moment you've had your dance. You haven't been as kind as you were before Miss Baird came. Come, Mr. Crane," she said, turning to her partner with an air of patient, pathetic, but undeserved sorrow. "Let us go and sit down somewhere. I don't think I care to dance this set."[87]

And she hangs on tightly. One morning "Maynard" appears at the "Turners'" door while they are at breakfast, and she—in dressing gown—slips quickly out of sight. After "Maynard" has delivered an official message to the captain and extended his apologies for not being able to call on "Mrs. Turner" at eleven, he turns to leave:

But a soft, silvery voice, a voice utterly unlike the petulant tones so recently heard at the breakfast table [as she defended herself against some deserved remonstrance by Captain Turner], comes from behind the *portiere* that hangs from the archway between the parlor and dining-room and halts him at the threshold.

"Don't look back, Mr. Maynard, I'm simply a fright this morning, but I couldn't help speaking to you. I'm so sorry you can't be here at eleven. Come this afternoon, you will get back in time, won't you? Come at three. That'll give you an hour before stables. *Do.*"

Maynard hesitated. "I'd like to, awfully, Mrs. Turner," he says, "but I—I've got an engagement at that hour."

"Ah, yes," answers Mrs. Turner. "No need to say where. I know who's expecting you at the Barrys'. I'm positively getting jealous, Mr. Maynard." And she was, too.[88]

As open and accepted as were the flirtations, there were restrictions designed to prevent triangles or home-breaking. One was that ladies would not receive gentleman visitors while their husbands were in the field. But "Mrs. Turner" archly ignores the rule, welcoming anybody day or evening, "though, as a rule, there was a sentiment against it, and the majority of the ladies—especially the elders—thought it wrong for the young matrons to receive the visits of young officers at any time when the head of the house was far away." Mere calls were frowned upon as it was, but the officers of King's —th Cavalry "wouldn't stand" for one of their own devoting himself to a lady while her husband was away.[89]

That some "innocent flirtations" turned into affairs is obvious, but there King drew the veil, acknowledging them merely by passing references. He mentions one "dashing lieutenant" who had made off with an officer's wife and resigned his commission. He also recalls that the commander of the "—th Cavalry" consigned a lieutenant to a remote one-company post when it appeared the lieutenant was becoming infatuated with a captain's wife.[90]

The play-acting of knight and lady fair did not entirely satisfy the actors' need for escape—if that was the psychological basis for it—and they also turned to amateur theatricals. Throughout the West, Army posts had amateur troupes with such names as the Fort Shaw

[Montana] Comedy Company, the Fort Sully Minstrel and Variety Troupe, and the Fort Keogh Dramatic Association. Some were composed entirely of officers and ladies, others of enlisted men. They seldom if ever mixed on the boards, but they all mixed in the audience.[91]

King captures the atmosphere, setting, and interaction of audience and players in the following description of the presentation of Thomas William Robertson's *Caste* at Ford D. A. Russell in the winter of 1876-77:

> ... the post theatre was crowded [usually plays were presented in the assembly hall or post school of army posts]. Immediately in front of the little stage with its flaring footlights the orchestra of the —th was seated. Then on camp-stools and low chairs the officers' children were chatting together, eager, excited, and full of joyous anticipation. Proud mammas and attentive nurse-maids were close behind their respective broods, the former now bending forward to restrain the impetuosity of some vigorous young soldier or to check the voluble tongue of the dainty fairy, "the image of her mother," then leaning back and looking over their shoulders to exchange confidences with garrison friends in the row in rear, where were seated mammas whose children were big enough to take care of themselves or so tender in years as to have no interest in the momentous proceedings of the evening. Here and there among the dames and damsels were scattered the officers of the post and masculine visitors from the neighborhood. Cheyenne had sent a large contingent of its *elite* [to cheer on the heroine, Mrs. Major Granger, wife of the commander of the quartermaster depot, who was both disliked and distrusted by the ladies of the —th]. Seven or eight rows of chairs extending, except for narrow aisles on each side, entirely across the hall were thus occupied by the families of the officers and their friends.... Then row upon row of benches, somewhat raised above the level in front, and here

swarmed the wives and children of the non-commissioned officers; and then the entire lower end of the hall was crowded by the troopers and infantrymen, keen critics and yet warm partisans; for, as was well known, there were probably a dozen among their number who could "give points" over and over again to any dramatically-inclined mortal among the shoulder straps. The management had carefully taken up the canvas covering of the floor so that the spotless dancing-surface should not suffer.... The orchestra had already played the overture to Massaniello and received its round of applause, and the leader kept glancing eagerly towards the hand-worn edge of the drop-curtain at the prompter's side, expectant of the signal to start the music which was to usher in act first of Robertson's famous comedy. But, though a hand appeared for an instant, it was hastily withdrawn. There was evident cause for delay, and once more the children, who had been hushed in expectation, began their tittering chat.

"Two to one they're waiting for Mrs. Turner," whispered Stannard to Mrs. Atherton. "She never was known to be ready on time."

It was fully twenty minutes after eight. The orchestra was playing a second overture, in obedience to signals from the stage, when Captain Truscott, holding his sabre in his hand [as officer of the day], so as to prevent its clanking, made his way quietly up the side aisle, and found a chair reserved for him next that of his wife.

But here the orchestra suddenly ceased; there was an instant of whirling over the leaves of music, and then, with a flourish of his bow, the leader signalled, and up went the curtain to an accompaniment of merry, tuneful air. Up it went a few feet at least, then there was a balk. One side hoisted higher than the other, and the painted town of "Irun on the Bidassoa" began to roll up askew, whereat there was a titter which increased to a general laugh as Mr. Wilkins was heard to call out, "Steady there! Dress to the left!" and then to a shout of merriment as "the Honorable George D'Alroy" brisky entered D. R. 2 E. only to find the curtain descending

151

for a straightening out, whereat he whirled about and came into violent collision with a tall eye-glassed swell, just appearing at the same door. When, after a moment's delay, the curtain was induced to go up straight and the two officers entered in conventional mufti, "the Honorable Mr. D'Alroy" could hardly keep his face straight, and the dawdling, languid "Hautree" was observed to have an unusual flush upon his cheeks...the coming of the heroine, and a gentle stir of welcoming applause greeted the timid, half-shy, half-joyous entrance of the lovely "Esther" [Mrs. Turner]. She swept forward as though to greet her lover, halted irresolute at sight of "Hautree," and then forgot them both, and smiled and bowed and smirked, and bowed again, and even essayed a stately Rosina Vokes courtesy [*sic*] in acknowledgement of a greeting which called for no such elaborate response. But, oh, why should the simple, modest, poverty-stricken London girl be attired in a tailor-made street suit of the latest fashion? Every woman in the audience saw the solecism at a glance.

"I'll bet ten to one that was the cause of the delay," growled Stannard to Mrs. Atherton, after it had been pointed out to him. And he was right. She had worn a very different garb at the dress rehearsal the night before, and had counted on escaping Blake's managerial eye until after the opening of the first act, and thus exhibiting the charming toilet just received from the distant East; but he had come upon her unawares, and then ensued a scene not down on the bills. Blake insisted that her costume was entirely inappropriate and begged her to change it. Mrs. Turner responded that when she saw what a guy the proper dress made her, she couldn't bring herself to wear it, and would not, and then "Legs" [a nickname for the long-legged Blake whom King once described as a grin atop a pair of bent dividers] made his fatal blunder.

"Good heavens, Mrs. Turner," he had exclaimed, "you looked lovely in it last night, and it was perfectly in accord with Mrs. Granger's, and she looks lovely in hers now. Do send right over and get it."

But this was just where the shoe pinched. Mrs. Granger

did look lovely in her simple but exquisitely-fitting costume. She had a figure whose beauty was actually enhanced by the plainness of her gown; whereas Mrs. Turner's strong point was her face, not her form, and it took consummate art to make the latter beauteous. Determined not to appear at a disadvantage, Mrs. Turner had planned this scheme, and now she would not budge . . . .

The overture was nearly finished . . . . Blake fairly pleaded with Mrs. Turner, but she was inexorable and even angry . . . by this time it was much after eight, and a moment's reflection convinced him that, after all, it was best to let her have her way; she could not change now inside of half an hour, and, if she were compelled to, would be apt to ruin the performance in some other way . . . and, with wrath in his heart, rang up the curtain.

The town coterie had applauded vigorously at [Mrs. Granger's] entrance; the fort had affably seconded, but a laughing nod was the only recognition. Her silvery voice rang out clear and resonant, compelling their sudden silence. She was through with the brief introductory scene in a moment, and then with infinite gusto fell to chaffing "Hautree." There was a shout of delight from the rear of the hall when "Polly" refused to recognize his rank, scouted the idea of his appearing in that house as a captain, and bade him be corporal or nothing.[92]

By making much of the gaucheries of that production King represents an Army theatrical faithfully. Fond recollections and flattering news reports made the plays sound like smashing successes, but actually many of them were pretty bad. During one play at Fort Concho a major burst out, "Oh, hell! That's too much for me," and walked out. A cavalry colonel said amateur theatricals, especially Negro minstrel shows performed by enlisted men, had "a sort of woodenness about them by no means pleasing."[93]

On other evenings one could tell where people had

gathered by the tinkle of banjo and guitar. Many evenings, indeed, were whiled away listening to some-one play and/or sing. Another form of tireless enter-tainment was the photograph album, over which guests would pore while listening to countless stories about the people in the photographs. Through such infer-ences there can be deduced an oral tradition in the Old Army by which much was known of individuals and events. "Lieutenant McLean" obeys "Mrs. Miller's" urgent request that he bring his scrapbook to a gather-ing at her quarters. "[In the scrapbook] he had a mis-cellaneous assortment of photographs of army friends and army scenes, of autographs, doggerel rhymes, and newspaper clippings, such as 'Spelling Tests' and 'Feats in Pronunciation,' and a quantity of others con-taining varied and useful information. It was a great stand-by and resource of his, and had helped to while away many an evening on the frontier . . . . Where three or four women are gathered together over an album of photographs or a scrap-book of which he is the owner, no man need hope to escape for so much as an instant."[94] Such passages lead to the further inference that isola-tion bred a need for company so intense that Army people did not tire of—or at least they tolerated—repe-tition in their social gathers much as children who ask to hear the same story over and over. Although that could have been just as true of family and neighbor-hood gathers in Eastern cities of the time, too.

Officers also amused themselves with poker, drink-ing, and pool at the post trader's store. "In modern par-lance it is simply 'the store.' The middle room of which, fitted up with a couple of old-fashioned billiard-tables, a huge coal stove, some rough benches, chairs, two or three round tables, and the inevitable bar and cigar-stand, bore on the portals the legend 'officers',' as distinguished from the general 'club-room' beyond."⁹⁵

The need for entertainment—any kind of diversion—was so great that one wife saw a Negro sergeant of the Tenth Cavalry skipping rope in full-dress uniform at the "forlorn and tumble-down adobe-built" Fort Quitman, Texas. "I felt rather shocked to see a soldier in uniform so disporting himself, but concluded if any one at Quitman could be cheerful enough to enjoy so innocent a pastime he was to be congratulated."⁹⁶

News reports indicate that the garrison became a complete family more at Christmas than at any other time, and King incorporated the excitement of Christmas preparations in several of his descriptions of post life. Sometimes all the children of the post received presents from the central Christmas tree; at other posts the officers' children received theirs at one party and the enlisted men's at another. "Dancing, games, and tempting bags of candy filled the measure of the little ones' happiness 4 till 6." At Fort Custer, Montana, officers' wives raised a hundred dollars to buy presents for all the children on the post, and officers played Santa Claus at the party. "It was a great pleasure to see the little ones step up and receive the toys, candies, and useful articles as plucked from the glittering, illuminated tree, or extract from the grab-bag the things of wonder and beauty to their young minds." For the grownups the glittering hour of any holiday season was the ball—Christmas, Fourth of July, it did not matter. In addition, Mrs. Roe found: "They have such a charming custom in the Army of going along the line [officers' row] Christmas morning and giving each other pleasant greetings and looking at the pretty things everyone has received. This is a rare treat out here where we are so far from shops and beautiful Christmas displays. We all went to the bachelors' quarters, almost everyone taking over some little remembrance — homemade candy, cakes, or something of that sort."[97]

Within the intricate web of relationships in such a seemingly simple society, certain forms governed manners. The snappy salute of the twentieth-century Army was absent when officers met. The requirement that officers salute each other was "far more honored in the breach" than in observance in the 1870's, although all officers saluted commanding and field-grade officers. However, it was no more than a doffing of the cap, "such salutation then being a fashion, not a regulation of the service." Few officers saluted line officers except when on duty; "It is sheer neglect," commented the prim and precise King in addressing Wisconsin National Guard officers. When a mounted woman rode by, officers raised their caps to her and she bowed in acknowledgement. Caught at rest, many officers shoved their hands deep into their pockets, but woe to the lieutenant who was caught at it.[98]

In meeting a lady, an officer lifted and lowered her hand, without the kiss, in the fashion of the day. In meeting a lady who had just arrived at the post, officers invariably inquired whether she rode or shot. Having heard that question from one officer after another, one young lady became irritated, but came to construe it "as being a mere cavalry platitude, corresponding somewhat with the question, 'How do you like our city?' asked of strangers back East." All officers were extremely attentive. No woman was allowed to go anywhere without an escort, not even from one room to another at dance or party. In his concern for a lady, a cavalry officer—when escorting her out of doors, as when taking her home from a dance—would throw his cape, known as the cavalry circular, about her. "In twenty little ways the officers spoiled us: they never allowed us to wait on ourselves, to open or shut a door, to draw up our own chair, or to do any little service that they could perform for us. If we ran to the next house for a chat ... we rarely got a chance to return alone, but [the officers] uniformly brought us back to our door!"⁹⁹

But in spite of the closeness, in spite of what others said about indissoluble bonds of friendship formed at frontier posts, in spite of the ideal of the garrison as family, there was a brittleness about garrison relationships. King expresses it through a veteran captain's injunction to a young lieutenant: "It is harder yet to say that friends in the army are a good deal like friends out of it; one only has to get into serious trouble to find how few they are."¹⁰⁰ Given the spirit of chivalry and self-sacrifice that indubitably was part of the Army code, one can find rationale for that condition in the slowness of promotion. Not even the most generous and great-hearted of men can turn his back on self-interest.

Gossip also corroded the family spirit of the garrison. Swinging into post life at Fort Lyon in 1871, Mrs. Roe gloried in the excitement and fun of riding and hunting and exclaimed that if the "stay-at-homes" would get the same exercise they would not "have time to discover so many faults in others, and become our garrison gossips!" Mrs. Custer said "the whole garrison was voluble in its denunciation" when someone said or did something deserving censure. But Custer, she said, would not allow anyone to speak to the detriment of another in his presence. "In vain I disclaimed being of that exalted order of females and declared that it re-

quired great self-denial not to join in a gossip." At
Fort Niobrara, Lieutenant Gonzalez Sidney Bingham,
Ninth Cavalry, fell in love with Antoinette Lynch,
daughter of Captain Edward Lynch, Eighth Infantry,
"and the post began to be on the *qui vive* to see how the
affair would end." It ended in an engagement.[101]

Surely a convenient device for King's stereotyped
plots, gossip nonetheless takes on lifelike dimensions
in his characterizations. Once again, "Fanny Turner"
becomes the embodiment of the gossip as of the flirt,
but she has able assistance in "Mrs. Raymond," "Mrs.
Gregg," "Mrs. Wilkins" and others. Nor did King spare
the men, for ". . . in the close comradeship and intimacy of frontier life men get to know one another so
well that the foibles, weaknesses, and waywardness of
the animal are apt to be far more prominently mentioned in garrison chit-chat than his sterling or lovable
traits."[102]

In King's novels, "the ladies very generally heard or
saw all that was going on," and spread the word. Servants are a fertile source of gossip. They will use any
excuse, such as borrowing a cup of sugar, to get into
another kitchen and tell their story. From the servant
the mistress hears the story, and from there it spreads.
"Now, it is a peculiarity of the ladies of the army that
the simple announcement of a fact is as stimulative of
conjecture and reflection as was the fall of Isaac Newton's apple." Another source of gossip is simply their
own observations. When the "—th Cavalry" is moving
into Fort D. A. Russell, an infantry officer says, "Mrs.
Whaling [wife of the post commander] has been helping
them unpack for the last three days, and telling everybody what they had and didn't have."[103]

"Mrs. Turner," however, carries the burden as the
symbol of all gossips everywhere. She "could . . . rob a

woman of her reputation and receive her with open arms almost in the same instant."[104] With her as a center-piece, King weaves in many aspects of Army life. In one scene he gives a classic description of the art of provoking interest as a preliminary to conversation. The setting is Crook's front porch at Fort Whipple where the ladies are sitting with the newly arrived "Mrs. Pelham" and dying to tell her of a strange, per-haps scandalous, relationship between "Truscott" and "Mrs. Captain Tanner." "Mrs. Tanner" passes them, and this conversation ensues:

"What a charming little woman!" said her ladyship after a pause, during which all four pairs of eyes had followed [Mrs. Tanner and her little daughter] out of earshot.

"Sweet," said Mrs. Turner, reflectively.

"So gentle and ladylike," said Mrs. Raymond.

"I've always admired her so much," said their companion [the unnamed wife of a staff officer]. Then came a pause.

"It is a perfect mystery to me how any one can help liking her," said Mrs. Raymond, softly and slowly. Another pause.

"And I supposed everybody did," said Mrs. Pelham, looking very intently at her two "subordinates," who there-upon became more intently interested in some distant ob-jects, waiting with well-assured shrewdness to be drawn out by further questioning.

"Has she been in to see Grace?" asked the staff lady.

"No," replied her ladyship promptly. "She went in to see Mr. Truscott [who lay wounded in the general's quarters].

Instantly Mrs. Raymond and Mrs. Turner exchanged glances of much significance, which Mrs. Pelham was quick to observe, and which, as soon as satisfied that she had ob-served, the two ladies discontinued and again became pre-occupied in manner.

The other lady said "Oh!"

Now, there are dozens of ways of saying "oh," each

eminently expressive of some different idea or emotion. This one was eminently expressive of, "Well, of course it's her own business, but if *I* were in *her* place," etc., and then there was a general lull of at least three seconds in the conversation. Just enough had been said, indicated, and acted to pique her ladyship's curiosity to the utmost.[105]

One after another, "Turner's" friends dropped away from him because of his wife's malicious tongue. The denouement comes in a split of the ladies at Russell in 1878, when "Mrs. Turner" spreads a rumor that "Mrs. Gregg" is ruining her husband financially. After a confrontation the two ladies part with the determination never to speak to each other. "Mrs. Gregg wrote a long, long letter to her husband [the companies were in the field], setting forth all the hateful, adominable things Fanny Turner had said; and, just as Turner had predicted, another old comrade and friend with whom he had campaigned all over the country . . . now coldly avoided him,"[106] King gets rid of "Mrs. Turner" by having her husband killed by an accident in the field.[107]

Once widowed, an officer's wife had no place on an Army post and had to leave as quickly as possible. Exceptions occurred on the Northern Plains where the hard grip of winter made travel impossible. Mrs. Lieutenant R. Frank Walborn, for example, had to remain at Fort Stevenson, Dakota Territory, during the winter of 1868-69 after the death of her husband. Mrs. Roe found the practice harshly unjust: "In civil life a poor widow can often live right on in her old home, but in the Army, never! Mrs. White [the fictitious name of a wife who had lost her husband immediately after she had given birth to a child] will have to give up the quarters just as soon as she and the little baby are strong enough to travel . . . to-morrow a number of us are to commence making warm clothing for her and the children."[108]

In such times of need the family spirit would cause the others in the garrison to buy the personal possessions of the departing widow for more than they were worth, as happens to "Mrs. Turner."[109] Departure sales also brought more than articles were worth when officers in straitened circumstances were transferred. But the sales could also be a burden on the departing couple when smallness and pettiness appeared in the garrison family. When Major Lane was ordered home from Fort Union for reasons of health in 1867, his wife prepared to auction all household goods not needed for the trip. "I was well aware how all the articles would be examined, by my army sisters for spots and specks." Therefore, she hired a man to work for several days, scrubbing everything to a spotless condition. She was thus incensed when an officer's wife, in a pre-auction inspection, whispered to her that things sold better *"when clean!"*[110] As a defense against smarting remarks, the ladies of the Third Infantry decided to hold a general auction when the regiment was ordered from Montana to Eastern posts in 1888. "As we did not desire to turn our houses into second-hand shops, where people could handle and make remarks about things we had treasured, it was decided that everything to be sold should be moved to the large hall, where enlisted men could attend to the shop business."[111]

From the accounts of garrison life one receives at least a hint of the dichotomy in the Army during the Indian-fighting period after 1865. The Army envisioned by the officers who wrote the regulations in Washington seemed to exist only in their minds. While these regulations specified quarters by rank, the frontier Army went its own way in providing what it could without regard to regulations. Regulations also specified that the inside measurements of an Army wagon were to be 22 by 42 by 114 inches. That hardly squares with the many references to the "massive blue Army wagons" that moved troops, families, and supplies from one post to another. It does come close to one type of wagon used on the Plains—the so-called Chicago wagon—which had approximately the same dimensions and could carry from 2,500 to 3,500 pounds. But the J. Murphy wagon would seem to have been the massive wagon described—beds sixteen feet long, six feet high, and rear wheels seven feet in diameter. Of course many different types of wagons were used in the West, and both the quartermaster and civilian contractors furnished wagons for Army transport.[112]

That garrison social life, as described by King, remained stable until at least the time of the Spanish-American War is shown in the memoirs of a latter-day Army woman. In 1894 she went to Fort Sill, Indian Territory, to visit a classmate, knowing no more of the Army than what she had read in the novels of "a certain Captain King." Almost all the elements of King's novels appear in her recollections. She was met at the railroad station in Rush Springs by her friend in an ambulance, escorted by two officers. The very next morning almost everyone on post called on her. There then ensued a constant round of parties and dances, with all the bachelor officers asking to be her escort. As time went on she came to focus more and more on a captain whom she finally married in 1896. Returning to Fort Sill as a wife, she encountered exactly the same social milieu that stands revealed in full detail in King's novels.[113]

5.
The Army Post

If one description could alone fit all frontier forts, it would be of a monotonous routine relieved only slightly by the color of periodic ceremony. All posts followed common customs and procedures, but there were always "ground rules"; that is, customs peculiar to a given post. The personality and psychology of post commanders, as well as those of subordinate officers, created different atmospheres.

At 5:30 A.M. the drummers and fifers sounded reveille, the drummer tapping out a quick-step on the same type of maple drum that had been used by the Continental Army, "not the modern rattlepan borrowed from Prussia." The fifers and drummers marched the garrison, parading down officers' row as well as in front of the barracks. In Arizona, the Apaches loved to hear fife and drum, but stopped their ears at the harsh notes of the trumpet when it was used.[1] At posts without a band, trumpet or bugle started the day.

For a quick eye-opener, cavalry officers downed a cocktail of whiskey, water, bitters and sugar.[2] In the meantime, the troops had tumbled out of barracks and answered to the first of three daily roll calls—reveille, retreat, and tattoo.[3]

At cavalry posts the next event varied. Some commanders wanted the horses cared for first, which meant that stable call was sounded almost immediately after reveille. Others reversed the two, giving the men about thirty minutes for both reveille and a quick breakfast of beef hash, dry bread and coffee.

Old Catnip [Pelham] was a firm believer in the theory that a soldier was far more apt to take an interest in the grooming of his horse when his own stomach was comfortably filled than when he was suffering for his breakfast. As a consequence, stable-duty was not the bugbear in the —th that it was in other regiments, where the men had to spend an hour or more, shivering and hungry and cross, spattering away with curry-comb and brush, and swearing *sotto voce* at their steeds in the same listless and perfunctory manner with which they would have cleaned several muddy pairs of boots. In Pelham's regiment the principal difficulty seemed to be that of restraining the men from whistling or singing at their work,—a thing which could not be permitted, because it was unprofessional from a military point of view.[4]

In either event, sleepy cavalry officers donned stable frocks—as did the men—and trudged off to the stables, while the infantry officers could slip back to their quarters for a short after-sleep.[5] When the work was done outdoors, the scene at stables appeared thus:

Lashed tight to the heavy picket rope, the horses were revelling in the keen morning air and slanting sunshine, nipping at each other's noses, challenging, with sparkling eye and tip-tilted ear, each well-known face and form of officer or man to caress or frolic, snapping and squealing at each other across the line, occasionally rearing and plunging in uncontrollable jollity. Bending to their work in their white stable frocks and overalls, the men were making brush and currycomb fly over the shining coats of their pets, carefully guarding, however, the long, thick winter crop of hair, for no man could say how soon they might have to take the field and face unsheltered the keen Dakota blasts. The frosty quadrangle was merry with musical tap, tap of the metal comb, and the snort and *"purrr"* and paw of hoof of the spirited bays. [Lieutenant] Sanders, an enthusiastic horseman, was darting in and out among his charges, praising this man's work, condemning that, and occasionally seizing brush and comb himself and giving a practical lesson to some comparative novice.[6]

Before the company was released from stables it had to "stand to heel" while the stables were inspected, too.[7]

Once on the picket line, the horses had their own ideas of what a proper morning routine should be:

...there was no one exploit that seemed to give the younger animals keener delight,—nothing that made the perpetrator a bigger hero in his own eyes or the object of greater envy among his fellows,—and as a consequence every device of which equine ingenuity was master was called into play, regularly as the morning came around, to break loose either from the controlling hands of the troopers or from the taut and straining picket rope.[8]

Ordinarily, the horses were then turned out to graze, under the watchful eyes of a herd guard.[9]

After stables, the officers hurried back to quarters, threw off the "strongly-scented stable rig," and had a quick, cold "plunge bath," followed by a brisk rub.[10] There then was an interlude in which the cavalry officers could catch up with the infantry officers who by then had had time for breakfast.

Next came guard-mounting. Marching the parade ground, the band brought forth in good weather every woman, child, and dog to watch. Fully uniformed in helmet and sabre, the new officer of the day marched on with the guard for that day, and the old guard marched off. Together the old and new officers of the day visited the guardhouse; checked the roster of prisoners; and the one turned the roster over to the other. With them were the officers of the guard, old and new; during a tour of guard duty the officer of the guard had to spend his entire time at the guardhouse.[11]

[The guardhouse at Fort D. A. Russell had both cells and] what was known as the garrison prisoners' room on the east side of the building. A big coal-stove stood in the middle of the large apartment and a wooden shelf or bunk extended around two adjacent sides. A single window at the east gave light to the room in the day-time, a swinging lantern at night. The members of the guard were gathered in a big room separated from this one only by a thin partion of boards. . . . despite the big stove nearly red-hot at the globe, the bitter cold came driving through every cranny and chink.[12]

From frontier guardhouses several of King's characters engineered escapes, but that was entirely within probability. Many guardhouses were no more secure than frontier jails generally. For example, some horse thieves escaped from the Fort Lyon guardhouse by sawing a hole through the roof.[13]

The authoritative notes of adjutant's call then brought all officers to the C.O.'s office. Here again, practice varied according to ground rules. In one account King has a post commander assembling all officers for conferences and instructions, led off by the reports of the old and new officers of the day and the post surgeon. Even though the colonel might have nothing to tell them, the officers do not object to the meeting, because each there takes his after-breakfast smoke.[14]

Meanwhile, sick-call had sounded—after stables—

and then the fatigue call. The published schedule might call for drill both morning and afternoon, but frontier soldiers spent a large amount of time on fatigue details as common laborers. That was one of the causes for the high rate of desertion. Both drum and trumpet sounded mess call for dinner—the noon meal—which usually was no more varied or appetizing than breakfast had been.[15] After eating, the men either were drilled or put back to work. About 4:00 P.M. all officers and men responded to the evening stable call. Once again the troopers groomed and watered their horses. Then came supper, often only dry bread and coffee for the soldiers.[16]

The high point of the day came with the retreat dress parade at sundown, in conformance with army regulations which required one dress parade daily.[17] A composite description of parades—by one who, as adjutant, knew and delighted in every small detail of them—can be reconstructed from King's novels, as follows:

[The colonel] particularly prided himself upon the soldierly grace and style with which he presided at the most stately ceremony of the military day.... In all the yellow radiance of his cavalry plumage [he] strode forth from the veranda [of his quarters] and stood revealed in the rays of the westering sun ... putting on his white leather gloves and buttoning them at the wrist with much deliberation..... while the adjutant, hurrying on to where his sergeant-major was awaiting him at the edge of the greensward, signalled the band, and the stirring notes of "adjutant's call," followed by the burst of martial strains in swinging six-eight time, heralded the coming of the troops of the whole command.
Company after company, the cavalry from the west, the infantry from the east end of the quadrangle came marching forth upon the level green carpet, seemingly intermingling

in confusion as they neared the centre, yet unerringly and unhesitatingly marching onward, until presently, with the solid blue and white battalion in the centre, and with the yellow plumed helmets of the cavalry parading afoot on both flanks, the long . . . line stretched nearly half way across the longest axis of the quadrangle. . . . [The cólonel] had with much deliberate dignity of manner marched out in front of the centre [and] now stood in solitary state with folded arms.

Company after company had taken the statuesque pose of "parade rest" and its captain faced to the front again, the adjutant . . . turned his head towards the band and growled, "Sound off!" The boom and crash of drum and cymbal . . . and the band went on thundering down the line, countermarched and came back to its post on the right, making the welkin ring with the triumphant strains of "Northern Route."

Then came the stirring "retreat" upon the trumpets, the roar of the evening gun, the fluttering folds of the great garrison flag to the ground as though its hilliards were shot away. . . .

. . . the adjutant stalked his three yards to the front, faced fiercely to the left and shouted his resonant orders down the line, three hundred martial forms sprang to attention, and the burnished arms came to the "carry" with simultaneous crash, ranks were opened with old-time precision, the parade "presented" to the colonel, the manual was executed . . . first sergeants reported, orders were published, parade formally dismissed . . . the officers closed on the centre, and some sixteen of them came marching to the front to the stirring music of *"En Avant"*. . . . the line of officers marched solidly to the front, halted, and made its simultaneous salute to the colonel, who slowly raised and lowered his white-gloved hand in recognition.[18]

Leaving the retreat dress parade, officers unbuckled belts and removed helmets as quickly as they reached their doors, "in eager haste to get out of the constraint of full dress."[19] For most of the officers the day's work was done, and they could turn to family life, or cards at the trader's store, or whatever social event had been scheduled for the evening. For the enlisted men there then ensued a period of free time until tattoo, anywhere from 8:00 to 9:30 P.M.[20]

Tattoo, marked by the cavalry band playing "The March of the Bear," brought all enlisted men and some officers out again.[21]

Then soft and clear there rose from the flagstaff the trumpet signal for "first call;" and, as the mellow notes were repeated, the doors of the men's quarters across the parade were opened, and, with jest and laughter and merry talk, the troopers came sauntering out. Here and there lights flitted to and fro,—the lanterns of the first sergeants. Then the trumpeters of the entire command, having united, began their march around the garrison, sounding their stirring quicksteps. Door after door along officers' row opened and gave exit to some muffled figure, and the lanterns of the company officers danced away across the dark parade... then the assembly rang out upon the still air, and the "here," "here," of the men could be distinctly heard, and the gruff voices of the sergeants calling their rolls; then the lanterns all seemed to be converging towards a solitary light that stood under the flagstaff [that of the adjutant, to receive reports from company officers], each halting short some few paces from it, and such communications as "Company 'B,' present, or accounted," "Company 'F,' Private Mulligan absent," came floating along the chill night air.[22]

About fifteen minutes after tattoo the buglers or trumpeters would send across the garrison the gentle but magisterial imperative of taps—what one wife considered the most beautiful call in the world.[23] From the barracks windows the lights would suddenly fade, leaving large, bulky shadows in the dark. Across the parade lights still shone in officers' quarters, as did turned-down lamps in the hospital and a few lanterns that burned all night at postern and guardhouse. The day was done. All could sleep safely, for the sentries around the perimeter called out the hour at thirty-minute intervals. Starting with Post No. 1 at the guardhouse, the call was taken up by each sentry in turn, giving the hour and the drawn-out assurance of "All's well!"[24]

In addition to the prescribed daily routine, officers and men were occupied in work details, drills, garrison courts (before summary courts-martial were introduced in the 1880's to handle minor infractions), boards of survey, large general courts-martial that dispensed justice for more serious breaches by officer and soldier alike, "and the long list of minor but nonetheless exacting demands on the time and attention of the subalterns and company commanders."[25]

King said honestly that "a junior in the line is apt to find life more or less monotonous," and made worse by the "stagnation of promotion."[26] It became particularly bad in the North when life settled into "the usual midwinter plane of monotony."[27] On the other hand, the wives appreciated the winter, for it kept the men at the post—usually—and gave them abundant free time for family and social life. As one who loved the invigorating life of the field, King nevertheless conceded: "Our truest heroes are those who bear with equanimity the heat and burden of the long monotonous round of garrison life with its petty tyrannies, exactions, exasperations, and bear them without a break or murmur."[28]

The week-long sameness of the days was broken by the pomp of full-dress inspection on Sunday, "a long and intricate ceremony." As part of the overall repetition day by day, it merely helped mark the passage of time.[29]

First call for inspection in full dress had "gone," as the soldiers say, as the colonel appeared in the panoply of his profession upon the front piazza [of his quarters], glancing modified approval at the glistening surface of his top-boots and the brilliant polish of his spurs. Down at the front gate his orderly stood, every item of his dress and equipment a model of soldierly trimness. Out in the centre of the parade a little party of the guard had just lowered the storm-flag that had been hoisted at dawn,[30] and were running up in its stead the great garrison standard, whose folds of scarlet and white lapped out lazily in response to the soft breeze now rising from the westward bluffs. Over at the barracks the men had come pouring forth, the neat dark blue and white of the infantry at the east side contrasting favorably with the glaring yellow trimmings of the cavalry battalion, swarming along the walk and streaming from the stairways and galleries of their crowded quarters, like so many full-plumaged hornets. On the verandas across the parade, helmeted officers and ladies in dainty muslins began to appear.[31]

After the morning inspection, officers and troopers had the rest of the day off. In most posts there was no conflict between the inspection and religious services, because the Army's small corps of chaplains were assigned, as a rule, only to regimental headquarters posts and not always then. In moving about the West through a period of years, one wife recalled that she had spent those years "in a heathenish manner, as regards all church observances." At some posts, though, some ladies made arrangements for civilian clergymen to conduct services on post. One was Mrs. Lieutenant J. P. Martin, Fourth Cavalry, who arranged for a clergyman of Silver

City, New Mexico, to preach in the post library of
Fort Bayard on alternate Sundays. Describing the
Eighth Infantry's move to Fort Niobrara, in 1886, a
wife said: "Being nearer civilization now, Uncle Sam
provided us with a chaplain ... a weekly service was
held ... and it was a great comfort to the church people
to have this weekly service." But as an indication of
values, she described the chaplain as one who "as far as
looks went could hold his own with any of the younger
officers." Chaplains wore the uniform of the Army with
the status—not the rank—of captain. On their shoulder
straps they wore only a shepherd's crook. When service
was held in a post chapel (usually the combination
chapel, dance hall, and theatre), officers frequently
wore full dress uniform and sword to the service. However, an indication that a chaplain's services were
limited and perfunctory in many ways can be seen in a
communication from Chaplain G. W. Simpson of Fort
Laramie in 1883; he wrote the *Army and Navy Journal*
that he had served communion the preceding Sunday,
which was seldom done, and that he saw no reason
why it should not be done regularly inasmuch as
chaplains were ordained ministers.[32]

Whereas chaplains come into King's accounts only
sporadically and briefly, the Army doctor is a major
presence throughout his works. Perhaps King was reflecting a general attitude among the officers when he
described a doctor as "one of the best men in one of the
very best corps, personally and professionally, in our
little army." Interestingly, the Army doctor almost always appears as something of a father figure—a professionally qualified man in his field and a wise and
good human who fought for individual justice, acting
as a stabilizer of social relations at an Army post.[33]

Doctors who specialized in illnesses of women and children were of "vital importance . . . in our large garrisons." One wife swore by Army doctors because of their interest in her children. When troops were in the field, and the women under corresponding strain, the doctor "was our mainstay . . . to whom we rushed if only a finger ached." Another wife gave full credit to a doctor at Fort Craig, New Mexico, for having cured a baby who had been stricken with croup during a march in a rainstorm. Still another recalled that Dr. Henry Lippincott happened to pass through Ehrenberg en route to a post while she was ill, and "it is to him that I believe I owe my life." A physician at Camp McDowell was remembered as such a good doctor that "we never had a moment's anxiety, as long as he staid [sic] at Camp McDowell." Like the old family doctor, the Army doctor came whenever needed. To serve troops at Fort Fillmore, New Mexico, in 1861, a doctor would come from a post forty miles away. He would come at any time of night in his own garrison. In 1867 two white girls, who had been recaptured from Indians, stayed the night in the home of Lieutenant and Mrs. Frank Baldwin; the doctor came to their house and stayed throughout the night with one of the girls who had been driven to insanity because of her treatment at the hands of her captors.[34]

The heart of post operations, of course, was post headquarters; King describes a small post in Arizona in the following way:

The little office had barely room for the desks of the commander and his adjutant and the table on which were spread the files of general orders from various superior headquarters—regimental, department, division, the army, and War Secretary. No curtains adorned the little windows, front and rear. No rug or carpet vexed the warping floor. Three chairs, kitchen pattern, stood against the pine partition that shut off the sight, but by no means the hearing of the three clerks scratching at their flat-topped desks in the adjoining den. Maps of the United States, of the Military Division of the Pacific, and of the Territory, as far as known and surveyed, hung about the wooden walls. . . . But of pictures, ornamentation, or relief of any kind the gloomy box was destitute as the dun-colored flat of the parade. Official severity spoke in every feature of the forbidding office as well as in those of the major commanding.[35]

. . . the colonel and [the adjutant] remained at their desks in the office, the former occasionally addressing some question to his silent subordinate, and then going on in his methodical way with his letters. From time to time the sergeant-major or a clerk would enter with a fresh batch of papers, which would be noiselessly deposited on the adjutant's desk, and those already signed were as quietly removed, and in the adjoining room, where the clerks were busily at work, made ready for the mail.[36]

To summon clerks from the other room, the "old man" —as the C.O. was known even in the 1870's—used a push-gong bell of the type once familiar at hotel registration counters. Throughout the day the orderly trumpeter sat at post headquarters, with one eye on the clock, waiting to sound the calls prescribed by post rules. Ordinarily, the trumpeter would stride to the bandstand to sound his call.[37]

Considerable responsibility rested upon the two officers in that office. In addition to ultimate responsibility for his quartermaster, commissary, and ordnance officers, the post commander also had to worry about fires, which plagued almost every wooden frontier post. When high winds buffeted Fort D. A. Russell, the colonel "ever on the defensive against fires, bade the troop officers look well to their company kitchens and see that all the ranges and stoves were securely banked." He also was required to make a monthly inspection of the garrison.[38]

We all know what the adjutant should be,—a soldier in everything, in carriage, form, voice, and manner, the soul of parade and guard-mounting, the reliable authority on tactics and regulations, the patient student of general orders, the rigid scrutinizer of returns and rolls, the scholarly man of the subalterns, the faithful adherent and executive in spirit and in letter of the commanding officer.[39]

Too, there was always the danger of theft from a post's valuable stores of ammunition, weapons, food, and grain. When King made such a theft a major part of a plot,[40] he was dramatizing an experience of his own. As adjutant at Fort D. A. Russell in 1876-77 he also was loaded down with the job of ordnance officer to oblige the departing commanding officer who was anxious to begin a leave.

A vast quantity of ordnance stores, arms, ammunition, and equipments of every kind had been sent to the fort during and after the Sioux campaign, the officials of that most level-headed [Ordnance] department finding it far easier to ship in bulk from the great arsenal [at Rock Island, Illinois, than to break down shipments to the size required by the post].[41]

[As a result, six hundred thousand rounds of ammunition were stored in a magazine a mile and a half away from the post, plus about one thousand sets of infantry and cavalry equipments in post warehouses.] Then [the magazine] was robbed. A party of citizens from the neighboring town sallied forth one bitter cold night and helped themselves to what they could carry. X. tracked them through the snow to town on the following day, and after some detective work succeeded in securing the arrest of one of the parties who had a lot of the stolen property in his cellar.[42] [But the jury acquitted him.]

A highlight of the week or month was the arrival of the mail. At Fort Stanton in 1870-71, the arrival of the weekly mail "made that day a red-letter one in our quiet lives. It was always devoted to eager anticipation and close watching of the long line of road over which the mail rider came. If overdue, nothing else could be thought or talked of until he arrived, and we received our news from beyond the border." Things had not changed much at Stanton since 1858 when the monthly mail arrived the same way; then, most people devoured their month's backlog of newspapers immediately, although one wife gave her husband one paper a day, putting it beside his place at table each morning to create the illusion of reading the "news." At Fort C. F. Smith in the winter of 1867-68 Indian couriers took and brought the monthly mail. "The day appointed for their return, everyone listened anxiously for the signal from the sentinel which would announce the approach of the mail as it would appear in sight coming over a high hill a few miles from the post. On pleasant days we were allowed to go to the south bastion as a great privilege to watch for the arrival." The manner of distributing the mail varied. On some posts the commander took the mail to his office immediately; King has one commander examine the mail first to see who was writing to whom. At others, the mail was distributed to officers' families in the office, or by an orderly who marched down the row, filled with the importance of his duty as he delivered mail to each home.[43]

For official communications, a number of posts had telegraph offices by the mid-seventies and many more by the eighties. Since most of the traffic was military, the operators were soldiers. They were not required to work past 9:00 P.M., but many slept by their instruments in case of emergency. When a message came in, the operator delivered it in an "ugly brown envelope" to the post commander. But the fact that a message was official did not mean it was secret. "Telegraph offices 'leaked' on the frontier in those days [about 1875]. The operators at the military stations were all enlisted men ... not bound by the regulations of the Western Union, and who could not keep to themselves every item of personal interest." Although King was generalizing when he wrote that passage, a specific example can be drawn from Crook's experience at Fort Laramie in the spring of 1877. While he was then waiting for word from Spotted Tail, the Brulé Sioux chief who had gone onto the Plains to try to persuade Crazy Horse to surrender, an emissary from the chief reached Deadwood whence a telegram was sent immediately to Laramie. A Chicago *Times* correspondent at Deadwood said Crook had not received the awaited and critical message telling him Crazy Horse was coming in because he had been out fishing. Since Crook did not react until the next day, the version would appear to be correct, and—in keeping with King's reference to gossipy telegraph operators—it also would appear that the Laramie operator had told the Deadwood operator where Crook was.[44]

As a matter of fact, ordinary discipline was sometimes lax in frontier posts, especially in Arizona where troopers concentrated on scouting rather than spick-and-span crispness in garrison. Observing that frontier posts were often remiss in some forms, King describes his "—th Cavalry" as having had several years of "go-as-you-please work" in Arizona, where the regiment had been broken into scattered detachments. But in Kansas as of 1876 they were beginning to shape up, especially in posts where several companies were gathered. He said the same thing, in a factual account, of the Fifth Cavalry. By 1877, he wrote, the Fifth had fallen into a lack of uniformity, even at parades, because they had been so scattered. But the companies eventually were brought into uniformity through intensive training at Fort D. A. Russell.[45]

King thus brought into focus the marked differences between campaigning in Arizona and on the Northern Plains. And his opinions were repeatedly substantiated by other writers, especially by a regimental commander who wrote:

The hardships of campaigning in Wyoming Territory contrast strangely with those of Arizona. On the one hand there are thick-ribbed ice, fearful snow-storms, and wintry winds that chill the marrow in one's bones; while on the other hand there are stifling heat and parching sand-storms.

I believe I know what heat is, and the deaths that some of our people die on the white sand plains of Arizona must be the most dreadful of all. Without water, without shade, without hope, the rocks so hot as to blister the hand if it touches them, these men lie down in a fearful state of delirium, and nothing is ever known of them again except perhaps when their bleached bones are found. I have seen soldiers staggering along the road like so many drunken men, and known of their minds deserting them, leaving only shattered wrecks. This is not a very pleasing view of "the pomp and circumstance of war," but it is a true one, as all old cavalry campaigners know, though as a general thing they say but little regarding it.[46]

Most Army people dreaded service in Arizona, looking upon it at the time as "exile" and "dry-rotting." Later, they referred to the campaigns of the 1870's as the "days of the Empire" in Arizona.[47] Two of King's descriptions follow:

Arizona was an interesting region in those days of development that followed close on the heels of the war. Hundreds of experienced hands had been thrown out of employment by the return of peace, and the territories overflowed with outlaws, red and white, male and female. It was taking one's life in one's hands to venture pistol shot beyond the confines of a military post. It was impossible for paymasters to carry funds without a strong escort of cavalry. The only currency in the territory was that put in circulation by the troops or paid to contractors through the quartermaster's department. Even Wells-Fargo, pioneer expressmen of the Pacific Slope, sent their messengers and agents no further than the Colorado River, and Uncle Sam's mail stage was robbed so often that a registered package had grown to be considered only an advertisement to the covetous of the fact that its contents might be of value.[48]

Indeed, the *Army and Navy Journal* received a letter from Arizona in 1882 which had been forwarded from the San Francisco post office, opened, and marked "robbed by highwaymen, September 19, 1882."[49]

There was little duty doing at Sandy at the time whereof we write [c. 1875]. Men rose at dawn and sent the horses forth to graze all day in the foothills under heavy guard. It was too hot for drills, with the mercury sizzling at the hundred mark. Indian prisoners did the "police" work about the post; and men and women dozed and wilted in the shade until the late afternoon recall. Then Sandy woke up and energetically stabled, drilled, paraded under arms at sunset, mounted guard immediately thereafter, dined in spotless white; then rode, drove, flirted, danced, gossiped, made mirth, melody, or monotonous plaint till nearly midnight; then slept until the dawn of another day.[50]

Arizona officers wore white cotton uniforms made by company tailors. In garrison or on the trail, troopers habitually closed their eyes to slits in the daytime, although green goggles were worn by some officers in the West. As they traveled from post to post they followed roads that "twisted as only Arizona roadways can." En route from Yuma to Tucson they could stop at road ranches where the unvarying menu for breakfast was bacon, beans, and fried eggs for one dollar. In all the territory, Tucson was the closest approach to a town (Prescott notwithstanding). One officer recalled: "Tucson was known to us of the old army as the 'jumping off' place, and together with the two other habitations south, on the road to Mexico, when alluded to, were summarized as 'Tucson,' 'Tubac,' 'tumacacari' [*sic*], and 'to hell.'" For refreshment they drank California wine, for "Arizona whiskey is of the vile vilest." Added to the exasperations of heat and dreariness, officers found that their watch mechanisms went awry because of the hot, dry climate.[51]

Once their "exile" was over, soldiers could not get out of Arizona fast enough. When the Third Cavalry was rotated out in 1871, Captain Anson Mills and other officers went aboard a steamboat at Yuma and then "took off our shoes and beat the dust of Arizona over the rail, at the same time cursing the land." When, after four years, the Eighth Infantry was transferred, a wife was elated: "Ordered 'out' at last! I felt like jumping up onto the table, climbing onto the roof, dancing and singing and shouting for joy!"[52] At the same time, there were some compensations, as King has a captain explain to a lieutenant just out of West Point:

> You can live like a prince on bacon and *frijoles,* dress like a cowboy on next to nothing or like an Apache *in* next to nothing, spend all your days and none of your money in mountain scouting, and come out of it all in two or three years rich in health and strength and experience and infinitely better off financially than you could ever have been anywhere else. Leave whiskey and poker alone and you're all right.[53]

Both the good and the bad of Arizona came out in a controversy among the officers of the Sixth Cavalry in 1882-84. The schism appeared when Washington received the impression that the Sixth wanted to stay in Arizona. When that error came to light there was a quick retort that most wanted to leave, but "the few who wish to remain for pecuniary reasons" [mining, by implication] had fixed the belief the entire regiment wanted to stay. "The keeping of this regiment here in this unhealthy locality so long, just to suit a few holiday soldiers, who never do any field duty, and a few speculators, who have become inefficient and worthless as soldiers is one of the worst abuses that has occurred in the Army for many years." That brought a retort from Captain Adna R. Chaffee that there were no holiday soldiers or officers who escaped field duty in the Sixth. However, he added: "I believe it is true that a number of our officers find their health breaking down, and a change of station is now considered desirable by a good many." Still another correspondent said the question agitating the "scouting part" of the Sixth was whether the regiment should "swelter on for seven years longer and wear itself out tramping over the hot and arid plains and mountains, or will it get what it justly deserves, a change of station?" The Sixth, as of 1882, had already been there for seven years. And there were officers who wanted to stay longer. One of them said: "Arizona is the best Department in the country. To-day it is the only department in which one gets what ought to be expected of an Army man — work in the field. If any one — officer or enlisted man — wants glory there is the only place he can get it." What the Sixth finally got was a transfer to New Mexico, known as the "Trooper's Paradise," in 1884.[54]

There was not the same depth of feeling about service in northern posts, probably because the desert makes an impact all its own on people who are accustomed to greenery and regular changes of season. But against the heat of Arizona there was the biting, stinging cold of ferocious winds on the Northern Plains. With more mellowness, King describes a pleasant winter day at Fort D. A. Russell:

It was one of those rare late winter days that sometimes dawn upon the eastern slopes of the Rockies. The frosty air was full of ozone, stimulant, and sparkle, and so still and serene that the smoke from every chimney sailed slowly aloft, straight towards the zenith. The sunshine poured down from an unclouded sky, warm, rich, and mellow. The prairie roads were hard and beaten. The prairie sward glistened and glinted with innumerable tiny globules where the sharp touch of the night frosts had fringed every little blade of bunch-grass. Thin, brittle sheets of ice overspread the little pools, where the dancing waters of the *acequia* had been checked in their rapid flow; and under every pole of the military telegraph line a musical hum, like that of some huge single-stringed aeolian harp fell upon the ear.[55]

Then came spring:

... the late, reluctant spring was breaking. The days were getting longer, warmer, and more laden with the sweet south wind. Tiny little flowerets, snow-white,—the Star of Bethlehem,—began to peep out among the clumps of bunch-grass; the snow had softened and moistened the soil and gone its way; even in the deepest ravines it was disappearing ... the little starry flowers speedily covered the rolling waves of prairie like a snowy fleece, and so long as the sun was high the children and their mothers strolled out over the broad expanse north and east of the post, gathering the dainty blossoms by the handful, and all the garrison seemed rejoicing that the spell of [winter] was broken.[56]

Who can welcome spring as could those exiles of the old days on the frontier? How those fair women, those restless little ones, seemed to glow and gladden after the long, long months of seclusion when, snow-bound, they were penned within the stockade or limited to the sentry lines of some struggling prairie post![57]

Part of the post day was given to training, or drills, in the term of the day. Sometimes, that is, for most enlisted men of the Indian-fighting Army received precious little training beyond the use of their weapons (in which they were not always proficient), guard duty, and military courtesy. Most of what they learned came through the hard experience of campaigning. During the winter, officers at various posts met for one or two evenings a week for recitations in regulations or "Tactics"—the only "'book-schooling' to which they were then subjected."[58] Also during the winter there was

183

time—when work details permitted—for company and battalion drills:

> ...as the various troops of the —th, with fluttering guidons and glistening sabres came dancing up the slopes from the stables in the valley,—the men simply could not make their horses walk on such a [beautiful winter] day,—and adjutant's call rang out from the squad of trumpeters stationed in front of the old brown hospital [at Russell]. "In such glorious, faultless weather," said the colonel, "horses and men would be all the better for a brisk battalion drill." Fingers and noses might suffer a trifle at first, but the exercise would soon send the blood bounding through the veins and make it joy to be in saddle. And he was right. Presently, in long extended rank, the six troops were drawn up in line of battle, the sabres flashed their salute to the commanding officer ... the rapid manoeuvres of the battalion, heralded by stirring trumpet calls.
>
> The men had been doing their best, but in that keen, exhilarating air the horses were almost wild with high spirits, and several of their movements at rapid gait had degenerated into impetuous rushes, almost like those of a flock of sheep, which the troop commanders had labored in vain to prevent. Every time the gait was increased to the gallop some luckless troopers, tugging manfully at the reins, would be whisked away by their plunging steeds, and, to the colonel's intense disgust, half a dozen hard-mouthed chargers at this very moment were dashing about the prairie in big sweeping circles, despite every effort of their riders to restrain them.[59]

Although King made that drill part of a contrived incident, such confusion might have been quite frequent. "Cavalryman" disgustedly wrote that troopers could not handle their horses; ranked near the bottom in the annual target competition among regiments; were so inefficient with pistols that the weapon was more dangerous to horses and themselves than to

Indians; and could not swing the sabre. Indeed, he said, watching cavalry drill was as good as going to a "circus."[60]

On balance, the frontier post was mostly a wintering place for troops and a logistical support station. Troopers performed their main job in the field, usually between April and October, but also throughout the winter where climate and need permitted or dictated.

6.
War Parties

Frontier Army people may have had more in common with Indians than with their own kind, east or west. Both Indian and soldier were nomads—one from the force of environment, the other under force of orders. The rituals of the post were parallel—very roughly—to the ritual of the dance. The trumpet calls for the daily post activities could be likened to the village crier. For both Indians and soldiers gallantry in battle was a mark of superior manhood. Both periodically sent out their war parties, one to defend against invasion, or drive off other Indians, or count coup on traditional enemies, or steal horses; the other, as the agents of a government that was taking land from the Indian and forcing him onto smaller and smaller reservations. Both left their women behind (the Indians, not always) and returned to a hero's welcome. The Army's incursions into Indian lands are labeled campaigns or expeditions in the Anglo lexicon, but they were war parties, as surely as were the Indians'. The Army sent out some large expeditions, of course—such as the columns of Crook and Terry consisting, in 1876, of several thousand men—but small troop units fought sixty-three per cent of the Indian battles between 1865 and 1890.[1]

When troops took the field for a routine patrol, the scene could be like the start of this Arizona scout:

Soon after retreat that evening, while yet the lingering hues of crimson and royal purple mantled the jagged rocks that hemmed in the valley from the east [at "Camp Sandy"], a busy throng had gathered in the open space between the quarters and the stables. Drawn up in single rank were the horses of the two companies,—Tanner's and Ray's,—while the men in their rough and serviceable scouting-dress were nimbly darting about their steeds, tightening "cinches," or more snugly strapping the blankets or canteens that swung on the saddles. A little distance away, huddled together in silence, were the Apache scouts who were to accompany the command, and behind them all, scattered here and there over the sandy level, or clustering about the bell-horse of the half-breed leader, were the hardy, devil-may-care-looking little pack-mules.

Thronging about in their undress uniforms and overcoats (for the December air was chill) were the men of the four troops who were not so lucky as to be of the detail, all envious of their departing comrades, and, soldier-like, nearly all indulging in much good-humored chaff at the expense of the envied ones.

"It's old Skinnin' Jim [Eskiminzin, the Apache leader] ye're after this time, Micky. Luk out fur that beautiful crop o' yours." An allusion to the vivid hirsute adornment of Private Michael Mulligan that called forth a roar of applause. "Will ye lave me your boots, Hoolihan? It's the other end of ye that'll need a bomb-proof." "Don't you get kilt, Kelly; it'll ruin the sutler entirely," etc. All of which seemed to give infinite delight to the surrounding crowd, and not at all to discompose the martial objects of the sallies.

Presently Lieutenants Ray and Dana rode up and commenced a leisurely inspection of their commands, putting an end to the fun and laughter. Darkness was beginning to settle down upon the garrison, and lanterns were called into requisition.[2]

187

When cavalrymen grasped the mane with the left hand and swung into the saddle for the start of a campaign that might last weeks or months, their wives responded to the separation as variously as their emotional traits varied. Some had burst into tears when the orders came. Others had met it with a superficial composure for the sake of their husbands, saving their tears for the first lonely hours after his departure. Occasionally a wife became hysterical. Given human nature, it is likely that some, too, rather welcomed a temporary separation.

Something of the general attitude of Army wives was summarized by Mrs. Boyd who wrote: "No murmur was ever heard at the order to move, if women were to be included; for no matter how hard, long, or wearisome the journey they were content if permitted to accompany their husbands. But when the officers were sent away on the many expeditions cavalry service demanded, where their wives could not go with them, then they were indeed wretched; hours and days seemed endless until the return of the loved ones."[3] Mrs. Custer still was not inured to "those agonizing good-bys" (if she ever became accustomed to them) when the Seventh Cavalry left Fort Riley on the Hancock expedition to the Southern Plains in 1867. "There was silence as the column left the garrison... the closed houses they left were as still as if death had set its seal upon the door; no sound but the sobbing and moans of women's breaking hearts."[4] Mrs. Burt recalled the leave-taking for summer campaigns: "These partings were always great trials to me. Our family farewells were always made in quarters behind closed doors. Then he to his duty and I in a back room to my tears and prayers. I would choose a back room to shut out the tune the band played, 'The Girl I Left Behind Me.'"⁵ When the as yet uninitiated Katherine Garrett heard Seventh Cavalry wives speak calmly of the regiment's campaigns of the past, she asked if they were not afraid for their men. "Of course we are," they replied unanimously. A few days later, in 1874, she watched Custer lead his troops out on the march to the Black Hills. She asked if anything would happen to her fiancé. "Not likely," Mrs. McIntosh replied, "but you never can tell. That's what we army women are confronted with—uncertainty."⁶

Writing from his own experience, King's accounts of these separations are emotional. "Ladies there were in the —th who spent several days in prayers and tears [at Fort D. A. Russell in 1876] after they had seen the last of the guidons as they fluttered away over the 'divide' towards Lodge Pole [Creek]." Others met the situation with resignation. "Mrs. Turner" quickly accepts her captain's departure, looking forward to the dances that will still be possible with the few officers left at Russell. King defends her attitude, saying, "... but heavens! if one had to go into deep mourning every time a husband had to take the field, there would be no living in the cavalry at all!"⁷ Once the men were gone, women made peace with reality and went about their daily lives, wrapped in gossip and desperate efforts at diversion. If the campaign were to be prolonged, "it became quite the thing for some of the ladies ... to club together, share expenses, and thereby economize."⁸

Using an imaginary Fort Scott, city of Braska, and Braska County, Nebraska, as the setting, King describes the scene of the "girls they left behind them." Civilian "gallants" come out from town and ranchmen from the county to dance with the ladies or take them driving.

"Really," said one of the ladies, "if it hadn't been for our friends from town and the ranches I don't know what we should have done." What some of them,—ay, many of them,— did was to gather their little broods about them morn and night and pray ... for the life and safety of the father in the field.... What others did was to accept most liberally the parting injunction, "not to mope, but try to have a good time and be brave and cheerful," while the soldier went his way.[9]

The autobiographical accounts are more shallow than King's, and perhaps less truthful in the round. Given the mores of the late nineteenth and early twentieth centuries, when the ladies' memoirs were published, it is not to be expected that they would have admitted in print to any gaiety while their men were on combat duty. But Mrs. Summerhayes felt no compunction about saying that she was entertained with daily drives to Cheyenne, with small dances, and with theatricals at Fort D. A. Russell while her husband was on detached duty at the Spotted Tail Agency for two months in 1874.[10] During a similar separation, when two lieutenants left Fort Concho for a brief rotational tour at Grierson Springs, their wives wore "their temporary widowhood becomingly and soldierly."[11]

It was quite different, however, when troops were known to be moving toward hostile Indians. The ladies at Fort Laramie were unsettled when Crook announced plans for a winter campaign in 1876 (the one that ended with the botched attack on Crazy Horse's village in March 1876). "... the harmony of our pleasant garrison life received a dreadful shock when a winter campaign was announced. Fortunately for us 'Infantry' wives, the expedition was to be composed of cavalry with only two companies of infantry." All that changed a few weeks later when Crook mobilized his forces and marched northward on the major campaign of 1876. Those orders "gave us wives ample cause for sorrow," because it took a number of infantry officers away from Laramie. "With aching hearts we watched the soldiers march away," on May 22, 1876.[12]

While the men were gone, the women were hungry for news of the expedition. While Custer was exploring the Black Hills in 1874, the ladies of Fort Lincoln brought their husbands' letters to their daily sewing bees and compared notes because no husband covered all the details in his letters.[13] When a dispatch reached the post commander, by means of the couriers who maintained regular communication between the column and the post, he immediately let the ladies know at least the most important details. Also, officers going forward called on the ladies to see if they could take letters to their husbands; the couriers also took letters to the field. But their husbands' letters usually did not tell of troubles with the Indians. Not until the men came home did the wives learn of their fights and hardships.[14] When an officer was detached from the column —wounded or as a courier, for example—and reached the post, he was plied with questions, and not always about the welfare of husbands or regiment. "Mrs. Turner" hammers a returning officer with these questions: "Was it true that Mr. Crane was drinking hard again? Was it true that there was a game of poker going on all the time? Was the Colonel as exacting and horrid as he was at the post?"[15]

In the summer of 1876 all too many wives learned what it meant when the uncertainty of separation turned to certainty. Mrs. Gibson was by then stationed at Fort Rice, where some companies of the Seventh were based. She and other ladies were sitting on a porch one July evening when an Indian scout, Horn Toad, brought news of the Custer disaster. "The guitar slipped from my knees to the floor, the pink ball of knitting fell out of Charlotte Moylan's hands, rolling across the porch, the letter ... in Mrs. Benteen's lap fluttered over the rail." The three women spent the night together, sleepless, and the next day received official confirmation. Fortunately for them, Captain Myles Moylan, Captain Frederick Benteen, and Lieutenant Gibson came out of the fight alive. "And how this little band [of women] clung together! Some of us could have returned for a few months to our family homes, but we chose to remain and share everything, good or bad, that came to one or all of us."[16] News of the Custer disaster filled the women at Fort Laramie "with an increased dread of what might follow." Mrs. Burt added: "Naturally we at Fort Laramie were a profoundly depressed collection of women.... You can well imagine how hard and sorrow-breeding it was to sit and think and think and think and imagine all kinds of disasters."[17]

King dramatizes the situation at Fort D. A. Russell:

Mrs. Whaling permeated the post in an ecstasy of soulful comfort, shedding prayers and prophecies of similar fortune for the —th with the impartiality of a saint. She even succeeded in scaring Mrs. Turner half to death and exasperating Mrs. Wilkins to the verge of a tirade, but the latter had contented herself with the spirited though ungrateful announcement that when it came to having hearses and mutes it wouldn't be Mrs. Whaling they'd inquire for. "Matters are bad enough without your making 'em worse, ma'am," she said in her decided way. And the good lady, longing to deluge somebody with sympathetic tears, was compelled to confine herself to the rounds of the infantry quarters, where, with the ladies of her own regiment, she could bemoan the un-fathomable ingratitude and lack of appreciation of their sisters of the —th.[18]

The next year many Army wives faced the even more certain prospect that their men would go into battle when troops were mobilized in Oregon, Idaho, Wyoming, Nebraska, and Montana to halt the flight of the Nez Percé. Mrs. Lieutenant Frank Baldwin, who ten years before had become hysterical when her husband had taken the field from Fort Wingate, now met with composure her husband's departure, as did the other ladies at Fort Keogh.[19]

Much closer to the scene, the ladies at Fort Lapwai were set on edge as the prospect of a war with the Nez Percé had become daily more certain throughout May and June. It particularly agitated Mrs. Captain David Perry, whose husband had seen much campaigning. In May, the wife of Dr. FitzGerald had written her mother: "It would seem sort of funny to you that the people here take things so quietly. I am continually wondering why no one [except Mrs. Perry] seems excited ... we fuss over our dinners and clothes, etc., as if it was the most usual thing in the world to have trouble with the Indians. Oh, how I hate them. I wish they could be exterminated, but without bloodshed among our poor soldiers." A month later, it appeared still more definite that troops would have to take the field against Chief Joseph and the other nontreaty Nez Percé. On that afternoon, June 15, 1877, Mrs. Major W. H. Boyle "just ran down the back way for a minute to discuss the matter for a little." That afternoon came the news of the outbreak. "Mrs. Boyle and I have just been sitting looking at each other in horror." Orders for Captain Perry to lead his men against the Nez Percé sent his wife into hysterics.[20]

That same afternoon, Mrs. Lieutenant E. R. Theller packed her husband's mess chest for the campaign. Three days later she learned he had fallen in battle. Mrs. FitzGerald and Mrs. Boyle spent much time comforting her; the former also took into her home a "poor little laundress, who has also lost her husband." During succeeding weeks, officers passing through Lapwai to join commands in the field left with Mrs. FitzGerald and Mrs. Boyle personal mementos to be sent to relatives in case they should not return—a watch to be forwarded to a wife, the photograph of a son, other cherished belongings. All of which drove Mrs. Fitz-Gerald to the outburst: "Oh, the government, I hate it! Much it respects and cares for the soldier who, at a moment's notice, leaves his family and sacrifices his life for some mistaken Indian policy." During the enforced wait of long weeks while her husband was in the field, she wrote her mother: "I don't know how much more of this waiting and waiting I can bear. It does seem to me sometimes that I will go crazy and cannot wait another day to see my husband." She waited, though, and when he came home in the fall, they returned to their home in the East. Ironically, Dr. FitzGerald died soon after reaching the East from a Civil War wound which had been worsened by a lung infection contracted in the pursuit of the Nez Percé.[21]

Once on the trail, the cavalry column marched with a distance of one yard between croup and head of the horses. And "by inexorable rule of the cavalry the shorter men rode at the flanks of the troop."[22] A thirty-man troop marching in Wyoming appeared thus:

Out some three hundred yards to their right and left rode little squads as flankers. Out beyond them, further still, often cut off from view by low waves of prairie, were individual troopers riding as lookouts, while far to the front, full six hundred yards, three or four others, spreading over the front on each side of the twisting trail, moved rapidly from crest to crest, always carefully scanning the country ahead before riding up to the summit.[23]

A larger column on the Plains:

The October sun is hot at noon-day, and the dust from the loose soil rises like heavy smoke and powders every face and form in the guarding battalion [of the wagon train] so that features are wellnigh indistinguishable. Four companies of stalwart, sinewy infantry, with their brown rifles slung over the shoulder, are striding along in dispersed order, covering the exposed southern flank from sudden attack, while farther out along the ridge-line, and far to the front and rear, cavalry skirmishers and scouts are riding to and fro, searching every hollow and ravine, peering cautiously over every "divide," and signalling "halt" or "forward" as the indications warrant.[24]

Many times the men did not look like soldiers at all. While they sometimes wore regulation undress uniforms in the field, King constantly represented the troops as wearing whatever they chose. With hardly a regulation uniform to be seen in his columns, the men wore slouch hats, buckskin or woolen trousers and shirts, and, especially in Arizona, Tonto moccasins rather than boots. Officers usually wore blue flannel shirts. Preferring broad felt hats to forage caps, the men bought their own from the post trader at considerable personal expense. From King's accounts, it would seem that the custom of dressing as irregulars dated from the commencement of Crook's first tour in Arizona. When the Fifth Cavalry moved from Nebraska to Arizona in 1871, the regiment "began a campaign such as it had never heard or dreamed of. 'Stow away your sabres, your sashes, plumes and even your uniforms; you won't need them,' were the orders. They found the department commander [Crook] and his staff in rough hunting suits, and garbed themselves accordingly."[25] In an autobiographical passage, King (Billings, below) describes his reaction to the dress of troops when he reported at Camp Verde in 1874:

Coming, as he had done, direct from a station and duties where full-dress uniform, lavish expenditures for kid gloves, bouquets, and Lubin's extracts were matters of daily fact, it must be admitted that the sensations he experienced on seeing his detachment equipped for the scout were those of mild consternation. That much latitude as to individual dress and equipment was permitted he had previously been informed; that "full dress," and white shirts, collars, and the like would be left at home, [he] had sense enough to know; but that every officer and man in the command would be allowed to discard any and all portions of the regulation uniform and appear rigged out in just such motley guise as his poetic or practical fancy might suggest, had never been pointed out to him; and that he, commanding his troop while a captain commanded the little battalion, could by any military possibility take his place in front of his men without his sabre, had never for an instant occurred to him. [Regulations required officers to wear swords whenever with troops, except on stable duty and fatigue details.] As a consequence, when he bolted into the mess-room shortly after daybreak on a bright June morning with that imposing but at most times useless item of cavalry equipment clanking at his heels, the lieutenant gazed with some astonishment upon the attire of his brother-officers there assembled, but found himself the butt of much good-natured and not over-witty "chaff," directed partially at the extreme newness and neatness of his dark-blue flannel scouting shirt and high-top boots, but more especially at the glittering sabre swinging from his waist belt.

"Billings," said Captain Buxton, with much solemnity, "while you have probably learned through the columns of a horror-stricken Eastern press that we scalp, alive or dead, all unfortunates who fall into our clutches, I assure you that even for that purpose the cavalry sabre has, in Arizona at least, outlived its usefulness. It is too long and clumsy, you see. What you really want for the purpose is something like this,"—and he whipped out of its sheath a rusty but keen-bladed Mexican *cuchillo*,—"something you can wield with a deft turn of the wrist, you know. The sabre is apt to tear and mutilate the flesh, especially when you use both hands." And Captain Buxton winked at the other subaltern [*sic*] and felt that he had said a good thing.

But Mr. Billings was a man of considerable good nature and ready adaptability to the society or circumstances by which he might be surrounded. "Chaff" was a very cheap order of wit, and the serenity of his disposition enabled him to shake off its effect as readily as water is scattered from the plumage of the duck . . . .

If Mr. Billings was astonished at the garb of his brother-officers at breakfast, he was simply aghast when he glanced along the line of Company "A" (as his command was at that time officially designated) [actually, King was with K Company] and the first sergeant rode out to report his men present or accounted for. The first sergeant himself was got up in an old gray-flannel shirt, open at and disclosing a broad, brown throat and neck; his head was crowned with what had once been a white felt *sombrero*, now tanned by desert, sun, wind, and dirt into a dingy mud-color; his powerful legs were encased in worn deer-skin breeches tucked into low-topped, broad-soled, well-greased boots; his waist was girt with a rude "thimble-belt," in the loops of which were thrust scores of copper cartridges for carbine and pistol; his carbine, and those of all the command, swung in a leather loop athwart the pommel of the saddle; revolvers in all manner of

197

cases hung at the hip, the regulation holster, in most instances, being conspicuous by its absence. Indeed, throughout the entire command the remarkable fact was to be noted that a company of regular cavalry, taking the field against hostile Indians, had discarded pretty much every item of dress or equipment prescribed or furnished by the authorities of the United States, and had supplied themselves with an outfit utterly ununiform, unpicturesque, undeniably slouchy, but not less undeniably appropriate and serviceable. Not a forage-cap was to be seen, not a "campaign-hat" of the style then prescribed by a board of officers that might have known something of hats, but never could have had an idea on the subject of campaigns. Fancy that black enormity of weighty felt, with flapping brim well-nigh a foot in width, absorbing the fiery heat of an Arizona sun, and concentrating the burning rays upon the cranium of its unhappy wearer! No such head-gear would our troopers suffer in the days when General Crook led them through the canons and deserts of that inhospitable Territory.[26]

There are many factual references to the nondescript appearance of troopers in the field, such as John F. Finerty's statement that little attention was paid to uniform in the field.[27] But King's emphasis indicates that he considered the free choice of clothing both picturesque and sensible. On the other hand, a regimental commander thought the men tried "to make themselves as outlandish as possible."[28] In addition, both officers and men allowed their beards to grow because a mass of hair protected their faces against sunburn and windburn.[29]

As of the early 1880's King described a column in Wyoming as being in prescribed uniform. Their great coats were rolled and strapped at the pommel, covered by a poncho. Blanket and sidelines were strapped behind the cantle, while the lariat and picket pin were fastened on the left side of the pommel with the canteen on the right. Saddlebags contained extra horseshoes, nails, socks, underwear, brushes and combs for grooming the horse, and ammunition. The broad carbine sling rested over the left shoulder, with the muzzle of the weapon thrust into a socket on the right side of the saddle. Generally, cavalry throughout the period carried the carbine in the sling, but King emphasized several times that in Arizona troopers carried the carbine on the pommel; Remington's drawings of a later period show Arizona troopers with the sling. Although the men in the Wyoming column wore boots, they had moccasins in their saddlebags, waiting for their Arizona-trained officer to tell them they could change. Buckskin gauntlets set off the blue flannel shirt and blouse. By that time, cavalry wore a regulation brown campaign hat with a prescribed crease.[30]

Officers also carried scouting notebooks in which they kept a log of the campaign as well as information about the country. Part of their responsibility was to help develop detailed knowledge of topography. Mapping or learning the country was, in Army slang, "topogging."[31] On the basis of the data thus obtained, maps were drawn by engineer officers at department and division headquarters.

Troops not only improvised uniforms but some equipment as well. In particular they developed for themselves a much more efficient means of carrying ammunition than the Ordnance Department provided, through the so-called "prairie belts," similar to the thimble-belts mentioned earlier. The Army supplied a cartridge box to be suspended from the belt, but the clank of metallic cartridges not only was irritating but could give away a soldier's position when creeping upon the enemy. An improvised cloth cartridge belt may have resulted through polygenesis, but in 1866 Captain Anson Mills had the post saddler make leather cartridge belts for his infantrymen at Fort Bridger; he was an infantry officer before he transferred to the Third Cavalry. Some made belts of leather with canvas loops; others, belt and loops both of leather. By 1876 an ordnance officer reported that neither officers nor men would use the cartridge box, insisting upon their home-made belts. With that the Ordnance Department began to supply the "prairie belts" of leather with canvas loops, but they proved defective. An inspector general's report in 1880 said the loops worked loose and troops lost five to ten per cent of their cartridges — the infantryman when throwing himself on the ground, the cavalryman at more than a walk. By the mid-80's, Mills introduced the now standard web equipment that made his fortune.[32]

As they had done in the Civil War, infantrymen discarded some of the equipment they were expected to carry. By regulation a doughboy was expected to lug about fifty pounds of gear, including knapsack, one-half of a shelter tent, a blanket, extra shoes and clothing, and food. But, as soldiers will, they discarded so much of it that Colonel Edmund Rice of the Fifth Infantry designed a new combination cartridge belt and jacket — a one-piece garment that was never adopted by the Army — about which Frederic Remington commented: "... he has never seen United States infantry in active field-work carry what is loaded on to them by the army regulations. He knew that they ought to carry all the things prescribed, but he also knew that they never did."[33]

Officers disregarded the rules, too. In regulations written for warfare between nations, officers were permitted to discard any prominent insignia that might make them targets for sharpshooters, but were required to wear shoulder-straps to show rank. On Indian campaigns, however, officers frequently wore blue flannel shirts without rank insignia of any kind.[34]

As with quarters and the size of Army wagons, the difference betwen practices of the Indian fighters and the prescriptions of Washington officers suggests again the dichotomy of two armies. And King had quite a bit to say about officers in the East, especially officers of the "scientific corps"—artillery and engineers—who looked down on the cavalry's handling of Indian fights. "Odd as it may seem, it is the men who have had the least to do with Indians and Indian-fighting who have apparently the most ideas on the subject. This is not a paradox. Those who have spent several years at it probably started in with just as many, and exploded them one after another."[35] More caustically, he said there were officers in the War Department "who regarded Indian warfare on the frontier as a matter quite beneath their notice [and one that] could be of small moment to the army,—that is, the Army as known to society, as known to the press, and, 'tis to be feared, as understood by Congress,—the Army in its exclusive and somewhat supercilious existence at the national capital."[36]

A much fuller passage re-enforces the impression of a dichotomy in the two armies just as it also brings to light Army politics, the front-line soldier's distrust of the rear echelon, and the sense of conspiracy that is apt to grip the mind of anyone who thinks he is being held back by someone else. An adjutant, "Lieutenant 'Black Larry' Leonard," is in conversation with an unnamed chaplain:

"One learns to be something of a courtier even in Chicago [headquarters of the Military Division of the Missouri], and as for Washington, service there is a liberal education in diplomacy. One never knows who may have the strongest pull with the President in the event of a vacancy in the staff corps."

"Leonard," said the chaplain, gravely, "you're a born cynic and a pessimist to boot. Have we no generous impulses in the army?"

"Lots of 'em. Lots of 'em, chaplain, especially in the line and on the frontier, where we can afford to pat a fellow on the back, since we know that's about the extent of the reward he'll ever get. It's when we're in big society in the East, above all in Washington, one has to be guarded in what he says, or first thing he knows he'll be hoisting some fellow over his own head in a moment of enthusiasm. No. I know just how you regard me, but I spent six weeks of a three months' leave in Washington last winter, and sat night after night at the club, or day after day among the army crowd at the Ebbitt, or in some fellow's den at the Department, and never once did I hear one word of frank, outspoken, fearless praise of some other fellow's work or deeds, unless it were to his face. Ask a man flat-footed if that wasn't a capital scout of Striker's last winter in the Tonto Basin, or if Jake Randlett hadn't done a daring thing in going all alone through the Sioux country to drum up Crow scouts for Crook's command, or what he thought of Billy Ray's cutting his way out through the Cheyennes to bring help to Wayne last June, and ten to one he'll hum and haw and say yes, he *did* hear something about that, and now that I mentioned it he believed Striker or Jake or Billy had really behaved quite creditably, but the whole tone was significant of 'nothing like what some other fellow I might mention, modesty only forbidding, would have done under similar circumstances.' It's just the damnation of faint praise. The trouble with the whole gang of those fellows seems to be a mortal dread lest somebody's eyes should be deflected from the valor of the warriors at Washington to that of the warriors on the plains. What recognition do you suppose Ray will ever get for that feat? General Crook says it's useless to recommend him for brevet, because the Senate wouldn't confirm it, and the reason they won't is that those hangers-on about the capital don't mean to let such rewards be given to the men on the frontier. And yet this sort of thing doesn't happen only in Washington. It was a cavalry officer who said of that very affair that Ray was simply a reckless fellow under a cloud, with everything to gain and nothing to lose, and that doing a reckless thing was just as much a matter of instinct with him as battle is to a bulldog."[37]

Although the nature of campaigning was much the same in different areas, troops had to adjust to sharp differences imposed by environment. Again, the contrast between service in Arizona and the Northern Plains, as reported by a regimental commander, is illustrative:

In the autumn of 1879 a camp was established near Rawlins, Wyoming Territory, where the reserve troops of the Ute Indian expedition were halted for a considerable time. The men had no shelter, except such as was afforded by their white canvas tents, and there was a good deal of hardship. The nights were clear and intensely cold, and it seemed impossible to get clothing enough on to keep warm. Little stoves were put up in the tents, and all night long the men would endeavor to pass away the time by alternately piling in wood and diving under their blankets, where they would be quiet for a little while. But the frost would get the better of every thing, the wood soon consume in the flames, and then the process of firing up would be repeated. All outside was covered with a shining white mantle that glittered like steel. The horses groaned with cold as the fierce Rocky Mountain winds swept over them, and the howling wolves, that infest that region in great numbers, disputing possession with the big beaked ravens, seemed the only things that had any life left in them. The soldiers endured it as well as they could,

but the cutting frost sometimes got the better of their forti-
tude. This was as dreadful a picture of desolation as I ever
witnessed.

In May, 1882, during the Apache campaign in Arizona,
there assembled round a little water hole known as Cedar
Springs, between Forts Grant and Thomas, quite a respectable
force, all the men and animals of which were dependent on
the so-called spring for water. [Our] Apache Indian scouts
were, as usual, the first in, and they and their ponies, which
they had captured from the hostile Chiricahua Apaches in
Mexico, fared well enough. The headquarters and four troops
of the 3d Cavalry came next, many of the horses of the command being unable to get enough to drink. Afterward some
troops of the 6th Cavalry came up that were unable to get
anything whatever. The spring was a very small one, and over
five hundred animals surrounded it. The soldiers kept scrap-
ing the rocky bottom all through the night with their tin cups
to get a little more to prevent themselves and horses from
famishing.[38]

An Arizona patrol was usually made up of one or
two officers, thirty enlisted men, twenty Apache scouts,
and a pack train. Arizona campaigners placed great
reliance on Apache scouts, preferring Mojave Apaches
to Yuma Apaches. While Crook was in the department
in the early 1870's, his chief of scouts was Major George
M. Randall—as he would be later in the Department of
the Platte—whom the Apaches knew as "Big Chief
Jake." The Apache scouts guided them over many
rocky trails where only one Apache could have trailed
another. On the way, water in canteens became un-
drinkable because of the heat. "Lips, nostrils, eyelids
smarting with alkali dust, throats parched with thirst,
temples throbbing with the intense heat" made an
Arizona scout miserable. Officers had to learn the
country well, knowing just where "to turn for 'tanks' of

cool water for horses, mules, and men,—the cavalry order of precedence when creature comforts are to be doled out." Troopers came to hate what King called the weird, dismal call of the "raven-like Sierra hermit bird." Most of the fighting in Arizona involved small troop units and small groups of Apaches, but along the way the cavalry lost men to sunstroke, starvation, freezing, lightning, flood, fire, rattlesnake bites, explosions, thirst, arrow, and tomahawk.[39]

Troopers suffered from comparable hardships on the Northern Plains. If they drank alkali water, their lips would crack and bleed. But they would dig in dry stream beds to find water for their horses, even if they could not drink it themselves. On the Plains, soldiers also learned that the best way to watch for approaching men in the dark was to lie flat on low ground so that anything or anyone approaching would be silhouetted against the sky.[40]

In both areas, military "science" demanded that cavalry commanders conserve their horses by making marches of about twenty miles a day, ordinarily. When a battalion commander chose a place to camp for the night, the adjutant designated the area in which each troop was to camp and then directed the troop guidon-bearers to take station. Prior to 1890 cavalry guidons were swallow-tailed miniatures of the national flag but after 1890 they had a red and white stripe with the regimental and troop designation on the upper red stripe.[41] Each guidon-bearer then galloped to the designated location, and his company closed on him as a "living guide-post."

Each troop directed itself upon its own color; each in succession formed line to the left as its leading two [men, in a column of two's] came opposite the guidon; each was aligned to the right; then, without loss of time, the trumpets sounded, "Prepare to dismount;" the brown carbines were jerked from their sockets and tossed over the right shoulder as the odd-numbered troopers rode clear of the rank. "Dismount," clamored the trumpet, and down out of sight sank some fifty-odd blue flannel shirts and rusty old hats in each line. "Form rank." And out from under the chargers popped the vanished riders, each laying hold of the reins close to the bit as the line reformed and the captain said his brief speech: "Water as soon as you like, men, and graze well out to the north until nightfall . . ." And the next thing a dozen men were scampering like mad, lariats and picket-pins swinging, heading for the most promising patches of grass. Each picket-pin was stomped home, the lariats uncurled to their full length, and then back ran the troopers to unsaddle and lead to water. Ten minutes more, and the chargers . . . were being slowly driven . . . well out upon the northward slopes, where, after a preliminary roll, each horse set contentedly to grazing. Those preempted patches close at hand were reserved for their further use at night.

And then the little cook-fires began to blaze along the bank, and the pack-trains shambled in, and were unloaded in the twinkling of an eye. The mules went blinking off to water, and the [battalion commander], never quitting his saddle until his last trooper dismounted, slowly lowered himself to earth and went off in search of the colonel.[42]

The planting of picket-pin and lariat by each soldier was akin to staking a claim. "Trooper law reserved to the horse of the owner all space within lariat length of the firmly driven picket pin, and woe to the man that 'jumped the claim.'" Troopers also would steal food for their horses and share the scant bread ration with the animals, too. When feeding horses from the grain that often was carried in saddlebags, the trooper spread the oats on the dry side of the saddle blanket.[43] After dark

the horses would be hobbled and tied to a picket line
to prevent theft by Indians or white horse thieves. If
the column were accompanied by a wagon train, the
men slept in tents with the wagons forming a corral
within which the horses and mules were driven at
night. Sentries and herd guards kept watch through
the night.

The next day might bring battle. When it did, King
was at his best. Having fought in five engagements with
Indians and having undoubtedly listened to many
firsthand accounts by other officers, he imparted to his
battle descriptions a crispness and verve that would
meet the standards of good writing for any age.[44] His
first published battle description may have been a dispatch, which he once told an interviewer he had written
for the New York *Herald,* about Cody's fight with Yellow Hand on War-Bonnet Creek in 1876.[45] If true, that
would make him the originator of what became one of
the least important and overdramatized incidents of
the entire Indian wars. At any rate, his factual *Campaigning with Crook,* which covers that incident, is weak
tea compared with a novel, *Marion's Faith,*[46] in which
he describes much more vividly the march of the Fifth
Cavalry to join Crook.

The preliminaries to battle:

Daybreak again, and far to the east the sky is all ablaze.
The mist is creeping from the silent shallows under the
banks, but all is life and vim along the shore [where troops
were breaking camp in anticipation of battle]. With cracking
whip, tugging braces, sonorous blasphemy, and ringing shout,
the long train is whirling ahead almost at the run. All is
athrill with excitement, and bearded faces have a strange, set
look about the jaws, and eyes gleam with eager light and
peer searchingly from every rise far over to the southeast,

where stands a tumbling heap of hills against the lightening sky. . . .[47]

Many's the time a cavalry column, after an all-night march, finds itself jaded and drowsy just as a blithe young world is waking up to hail the coming day. Far different is the feeling when, refreshed by a few hours sound and dreamless sleep, warmed with that soldier comfort, coffee, and thrilled by the whispered news of "fight ahead," the troop pricks eagerly on. Then the faint blush of the eastern sky, the cool breath of the morning breeze, the dim gray light that steals across the view, all are hailed with bounding pulse and kindling eyes. . . .[48]

. . . brave men tremble oftimes until the first shot comes, and then the nervous strain is gone, for the hot blood leaps and tingles through the veins. . . .[49]

There is something in the sound of a single shot, fired at the break of day and in the midst of intense silence, that thrills the nerves and sets every sense alert and stirs the blood as even the crashing volleys of later battle fail to do. . . .[50]

Of his many battle scenes, the one below is cited because it is autobiographical. It describes the fight in Sunset Pass in which he was wounded: Billings is King, O'Grady is Sergeant Taylor, and the unnamed officer is Lieutenant Eaton:

One night [in October, 1874] some herdsmen from up the [Verde] valley galloped wildly into the post [Camp Verde, but not by name]. The Apaches had swooped down, run off their cattle, killed one of the cowboys, and scared off the rest. [Actually, Tontos had stolen cattle from the Verde Indian Agency, rather than from a ranch, as implied here.] At daybreak the next morning Lieutenant Billings with Troop "A" and about a dozen Indian scouts, was on their trail, with orders to pursue, recapture the cattle, and punish the marauders.

To his disgust, Mr. Billings found that his allies were not of the tribes who had served with him in previous expeditions. All the trusty Apache Mojaves and Hualpais were off with other commands in distant parts of [Arizona] Territory. He had to take just what the agent could give him at the reservation,—some Apache Yumas, who were total strangers to him. Within forty-eight hours four had deserted and gone back; the others proved worthless as trailers, doubtless intentionally, and had it not been for the keen eye of Sergeant O'Grady it would have been impossible to keep up the pursuit by night; but keep it up they did, and just at sunset, one sharp autumn evening, away up in the mountains, the advance caught sight of the cattle grazing along the shores of a placid little lake, and, in less time than it takes to write it, Mr. Billings and his command tore down upon the quarry, and, leaving a few men to "round up" the herd, were soon engaged in a lively running fight with the fleeing Apaches which lasted until dark, when the trumpet sounded the recall, and, with horses somewhat blown, but no casualties of importance, the command reassembled and marched back to the grazing ground by the lake. Here a hearty supper was served out, the horses were rested, then given a good "feed" of barley, and at ten o'clock Mr. Billings with his second lieutenant and some twenty men pushed ahead in the direction taken by the Indians, leaving the rest of the men under experienced noncommissioned officers to drive the cattle back to the valley.

That night the conduct of the Apache Yuma scouts was incomprehensible. Nothing could induce them to go ahead or out on the flanks; they cowered about the rear of [the] column, yet declared that the enemy could not be hereabouts. At two in the morning Mr. Billings found himself well through a pass in the mountains, high peaks rising to his right and left, and a broad valley in front. Here he gave the order to unsaddle and camp for the night.

At daybreak all were again on the alert: the search for the trail was resumed. Again the Indians refused to go out without the troops; but the men themselves found the tracks of Tonto moccasins along the bed of a little stream purling through the cañon, and presently indications that they had made the ascent of the mountain to the south. Leaving a guard with his horses and pack-mules, the lieutenant ordered up his men, and soon the little command was silently picking its way through rock and boulder, scrub-oak and tangled juniper and pine. Rougher and steeper grew the ascent; more and more the Indians cowered, huddling together in rear of the soldiers. Twice Mr. Billings signalled a halt, and, with his sergeants, fairly drove the scouts up to the front and ordered them to hunt for signs. In vain they protested, "No sign,—no Tonto here;" their very looks belied them, and the young commander ordered the search to be continued. In their eagerness the men soon leaped ahead of the wretched allies, and the latter fell back in the same huddled group as before.

After half an hour of this sort of work, the party came suddenly upon a point whence it was possible to see much of the face of the mountain they were scaling. Cautioning his men to keep within the concealment afforded by the thick timber, Mr. Billings and his comrade-lieutenant crept forward and made a brief reconnoissance. It was evident at a glance that the farther they went the steeper grew the ascent and the more tangled the low shrubbery, for it was little better, until, near the summit, trees and underbrush, and herbage of every description, seemed to cease entirely, and a vertical cliff of jagged rocks stood sentinel at the crest, and stretched east and west the entire length of the face of the mountain.

"By Jove, Billings! if they are on top of that it will be a nasty place to rout them out of," observed the junior.

"I'm going to find out where they are, anyhow," replied the other. "Now those infernal Yumas have *got* to scout, whether they want to or not. You stay here with the men, ready to come the instant I send or signal."

In vain the junior officer protested against being left behind; he was directed to send a small party to see if there were an easier way up the hill-side farther to the west, but to keep the main body there in readiness to move whichever way they might be required. Then, with Sergeant O'Grady and the reluctant Indians, Mr. Billings pushed up to the left front, and was soon out of sight of his command. For fifteen minutes he drove his scouts, dispersed in skirmish order, ahead of him, but incessantly they sneaked behind rocks and trees out of his sight; twice he caught them trying to drop back, and at last, losing all patience, he sprang forward, saying, "Then *come* on, you whelps, if you cannot lead," and he and the sergeant hurried ahead. Then the Yumas huddled together again and slowly followed.

Fifteen minutes more, and Mr. Billings found himself standing on the edge of a broad shelf of the mountain,—a shelf covered with huge boulders of rock tumbled there by storm and tempest, riven by lightning-stroke or the slow disintegration of nature from the bare, glaring, precipitous ledge he had marked from below. East and west it seemed to stretch, forbidding and inaccessible. Turning to the sergeant, Mr. Billings directed him to make his way off to the right and see if there were any possibility of finding a path to the summit; then looking back down the side, and marking his Indians cowering under the trees some fifty yards away, he signalled "come up," and was about moving farther to his left to explore the shelf, when something went whizzing past his head, and, embedding itself in a stunted oak behind him, shook and quivered with the shock,—a Tonto arrow. Only an instant did he see it, photographed as by electricity upon the retina, when with a sharp stinging pang and whirring "whist" and thud a second arrow, better aimed, tore through the flesh and muscles just at the outer corner of his left eye, and glanced away down the hill. With one spring he gained the edge of the shelf, and shouted to the scouts to come on. Even as he did so, bang! bang! went the reports of two rifles among the rocks, and, as with one accord, the Apache Yumas turned tail and rushed back down the hill, leaving him alone in the midst of hidden foes. Stung by the arrow, bleeding, but not seriously hurt, he crouched behind a rock, with carbine at ready, eagerly looking for the first sign of an enemy. The whiz of another arrow from the left drew his eyes thither, and quick as a flash his weapon leaped to his shoulder, the rocks rang with its report, and one of the swarthy forms he saw among the boulders tumbled over out of sight; but even as he threw back his piece to reload, a rattling volley greeted him, the carbine dropped to the ground, a strange numbed sensation seized his shoulder, and his right arm, shattered by a rifle-bullet, hung dangling by the flesh, while the blood gushed forth in a torrent.

Defenseless, he sprang back to the edge; there was nothing for it now but to run until he could meet his men. Well he knew they would be tearing up the mountain to the rescue. Could he hold out till then? Behind him with shout and yells came the Apaches, arrow and bullet whistling over his head; before him lay the steep descent,—jagged rocks, thick, tangled bushes; it was a desperate chance; but he tried it, leaping from rock to rock, holding his helpless arm in his left hand; then his foot slipped: he plunged heavily forward; quickly the nerves threw out their signal for support to the muscles of the shattered member, but its work was done, its usefulness destroyed. Missing its support, he plunged heavily forward, and went crashing down among the rocks eight or ten feet below, cutting a jagged gash in his forehead, while the blood rained down into his eyes and blinded him; but he struggled up and on a few yards more; then another fall, and, well-nigh senseless, utterly exhausted, he lay groping for his revolver,—it had fallen from its case. Then—all was over.

Not yet; not yet. His ear catches the sound of a voice he knows well,—a rich, ringing, Hibernian voice it is: "Lieutenant, *lieutenant! Where* are ye?" and he has strength enough to call, "This way, sergeant, this way," and in another moment O'Grady, with blended anguish and gratitude in his face, is bending over him. "Oh, thank God you're not kilt, sir!" (for when excited O'Grady *would* relapse into the brogue); "but are ye much hurt?"

"Badly, sergeant, since I can't fight another round."

"Then put your arm round my neck, sir," and in a second the little Patlander has him on his brawny back. But with only one arm by which to steady himself, the other hanging loose, the torture is inexpressible, for O'Grady is now bounding down the hill, leaping like a goat from rock to rock, while the Apaches with savage yells come tearing after them. Twice, pausing, O'Grady lays his lieutenant down in the shelter of some large boulder, and, facing about, sends shot after shot up the hill, checking the pursuit and driving the cowardly footpads to cover. Once he gives vent to a genuine Kilkenny "hurroo" as a tall Apache drops his rifle and plunges headforemost among the rocks with his hands convulsively clasped to his breast. Then the sergeant once more picks up his wounded comrade, despite pleas, orders, or imprecations, and rushes on.

"I cannot stand it, O'Grady. Go and save yourself. You *must* do it. I *order* you to do it." Every instant the shots and arrows whiz closer, but the sergeant never winces, and at last, panting, breathless, having carried his chief full three hundred yards down the rugged slope, he gives out entirely, but with a gasp of delight points down among the trees:

"Here come the boys, sir."

Another moment and the soldiers are rushing up the rocks beside them, their carbines ringing like merry music through the frosty air, and the Apaches are scattering in every direction.

"Old man, are you much hurt?" is the whispered inquiry his brother-officer can barely gasp for want of breath, and, reassured by the faint grin on Mr. Billings's face, and a barely audible "Arm busted,—that's all; pitch in and use them up," he pushes on with his men.

In ten minutes the affair is ended. The Indians have been swept away like chaff; the field and the wounded they have abandoned are in the hands of the troopers. . . .[51]

From his experience in the attack on the village of American Horse at Slim Buttes, Dakota, in September, 1876 and from what comrades perhaps told him of other charges, King drew graphic descriptions of attacks on villages—fairly common in the annals of Indian warfare—and observed: "Indeed, from a cavalry point of view it really is not a charge at all, not even a charge as foragers, but rather a wild dash into and through a straggling, swarming village of Indian lodges, every man for himself when once turned loose, the whole object being to carry terror, panic, and confusion to the half-waking warriors."[52]

While troops were in the far distant field, apprehension was just beneath the surface among the families left in garrison. Each time a courier came in sight there was immediate alarm, anxiety and curiosity.

The hoofs thundered across the rickety wooden bridge [as a courier rode into Fort Laramie], and the rider was hailed by dozens of shrill and wailing voices as he passed the laundresses' quarters, where the whole population had turned out to demand information.... No man in the group [of waiting officers] could catch the reply of the horseman to the questioners at "Sudstown," but in an instant an Irish wail burst upon the ear, and, just as one coyote will start a whole pack, just as one midnight bray will set in discordant chorus a whole "corral" of mules, so did that one wail of mourning call forth an echoing "keen" from every Hibernian hovel in all the little settlement, and in an instant the air rang with unearthly lamentations.

"D—— those absurd women!" growled [the post commander], fiercely, though his cheek paled at the dread of the coming tidings. "They'll have all the garrison in hysterics. Here, [Lieutenant] Hatton! run down there and stop their infernal noise. There isn't one in a dozen of 'em that has any idea of what has happened. They're howling on general principles. What the devil does that man mean by telling his news before he has seen the commanding officer, anyhow?"

Meantime, straight across the sandy flats and up the slope came the courier.... Reining in his horse, throwing his brown carbine over his shoulder and quickly dismounting, he . . . handed his commander a letter.[53]

It developed that he had merely shaken his head at the laundresses without telling them anything. "They are bound to make a row, whatever happens," he told the C.O.

Often the apprehension was needless, for expeditions sometimes turned into long camping trips. Especially in the mountains, a campaign provided much pleasure for healthy, muscular men who loved the outdoors. Except when warriors shadowed a column, soldiers could hunt and fish. The thrill of shooting a buffalo came to many, although some commanders held in check the senseless slaughter of the animals. Antelope, deer, and wild fowl added to the bag of the pothunter seeking variety in the standard field ration. But a tang in the environment made even monotonous fare satisfying. "The field appetite is a wondrous sauce, and soldier coffee with bacon, beans, 'Dutch oven' bread, and antelope steak have a relish in the keen October air known only to the frontiersman." And the "cold, clear trout streams and the bracing air" of the Big Horns made for genuine pleasure.[54]

The early summer months are the season for trout-fishing. . . . I know of nothing more pleasant than this sport. The smell of willows and sage-brush, the faint odor of the smoke from the Indian tepees or wig-wams near the stream, lull the senses, and everything appears peaceful. The red-throated robins, the yellow-breasted meadowlark, the flat-headed ducks, and the reddish-brown plumaged falcon hawks are enjoying themselves in bush and tree, and all seems gladdened by the merry rippling of the bright stream, as it dances over the pebbles by the velvet greensward.

215

Stretched at full-length on the grass, with the fly from one's fishing line daintily moving down the wrinkled waters, with here and there the black back of a trout visible way down in the dark depths—can anything be more charming than this? I fancy not. And all the wines of France or drugs of India never threw so fairy a mantle over the soul. Wild rose-bushes rise on every hand, fresh from their winter's sleep, and ready to adorn themselves with all their matchless loveliness. Earth has few pleasures equal to trout-fishing in an atmosphere which is perfumed with rose leaves![55]

King gave a similar picture when he described Crook's men in the Black Hills in October, 1876, after their trying march southward. The great relief experienced in finding sanctuary after weeks of hunger may have made his recollection more nostalgic than it would have been otherwise.[56]

October in the Black Hills of Dakota. Cloudless skies. Golden sunshine. Keen, crisp, invigorating air. Lovely vistas of romantic valley, hemmed in by rugged heights, rock-buttressed, pine-crested. Clear, sparkling waters rushing over rocky bed, browsing herds of troop horses scattered here and there over the billowy slopes. Bivouac fires twinkling everywhere through the timber, sending their curling smoke high aloft towards the zenith. Rich, resinous, balsamic odors floating on the faint breeze that whispers through the tree-tops. Here, there, and everywhere groups of gaunt, hardy, bearded men, whose rough garb of canvas, flannel or dressed deer-skin gives no evidence of their calling. Only the parallel rows of white tents gleaming in the sunshine in the middle distance and the stirring peal of the bugle tell of the probable presence of a military force. There, down the valley where it widens slightly, the strong battalions of infantry have stacked their long Springfields and pitched their canvas adobes after a tramp through mud and mire, over ridge and mountain, under weeping skies or blazing suns for two thousand weary miles; and now, blissfully drinking in this perfect air, they rest from their labors. Here, closer at hand, swarm their comrades of the cavalry, haggard and unkempt as themselves, for they have lived for weeks on what game they could find and upon the stringy flesh of such horses as they were not able to tow along to the Belle Fourche. It has been the roughest of rough campaigns. It has worn them down to skin and bone. It has been replete with suffering one day and sharp fighting the next [which is a monstrous exaggeration, as far as fighting was concerned]. But now, at last, in the recesses of the Southern hills, they are placidly waiting orders for the next move. . . . It has been a fortnight of lazy delight, in which men and animals fed and dozed by day and slept dreamlessly upon the turf at night,—a fortnight in which evening after evening the troopers gathered about their fires, sang, told stories, and compared notes upon the experiences so fresh in every mind.[57]

In season, the campaign ended and the troops marched back into the home post:

. . . the —th was home for good. What wondrous welcome had they when the column of bearded troopers, stalwart and sun-tanned, rode jauntily into the post. . . . The band played its most rollicking marches. The women and children from "Sudsville" fairly screamed with delight, as, one after another, some familiar and beloved face could be distinguished through the dust that coated the war-worn features. Over across the parade, along the verandas, the ladies were gathered in joyous bevies, while the little ones, gayly dressed in holiday garb, danced and shouted with impatient glee. The long line formed once more on the old, well-known parade. The colonel said brief words of commendation to his men. The standard was duly conveyed to headquarters. The troops were dismissed to stables, and then came the rush of officers to the waiting groups along the row. . . .[58]

Warm and beautiful were the mornings of that early

October, and there was gladness unspeakable in every face along the familiar old row in the week that followed the —th's return. All the livelong day the officers were busily occupied straightening out the troops after the dusty summer's campaign. Colonel, majors, captains, and subalterns were at work till evening gunfire.[59]

What the return of troops meant to the women is indicated by the recollections of three officers' wives. When read one way their remembrances show a strangely selfish concern with their own pleasure, but when read another way they indicate that wives had suppressed the tension and anxiety that went with having their husbands facing unknown dangers.

The absence from the post of the Infantry and Cavalry officers [on Crook's expedition of 1876] made a great vacancy in our social life [at Fort Laramie]. However, there were enough left to keep the gaieties and amusements going in the post to a certain extent. As was the practice . . . on the distant frontier . . . theatricals were very much resorted to. . . .
Of course it was very quiet for those wives left in the Post whose husbands were absent, but most of them were kept busy with children and household duties.[60]

Everyone is happy in the fall, after the return of the companies from their hard and often dangerous summer campaign, and settles down for the winter. It is then that we feel we can feast and dance, and it is then, too, that garrison life at a frontier post becomes so delightful.[61]

We were always delighted to welcome back the troops from their Indian reconnoitering, life was so dull without them. During their absence the garrison would consist of perhaps only one company of infantry, with its captain and lieutenant. . . . That summer [1871] even the band [of the Eighth Cavalry] was in the field, so we had no music to cheer us [at Fort Union]. All was, however, made up for on their return in November, when we inaugurated a series of hops that were delightful.[62]

At the same time, the women appreciated the dangers which their husbands had faced, and the men — by one account, at least — did not dwell on hardship or danger when they returned home. "The officers always had so many comical stories to tell on their return that even the bride [of an officer who had been whisked away immediately after bringing her to the post] failed to realize her husband's danger, and joined in the general laugh over those recitals."[63]

7.
Soldier and Citizen

After the sacrifices they had made on behalf of the
republic, the men of the Old Army were justi-
fiably embittered by the reactions of civilians—citizens or "cits," in the Army expression of the day. Public
attitudes ranged from indifference to scorn, and perhaps give a strong clue that Easterners did not pay
much attention to Western campaigns against Indians.
A young Connecticut girl who became an Army bride
in 1896 said the Army "was a distinctly unknown quantity in the East." It was so unknown that when she
married an infantry captain in her hometown of Mid-
dletown, Connecticut, her family's friends did not
know just how to entertain the groom and his best man;
a group of club men decided that soldiers must enjoy
drinking and therefore laid in a large supply of liquor
for the two officers; to their surprise the officers drank
sparingly. Another New England woman, after years
in the West, found herself alienated even from her kin
when visiting the East, because civilians and Army
people had so little in common. "Why, one-half of
them do not know the uniform and could not dis-
tinguish an officer of the Army from a policeman!"[1]
A more serious set of attitudes was reflected in this
commentary:

Soldier and Citizen

The people at large seem to think the Army composed of fugitives from justice, and whenever they hear that a neighbor's son has enlisted, break out into ejaculations of pious horror. The name soldier, as they use it, seems to be a synonym for all that is degrading and low, and whenever they meet a person bearing it they cannot forbear showing their contempt.

If a soldier be good-looking, they straightaway set him down as a libertine; if possessed of ordinary intelligence, they regard him as a bank defaulter; in short, they have an entire catalogue of imaginary crimes which are ingeniously fitted to every shade of character he may exhibit.[2]

Other attitudes can be inferred from various comments. The editor of the San Francisco *Report* said the Army should have "a recognized place in society," implying that it did not. Editors of competing newspapers in Columbus, Ohio, debated the charge that soldiers of the Regular Army were "outcasts of society, drunken dead beats, thugs, and thieves." One Louis Schlade asked the military affairs committees of both houses of Congress to investigate the Army, charging that German soldiers, as well as others, were turned into "pariahs and slaves," and that the Army had become a "refuge merely for such worthless characters who cannot make a living as freemen." Those conditions, he charged, arose from the "unsoldierly and penitentiary-like work" that was required of enlisted men.[3]

Those attitudes struck King full in the face, leaving a sting which he considered an insult to the uniform of which he was deeply proud and an indignity to himself. When he returned to Milwaukee on sick leave in 1878 (the shoulder wound was then getting the better of him after four years), he found that "the uniform that even the rebel South had treated with respect" was met on Milwaukee streets with "impudent and jeering comment." More infuriating, businessmen patronized him with the question, "Well, old fellow, how do you manage to kill time out in the Army—nothing but play poker and drink whiskey?" During the twenty-five years succeeding his retirement, he estimated, at least one hundred former soldiers had asked his help in finding jobs, but he had been able to find places for only three. One businessman told him frankly: "You see, it's this way. We naturally reason that a man couldn't have been of any account if the best he could get for himself all these years was a job at soldiering."[4]

It is easy to understand how civilians would have looked down on soldiers. In an age devoted to the rush for wealth, a man of "snap" could not have understood how anyone of character and ambition would devote his life to a career that offered so little in pay. The pay of enlisted men ranged from $13 a month for a private to $23 for a sergeant-major. Officers' pay ranged from $1,500 a year for an unmounted second lieutenant to $2,000 for a mounted captain.

But King made no effort to understand it. Instead, his resentment boiled to the surface in several novels. If his views cannot be accepted as representative of Army attitudes, they at least reveal how one acute observer saw the relationship of soldier and citizen. Especially in the aftermath of the sharp criticism the Army had received for the Wounded Knee fight, King's resentment erupted through a monologue by "Major Kenyon," a middle-aged cynic and realist:

   ... the great mass of the people have no conception whatever of the duties that devolve upon us, of the life we lead, of the trials we encounter ... they think ... we do nothing but loaf and drink and gamble. They are *taught* to think so by

the press of our great cities, and, never having a chance to
see the truth for themselves, they accept the views of their
journalists, who really know no more about it than they do,
but do not hesitate to announce as fact what exists only in
their imagination.

[Southerners] are all Americans. All through the North,
however, we have an immense foreign population that has
fled from the Old World to escape military duty. They hate
the very sight of a soldier. Three-fourths of the people of
some of our big cities are of foreign birth or parentage. The
papers seek their patronage, and in truckling to them they
prejudice northern Americans against their own friends and
relatives who have become idiots enough to become their
defenders.... People wonder how it was that it took the
North with three million soldiers so long to subdue the
South with less than a fourth that number. Now I see nothing
to wonder at whatever. The South has always respected the
profession of arms; the North has always derided it. Lee
with sixty thousand Americans at his back, and only sixty
thousand, knocked sixty thousand out of Grant's overwhelm-
ing force between the Rapidan and the James. Lee's sixty
thousand had the love of every Southern heart to sustain
them. How many of the North, think you, had no personal
interest in that struggle? How many thousands of the North
to-day care whatever for that flag ... and only ask to be let
alone to make money in their own way?[25]

Contact with civilian frontiersmen was much more
intimate than with Easterners, but there was antipathy
as well as fraternization in the relationship. For example, soldiers from Fort Dodge would go into Dodge
City on pass, get crazy drunk on vile whiskey, pass
out, and then, in a helpless condition, be stripped of
clothing and everything of value, whereupon the saloon
keeper would throw them into the street. From Fort
Douglas, Utah, a correspondent said the Army people
"lead a very quiet life out here at Salt Lake, not having

much intercourse with the Mormons, and desirable Gentiles not being numerous." From Fort Bayard another wrote: "Then our Mexican neighbors of Central City murder a colony of Chinamen within gunshot of the post, just to keep their hands in as it were. While highway robbery, mail robbery, horse thieving, etc., are minor every day occurrences, which nobody thinks it worthwhile to talk about." Another wrote: "It is common on the frontier for men who have been robbed by Indians or highwaymen, or reduced to want by the failure of a mining speculation, to apply to the military authorities for food.... When such applications are made to an officer of [the arrogant, overbearing type] they are invariably refused in rough and threatening terms." When a civilian was arrested by men of the Ninth Cavalry for murdering one of their comrades at Fort Sill and later brought to trial in Fort Smith, Arkansas, the defense attorney criticized the Army for having made the arrest. To which the prosecuting attorney replied that "from their argument a man, no matter how much of a scoundrel, if an American citizen, could wrap himself in his country's flag, anchor himself on the American Eagle, and snap his fingers at the military whenever it was their duty to arrest him."[6]

King was caustic in his portrayals of civilians in the West. Regarding Arizona in the years right after the Civil War, he wrote that a governor had been "duly expatriated to look after the interests of the United States" in that turbulent territory, and added:

Eventually, as a means of recruiting a population fast killing itself off, to the no great detriment of society in general, but the undoubted jeopardy of the commercial interests of those merchants who had shipped their goods thither ... a few lodes were duly "salted" by experienced hands of California education, the inflammatory announcement was made that Arizona was teeming with mineral wealth.... A swarm of eager adventurers rushed in ... and having invested their last shilling in the attempt were compelled to stick there and swindle others into coming.... finally it was brought about that three regiments and a brigadier general ... had to be scattered broadcast over this barren land to whip into subjection the Apache hordes, who looked with not undeserved hatred upon the original white invaders.[7]

The overall implication of this observation is, of course, false; King may have known of the salting of a given mine, but genuine mineral discoveries drew the first Americans into Arizona. He also was contemptuous of frontiersmen for their changes of place names. Of Laramie Peak he wrote, "Plainsmen to this day call it Larmie in that iconoclastic slaughter of every poetic title that is their proud characteristic." The "democratic intolerance ... of the free-born American" caused him to discard beautiful Spanish, French, or Indian place names and substitute American ones. Specifically, he was enraged that Monte San Mateo, the Arizona mountain named after Saint Matthew because of its bald top fringed by timberline, had become Baldhead Butte; that Monte San Pablo had become Bill Williams Mountain; that "the deep-vowelled Los Angeles of the last century" had become the *"Loss Angeles* of to-day"; that Yankees had changed the Purgatoire River in Colorado to the Picketwire; that the Mini Pusa (Dry Water) in Wyoming had become Muggins Fork; and that the War-Bonnet had become Hat Creek.[8]

When the paymaster appeared, even in the wilderness, "it was a duty all citizens owed to the territory to hasten to the scene and gather in for local circulation all that was obtainable of that disbursement; otherwise the curse of the army might get ahead of them and the boys would gamble it away among themselves or spend it for vile whiskey manufactured for their sole benefit." Two examples will illustrate the source of his concern. While Terry's command was scouting the Yellowstone country after the Custer defeat in 1876, traders came upriver by steamboat to sell goods of various types at inflated prices to the men in the field. The next year, payday at Fort Robinson—for both troops and Indian scouts—brought such a horde of harpies that the post commander locked a lot of them in the guard-house and then escorted them off the post en masse.[9]

Where frontier law and order was concerned, King displayed a bitterness and scorn that may have been representative of Army attitudes. "A territorial governor is not an awe-inspiring official ordinarily," he wrote. Besides that, "a frontier jury always decides in favor of the squatter and against the soldier." No local jury would hold a Wyoming citizen guilty when the offense was against "the peace or property of Uncle Sam." For that matter, ranchmen did not like soldiers, because soldiers "set too much value on government property." And when soldiers encountered ruffians they were at a legal disadvantage in that civil authorities forced on soldiers "the rule of the road" that they were not to defend themselves until hit and not to shoot until shot—"even a horse-thief had more civil rights than a soldier." Soldiers could not vote in territorial elections any more than they could arrest law-breakers without specific authority—other than those who had stolen government money or property. The Army, of course, had trouble with horse thieves who could change the "US" brand on a horse's shoulder into "0 8," or a toadstool, easily. Interestingly, in a

novel set on the Texas plains in the late 1880's (where
he had visited his old comrades of the Fifth Cavalry),
he said there were "few things the cavalryman holds
in meaner estimate" than fences.[10]

At the same time, there was fraternization between
officers' families and frontier people. At Camp Halleck
in 1869 the Boyds made friends with neighboring ranch
families; the "wives interested us greatly, they were
such perfect specimens of frontier women." The Boyds
also enjoyed contact with the townspeople of Silver City
a few years later. "The *elite* of the surrounding country"
attended a New Year's hop at Fort Stanton in 1882, and
Army people spent many happy days with the people
of Helena and Bozeman. That aspect of Army social
life came into King's novels but briefly, notably in one
instance in which Cheyenne civilians—but cast as
"prominent 'cattle-growers,'" be it noted—attended
dances at Fort D. A. Russell.[11] King just simply did
not have much use for civilians as a class, and that,
too, could have been a general attitude among Army
officers.

He and other officers especially disliked and dis-
trusted Indian agents. The many conflicts between
officer and agent form a well-known part of Western
history, but King gave them additional depth. Through
his novels he propagandized for the Army's point of
view which was, in brief, that Indian affairs should be
returned to the War Department. For Eastern readers
he identified the Indian agent "as one of the factors of
that mysterious and complicated piece of cabinet ware
known as the Bureau." With regard to the graft and
corruption that has stigmatized Indian agents as a
group, he quoted one agent in Arizona as having said,
"If it were not for those d——d army officers ... a man

might live like a gentleman even in Arizona." He always represented Indian agents as cowardly fools, ignorant of Indians. And there were many to agree with him, including a wife who said she had never once met an Indian agent who was the right sort of man.[12] As for the trouble the Army had because of civilian management of Indian affairs, King gave the following as the cause of an imaginary expedition:

> The old, old story again, and just as it had been time and time before. Absurdity in the Indian policy; mismanagement in the Indian bureau; starvation in the Indian villages; murmurings of discontent among the old warriors; talk of summary action among the young braves; emissaries from disaffected bands; midnight councils, harangues, dances, threats, an arrest or two, escape, and then a general rush to join the hostiles in the field.[13]

Although that description is in large part accurate, King really did not know any more about Indians than a Boston preacher. Nor did he evince any desire to know anything about people whom he described as being characterized by "innate sloth and restlessness."[14] But he did have opportunity to observe reservation Indians, probably during the brief time he spent at Fort Robinson in 1876 where both Brulé and Oglalla Sioux were on temporary reservations. Saying that "Indians would make splendid ward politicians," he said some Indian men obtained more than their share of rations by having their families overcounted at censuses. They borrowed children from a part of the camp already counted, or carefully covered a puppy in a blanket and presented it as a new baby, or used a "grandmother" who was passed from lodge to lodge to be counted. Wrapping a puppy in a blanket was,

Soldier and Citizen

indeed, discovered to be a ruse at Fort Sill in the late
1890's. "Agents might and did steal, but so did the
Indians, and many a rejoicing old sinner has been
credited with a family of twelve when his sole available
domestic assets consisted of two squaws and three
children.... Agents lent themselves to that sort of
thing because the more Indians they could show as
their especial wards, the more barrels and boxes and
bales were invoiced to that agency and deftly 'raked
off' *en route*."[15]

Otherwise, King simplistically re-enforced the
stereotype of the Indian in the late nineteenth century.
"The Apache lacks the magnificent daring of the Sioux
or Cheyenne. He is a fighter from ambush; he risks
nothing for glory's sake; he is a monarch in craft and
guile, but no hero in open battle." Or: "No Indian in
America can match the Apache in cunning, in planning
ambuscades and in sinewy strength and endurance.
Few four-footed creatures can scale mountains as he
can, and, in such an intricate maze of canyons, cliffs
and deserts, no troops on earth, campaigning on the
principles of civilized warfare, could, by any possibility, reach or punish him." He repeatedly represented Plains Indians as putting captives to death by
"fiendish torture."[16]

His treatment of Indians is one with a racism that
pervades all the novels and probably did represent
general Army attitudes, as it represented general Anglo
attitudes. Mexicans were always "greasers." Blacks
were "darkies," Africans, Ethiopians. And there was a
strong anti-Semitism in the novels, including a reference to the "shop-keeping Israelites, who had established the inevitable 'slop-shop'" in Prescott.[17]

Sketchy as they are, King's representations of civil-

229

ians can be taken as an indication of the alienation of the professional soldier in the predominant culture of America in the late nineteenth century. It can be reasoned that his novels could have been popular without veracity, but that he would not have commanded the respect of soldiers and critical reviewers if he had materially distorted the Army and its attitudes.

8.
Conclusions

The relationship of the novel to history is made a tricky piece of business by the preconceptions with which we historians are enfolded. Our scope of awareness has been considerably broadened in the last quarter-century by new methodologies and borrowings from the social sciences, but basically we still stagger under the von Rankean nonsense about "the sources" and their arbitrary, perhaps capricious, division into secondary and primary. The supposition that reality can be drawn only from factual documents overlays history like a thick skin covering a bucket of old paint. And yet we know that documents are themselves the relics of men who often had less concern with fact than with casting themselves in a favorable light. Still, documentary and archival materials impose a severe limitation upon our determination of what has happened and an even more severe limitation upon our understanding of it. Through the greater awareness that has resulted from criticisms of historical method and historians' own questionings of past assumptions, there is now the realization that the historian must work at several levels of observation, even when examining one manuscript.

At best, we must hold to the belief that there was a past and that it can still be comprehended.

Under certain circumstances—and they must be rigid—the novel can help us toward that comprehension. Indeed, the closeness between the "objective" historian and the novelist can be seen in R. G. Collingwood's observation that "the historian must re-enact the past in his own mind."[1] Collingwood certainly had no such connection in mind when he wrote that, but it is there nonetheless. The difference is that the historian can hope only to reconstruct a superficial "objective" account of the past. By contrast, the novelist can deal with both the objective and the emotional content of the past.

Historians have long made use of novels in certain educational contexts. Most frequently we pay attention to novels that have had an impact on their times, such as Upton Sinclair's *The Jungle*. Others provide insight into other times. Allan Nevins said that the reader can exhaust the authorities on eighteenth-century England but still must read Fielding's *Tom Jones* to learn of the manners, dress, speech, ideas, and ideals of that age.[2] That is, the novel—again within limitations—can help the historian understand another society in its own terms. Much more succinctly, comprehensively, and pragmatically, C. L. Sonnichsen phrased it as follows in discussing his work as a specialist in Southwestern literature and history:

> My objective . . . is to treat [novels of the Southwest] as social history. More than any other type of writing, they reveal what sort of people we were and are. From this point of view the incompetent novels, the amateur novels, the bad novels, are just as important as the good ones—sometimes more so. . . . Every novel, good, bad, and in between, is the product of a

human mind trying hard to say something important, and it reveals far more than its author usually realizes about the values and assumptions of the society he represents.[3]

That observation is particularly true when the novelist wrote of a life he had known intimately, of people he had known intimately, and who was — to treat Collingwood's phrase with license — re-enacting the past (his own past) in his mind. That was the case with King. His novels are unique.

We know much of the nineteenth-century Army from the historical accounts that have been culled from the mountains of material in the National Archives and elsewhere. But the official reports and government documents can never give us the feel, the atmosphere, the emotional tone of everyday life in frontier posts. King's novels have an enduring value in that they do provide that which is missing from the ordinary historical sources. That is, official documents and reminiscences (which are always distorted one way or another) provide the historian with only one level of observation. With King's work, another is provided, for the novels preserve a usably large body of unwritten records of the frontier Army.

Since this book was not intended to be — and shall not become — a literary criticism directed at the works of one man, there is no point in discussing the literary qualities of King's novels. Their worth to the historian is to be obtained by divorcing his picture of the Army — and a remarkably consistent picture it was through twenty-seven years of writing — from his mawkishly romantic story lines. The main configurations in his picture are corroborated by factual accounts. Where others skimmed over tantalizing aspects in memoirs, however, King brought to life those dedicated officers, unprincipled officers, dumbly obedient enlisted men, knavishly scheming enlisted men, mediocre women of integrity and devotion, empty-headed and frivolous women and bumbling men, as well as the "Plain Janes" who disappear in any group. For instance, the "art" of flirtation certainly would not have appeared in ordinary historical sources, beyond the few corroborative accounts already cited, but from King's pages we understand how important and ritualistic it was.

From the official accounts and memoirs we know of the highly successful as well as the spectacularly incompetent officers. From King's characterizations we know of the range of men in between, those who held their jobs with varying degrees of efficiency and those who guided the star of empire westward in their own mediocre way. The official routine is recorded in routine reports, but the everyday routine of human beings wrapped in the boredom of a frontier post would have been lost without King's preservation of it. No one would have written enough complaints about gossiping wives for us to know the extent to which gossip was a staple and a therapeutic in the social life of the garrison, nor of backbiting among officers except when it might have led to court-martial. In sum, King recreated the atmosphere of frontier Army posts. With a strong air of realism, he afforded a view from the inside—by one who knew every rip and patch and seam—and above all preserved for us its emotional realities.

To make use of the psychologist's situation-response theory—or SR—we can say that King described the situation as it existed and the responses it evoked from frontier soldiers, although to complete his SR pattern he had to invent fictional characters and contrived incidents to make the responses explicable. The latter, though, is of no moment here; the situation is, and it is one that the historian cannot elucidate from ordinary sources as readily as he can from this group of novels.

Sociologically, he represented Army officers functioning in an aggregative rather than merely a collective group. The picture is complicated by the many instances of individual deviation, which are believable in relation to empirical experiences with other humans and yet not contradictory. Seeing soldiers now as part of an aggregative group, it is easier to understand the code and the ease with which they moved from one garrison group to another, without being away from home. From his novels we also can see the frontier Army as a distinctive subculture, embracing a specialized group of people in a specific setting during one fleeting period of time. The webs of that subculture were strong enough to bind people scattered in small groups across a largely vacant land. At the same time, however, he made no attempt to give a balanced account in which he might have appraised and criticized the Army as an institution. Hence, we have a projection of the Old Army by one who accepted it and its objectives without question.

There was no confusion of values in King's representation.[4] Unlike most writers who created an image of the West, King wrote of what he had known personally, infusing into the accounts the values and bias of the professional soldier. When warfare was involved, the soldier was true and good; the Indian, crafty, sneaky, and unscrupulous. The frontier soldier, however, was just as much the victim of stupid and dishonest Indian policies as was the Indian; and while King made that clear repeatedly, he did not attempt to analyze it in those terms. A believer in direct action, and an opinionated man, he held in scorn both Eastern soldiers and Eastern civilians, bringing into clear view the alienation of the Old Army and the schism between the Army as envisioned by officers in Washington and that of the men in the West. He was aware of the Army's role in the opening of the continent, and took pride in it. But it is noteworthy that he saw nothing romantic, or even creditable, in civilian frontiersmen—in contrast to the romanticizers who created the myths of the heroic frontiersmen. But with army scouts, such as his good friend Buffalo Bill Cody—well, they were different.

His novels are a closely contained and accurate representation of one type of Westerner—the professional soldier there only because it was his lot to obey orders. Never does he endow any of his characters with truly heroic stature. Seldom does he attribute to any character any important status prior to his life as a soldier. Status is solely that of a soldier who excels at his profession. No one officer is imbued in equal measure with all the skills and functions required of a frontier commander. Never does he inflate a soldier into the military counterpart of Boone, Crockett, Cody, or Leatherstocking. Each is a believable man. So, too, his women. None of them is perfectly genteel, as required of the formula writers of his day.

From both his novels and memoirs it becomes clear that Army people moved as often as the squatters and riff-raff of the frontier, and frequently lived in conditions just as primitive. But they were caught up within the confines of a socio-professional institution that allowed neither for complete individualism nor for the deterioration in manners, bearing, and appearance that marked other Anglos in the West.

Conclusions

The Western has been written by many people, but only a few had the combination of literary skill and personal experience that made their work a social record rather than entertainment alone. Eugene Manlove Rhodes and Ross Santee were possessed of that combination, writing the cowboy Western. Only King wrote, authoritatively and extensively, the soldier Western. Many later writers have elaborated on his themes, writers more skilled than he but unable to place their conception within the realistic framework of personal experience. When an officer is referred to as an "institution," as General Harbord labeled King, he is a man whose interpretation of the Army commands attention.

Notes

Chapter One

1. Duane Merritt Greene, *Ladies and Officers of the United States Army; or, American Aristocracy. A Sketch of the Social Life and Character of the Army*, 3. Greene had resigned as a lieutenant in the Sixth Cavalry to which he had been assigned after service as a volunteer officer during the Civil War. Hereafter cited as Greene, *Ladies and Officers*.

2. Katherine Gibson Fougera, *With Custer's Cavalry. From the Memoirs of the Late Katherine Gibson, Widow of Captain Francis M. Gibson of the Seventh Cavalry*, 73-74. Hereafter cited as Fougera, *With Custer's Cavalry*.

3. Lt. Col. O. L. Hein, *Memories of Long Ago, by an Old Army Officer*, 126; hereafter cited as Hein, *Memories*.

4. Charles King, *Between the Lines; a Story of the War*.

5. *Army and Navy Journal* (October 5, 1889), 108.

6. *Ibid.* (August 17, 1889), 1052.

7. Brig. Gen. C. B. Devore to King, May 1, 1919, in Charles King Manuscript Collection, Wisconsin State Historical Library. Hereafter cited as King Papers.

8. Quoted by Acting Insp. Gen. Eli A. Helmick to King, August 25, 1921, King Papers.

9. Lt. Alvin H. Sydenham, "Captain King," *Buffalo* (N. Y.) *Express* [1893?], in Sydenham Manuscript Collection, New York Public Library.

10. Carl Van Doren, *The American Novel*, 193-94.

11. *Milwaukee Journal*, June 23, 1929, King Biographical File, Milwaukee County Historical Society. Hereafter cited as King Biographical File.

12. Charles King, *Memories of a Busy Life*, 2-8, 89.

13. Lt. Philip Reade, "Captain Charles King," *Lippincott's Magazine*, Vol. 42 (December, 1888), 856, 857.

14. King, *Memories of a Busy Life*, 22-23.

15. Reade, "Captain Charles King," 857-58.

16. King, *Memories of a Busy Life*, 23; Frances C. Carrington, *My Army Life and the Fort Phil. Kearney Massacre*, 212; hereafter cited as *My Army Life*. Frances Carrington was the second wife of Colonel Henry B. Carrington; her first husband, Lieutenant George W. Grummond, died in the Fetterman fight. The first Mrs. Carrington (Margaret) also wrote an account of their life at Fort Phil Kearny. After her death, Carrington and Mrs. Grummond began a correspondence that led to their marriage.

17. Reade, "Captain Charles King," 858; King, *Memories of a Busy Life*, 25.

18. Charles King, *Marion's Faith*, 26; King, *Memories of a Busy Life*, 27.

19. Adj. Gen. Robert C. Davis to King, May 28, 1924, King Papers.

20. King, *Memories of a Busy Life*, 28; Reade, "Captain Charles King," 861; Joseph L. Schott, *Above and Beyond*, 309; unidentified newspaper clipping, King Biographical File.

21. Charles King, *Campaigning with Crook*, ix, 124; Jack D. Filipiak, "A Biographical Sketch of General Charles King," *The Denver Westerners Monthly Roundup*, Vol. 22 (June, 1966), 9.

22. King, *Memories of a Busy Life*, 28; Reade, "Captain Charles King," 860.

23. King, *Memories of a Busy Life*, 29; Brevet Maj. Gen. George W. Cullum, *Biographical Register of the Officers and Graduates of the U.S. Military Academy at West Point, N. Y., from its Establishment, in 1802, to 1890*, 3d ed., Vol. 3, 71-72.

24. King, *Memories of a Busy Life*, 50; C. E. Dornbusch, *Charles King: American Army Novelist. A Bibliography from the Collection of the National Library of Australia, Canberra, passim*.

25. First published by the Milwaukee Sentinel Co. in 1880 and reissued in an enlarged edition by Harper's, New York, in 1890.

26. Charles King, *The Colonel's Daughter, or Winning His Spurs;* Charles King, *Marion's Faith;* Charles King, *Trials of a Staff Officer*, 185; unidentified newspaper clipping, King Biographical File; King to a Miss Mayer, December 20, 1932, King Papers; Charles King, "Thirty Years of Pencraft," *Lippincott's Magazine*, Vol. 86 (October, 1910), 471, 473-74; hereafter cited as "Pencraft."

27. King, *Trials of a Staff Officer,* 186.

28. "A Soldier-Novelist," unidentified newspaper clipping, King Biographical File; King, *Trials of a Staff Officer,* 185-97; Charles King, *The Deserter and From the Ranks. Two Novels.*

29. King, "Pencraft," 474; Charles King, *"Laramie;" or, The Queen of Bedlam. A Story of the Sioux War of 1876.* Hereafter cited as *Laramie.*

30. King, "Pencraft," 474.

31. "Brig. Gen. Charles King, the Soldier-Novelist," *Current Literature,* Vol. 27 (January, 1900), 20-21; unidentified newspaper clipping [1933?], King Biographical File.

32. Charles King, *Kitty's Conquest.*

33. King, "Pencraft," 469.

34. Reade, "Captain Charles King," 860-61.

35. King to K. C. Bullard, November 23, 1902, King Papers.

36. Sydenham, "Captain King," and King, "Pencraft," 470.

37. King, *Memories of a Busy Life,* 51.

38. Capt. E. R. Burroughs, Illinois Reserve Militia, to King, May 25, 1918, King Papers.

39. King Papers.

40. King, *Trials of a Staff Officer,* 19-29.

41. King, *The Deserter* in *The Deserter and From the Ranks.*

42. Elizabeth B. Custer, *"Boots and Saddles" or, Life in Dakota with General Custer,* 115; hereafter cited as *Boots and Saddles.*

43. E.g., *Ray's Recruit.*

44. Ellen McGowan Biddle, *Reminiscences of a Soldier's Wife,* 86-87; Charles King, *A Garrison Tangle.*

45. Charles King, *Captain Blake,* 370, 379-82.

46. Fougera, *With Custer's Cavalry,* 215-16.

47. Charles King, *Trumpeter Fred,* 55. The reward for apprehension of a deserter by any civil officer was raised to $60 by General Orders No. 145, December 19, 1890, in *Compendium of General Orders from the Adjutant General's Office Amending Army Regulations* [1889 to 1892].

48. Charles King, *An Apache Princess,* 168.

49. *Ibid.,* 222; Charles King, *The Way of the West,* 85.

50. King, *Trials of a Staff Officer,* 51.

51. King, *Captain Blake,* 232-34, 253.

52. Custer, *Boots and Saddles,* 116-17.

53. King, *Captain Blake,* ix.

54. King, *A Garrison Tangle,* 260, 263-71.

55. Alice Blackwood Baldwin, *Memoirs of the Late Frank D.*

Baldwin, 18; hereafter cited as *Memoirs.*

56. Charles King, *An Army Portia* in *A Soldier's Secret: a Story of the Sioux War of 1890; and An Army Portia. Two Novels;* hereafter cited as *A Soldier's Secret and An Army Portia.*

57. *Army and Navy Journal,* April 21, 1883, pp. 868-69; April 28, 1883, p. 886.

58. Charles King, *Rancho del Muerto and Other Stories from Outing,* hereafter cited as *Rancho del Muerto;* Charles King, *A Trooper Galahad;* Charles King, *Foes in Ambush.*

59. *Army and Navy Journal,* May 24, 1884, p. 885.

60. *Ibid.,* March 26, 1887, p. 692.

61. Charles King, *Warrior Gap, a Story of the Sioux Outbreak of '68;* hereafter cited as *Warrior Gap.*

62. *Army and Navy Journal,* May 5, 1883, p. 910; May 12, 1883, p. 931; May 19, 1883, p. 948; June 16, 1883, p. 1035; June 23, 1883, p. 1060; June 30, 1883, pp. 1081-1082.

63. Biddle, *Reminiscences,* 171-72.

64. King, *Marion's Faith,* 384-85.

65. Lydia Spencer Lane, *I Married a Soldier or Old Days in the Old Army,* 130; hereafter cited as *I Married a Soldier.*

66. Charles King, *The Story of Fort Frayne,* hereafter cited as *Fort Frayne.*

67. King, *Memories of a Busy Life,* 104; King, *The Colonel's Daughter,* 47, 73; Charles King, *A Daughter of the Sioux,* 283; Charles King, *Under Fire,* 284; Charles King, *Tonio, Son of the Sierras,* 308, hereafter cited as *Tonio.*

68. Martin F. Schmitt (ed.), *General George Crook: His Autobiography;* John G. Bourke, *On the Border with Crook.*

69. King, *Under Fire,* 284.

70. King, *Trumpeter Fred,* 175; King, *The Colonel's Daughter,* 371.

71. King, *Tonio,* 310.

72. King, *A Daughter of the Sioux,* 174, 184.

73. Charles King, "George Crook," in *War Papers Read Before the Commandery of the State of Wisconsin, Military Order of the Loyal Legion of the United States,* Vol. 1, 267.

74. *Ibid.,* 253.

75. *Ibid.,* 267.

76. *Ibid.*

77. *Ibid.,* 255-57.

78. King, *Tonio,* 308.

79. King, *Trials of a Staff Officer*, 35-43.

80. *Ibid.*, 44-45.

81. *Ibid.*, 47.

82. King, *The Colonel's Daughter*, 192; Charles King, *Sunset Pass or Running the Gauntlet Through Apache Land*, hereafter cited as *Sunset Pass;* Charles King, *Starlight Ranch and Other Stories of Army Life on the Frontier*, 94, hereafter cited as *Starlight Ranch;* King, *Fort Frayne*, 29; Charles King, *Trooper Ross and Signal Butte*, 67, 277; King, *Under Fire*, 5; King, *Marion's Faith*, 378-79.

83. King, "Pencraft," 473.

84. King, *Memories of a Busy Life*, 12-21; Mrs. Orsemus Boyd, *Cavalry Life in Tent and Field*, 13-23, 323-31, hereafter cited as *Cavalry Life;* Sydenham, "Captain King."

85. King to Maj. Gen. Thomas M. Anderson, April 13, 1902, King Papers.

86. *Army and Navy Journal*, March 24, 1883, p. 772.

87. King, *A Soldier's Secret and an Army Portia*, 86-92.

88. *Ibid.*, 252.

89. F. Tennyson Neely to King, August 17, 1898, King Papers.

90. Charles King (ed.), *An Initial Experience and Other Stories*, 3.

91. *Army and Navy Journal*, January 20, 1883, p. 555.

92. *Ibid.*, March 24, 1883, p. 781.

93. *Ibid.*, June 16, 1883, p. 1045.

94. Ibid., May 29, 1886, pp. 905-906.

95. *New York Times*, December 24, 1891.

96. *Ibid.*, June 3, 1899.

97. *Ibid.*, April 19, 1891.

98. *Ibid.*, July 24, 1893.

99. *The Story of Fort Frayne*, reviewed in *Bookman*, Vol. 20 (October, 1895), 147-48.

100. *Campaigning with Crook*, reviewed in *The Dial*, Vol. 11 (January, 1891), 293.

101. "General Gossip of Authors and Writers," *Current Literature*, Vol. 29 (August, 1900), 150.

102. King, *Lanier of the Cavalry.*

103. Charles King, *The True Ulysses S. Grant.*

104. King, "Pencraft," 469n.

Chapter Two

1. Ami Frank Mulford, *Fighting Indians in the 7th United States*

Cavalry, 60; Greene, *Ladies and Officers,* 16 and *passim;* Merrill J. Mattes (ed.), *Indians, Infants and Infantry: Andrew and Elizabeth Burt on the Frontier* (the recollections of Mrs. Lieutenant Andrew Burt), 180; Frances M. A. Roe, *Army Letters from an Officer's Wife, 1871-1888,* 81, 166, hereafter cited as *Letters;* King, *Under fire,* 296.

2. Don Rickey, Jr., *Forty Miles a Day on Beans and Hay: The Enlisted Soldier Fighting the Indian Wars,* is the only study of enlisted men. Rickey did a masterful job in ferreting out what was available, but the enlisted man left so few personal traces that he remains a shadowy figure.

3. Greene, *Ladies and Officers,* 17-18, 20, 61-62.

4. Charles King, *Two Soldiers and Dunraven Ranch, Two Novels,* 12-13.

5. *Ibid.,* 17.

6. Roe, *Letters,* 166.

7. *Ibid.,* 81.

8. King, *A Garrison Tangle,* 78.

9. Custer, *Boots and Saddles,* 105, 106; Boyd, *Cavalry Life,* 142; *Revised Army Regulations, 1873,* House Report No. 85, 42d Congress, 3d Session, p. 41; hereafter cited as AR 1873; *Regulations for the Army of the United States, 1889,* p. 115, 156-57; hereafter cited as AR 1889; *Chicago Times,* March 31, 1877.

10. Greene, *Ladies and Officers,* 31; King, *Marion's Faith,* 247; King, *Under Fire,* 143; King, *Captain Blake,* 15, 64, 353; King, *The Colonel's Daughter,* 332; Boyd, *Cavalry Life,* 177.

11. King, *Marion's Faith,* 21.

12. Boyd, *Cavalry Life,* 141-42, 149-63, 244-53.

13. [Colonel A. G. Brackett], "Our Frontier Forts," *Chicago Times,* September 13, 1879, p. 14. The *Times* article did not carry Brackett's by-line, or identify the author in any way, but Brackett was identified as the author by the *Army and Navy Journal,* October 18, 1879, p. 198.

14. Mulford, *Fighting Indians,* 69-70.

15. Col. Henry B. Carrington, *Ab-sa-ra-ka, Land of Massacre: Being the Experience of an Officer's Wife on the Plains,* 42-43; hereafter cited as *Ab-sa-ra-ka.* This is the fourth edition of a book by Mrs. Margaret Carrington; this edition carried her husband's name because he had added to it materially.

16. Capt. Robert G. Carter, *On the Border with Mackenzie,* 416-17.

17. King, *Under Fire,* 163.

18. King, *The Colonel's Daughter,* 21-22, 49, 238, 283; King,

Marion's Faith, 20.

19. King, *The Colonel's Daughter,* 151, 238; King, *Marion's Faith,* 22-23.

20. King, *Captain Blake,* 42, 43, 62-63.

21. *Ibid.,* 24, 71, 418.

22. King, *The Colonel's Daughter,* 50-51.

23. *Ibid.,* 137, 328; King, *Captain Blake,* 72, 207, 211-14.

24. King, *The Colonel's Daughter,* 328; King, *Captain Blake,* 73-74; King, *Marion's Faith,* 126.

25. King, *The Colonel's Daughter,* 23, 49; King, *Captain Blake,* 413.

26. Greene, *Ladies and Officers,* 42.

27. Custer, *Boots and Saddles,* 115.

28. *Army and Navy Journal,* May 21, 1887, p. 852; Hein, *Memories,* 126.

29. King, *Marion's Faith,* 34, 36, 39, 108, 116, 126; King, *Captain Blake,* 20; King, *A Garrison Tangle,* 76.

30. King, *Marion's Faith,* 119-20.

31. Martha Summerhayes, *Vanished Arizona,* 36, 65.

32. *Ibid.,* 35, 36; Biddle, *Reminiscences,* 166.

33. *Army and Navy Journal,* January 28, 1882, p. 563-64, January 6, 1883, p. 507.

34. King, *Captain Blake,* 61, 79, and *passim;* King, *Marion's Faith;* Reade, "Captain Charles King," 861.

35. King, *Tonio.*

36. King, *The Colonel's Daughter,* 114, 273-75; King, *Marion's Faith,* 120; King, *Captain Blake,* 21, 13-14, 66; Roe, *Letters,* 50. The difficulty with Mrs. Roe's collection of letters is that she used fictional names throughout; in the text, even her own name appears as Rae.

37. King, *Marion's Faith,* 113-14, 165-66.

38. *Ibid.,* 165-67.

39. King, *Captain Blake,* 79 and *passim;* King, *Ray's Recruit;* King, *Under Fire;* King, *Laramie;* King, *Dunraven Ranch,* in *Two Soldiers and Dunraven Ranch.*

40. King, *The Colonel's Daughter,* 104; King, *Laramie,* 50.

41. Summerhayes, *Vanished Arizona,* 254-55.

42. Abe Laufe (ed.), *An Army Doctor's Wife on the Frontier,* 238.

43. Carrington, *Ab-sa-ra-ka,* iii, 41; Mattes, *Indians, Infants and Infantry,* 5.

44. Boyd, *Cavalry Life,* 65-66.

45. Diary of Lt. John Gregory Bourke, Vol. 19, pp. 1845, 1847-

48; hereafter cited as Bourke Diary.

46. *Army and Navy Journal,* April 30, 1887, p. 791; April 16, 1887, p. 750.

47. King, *Marion's Faith,* 138; King, *Captain Blake,* 24.

48. Custer, *Boots and Saddles,* 16.

49. King, *Under Fire,* 397, 399; Mattes, *Indians, Infants and Infantry,* 20-21, 103-105; Laufe, *An Army Doctor's Wife on the Frontier,* 194.

50. Custer, *Boots and Saddles,* 180; Elizabeth B. Custer, *Following the Guidon,* 132-33.

51. King, *The Deserter and From the Ranks,* 26.

52. King, *The Colonel's Daughter,* 369-71.

53. Summerhayes, *Vanished Arizona,* 43.

54. King, *A Garrison Tangle,* 5; Custer, *Following the Guidon,* 261, 309; Lane, *I Married a Soldier,* 86; Boyd, *Cavalry Life,* 100.

55. Fougera, *With Custer's Cavalry,* 44-61.

56. Roe, *Letters,* 357; Boyd, *Cavalry Life,* 29, 181, 188, 191.

57. Boyd, *Cavalry Life,* 82; Lane, *I Married a Soldier,* 51, 62, 67, 72, 82. Mrs. Lane was also a daughter of Maj. Blaney.

58. Boyd, *Cavalry Life,* 215; Summerhayes, *Vanished Arizona,* 158, 234.

59. Lane, *I Married a Soldier,* 154.

60. Boyd, *Cavalry Life,* 29, 68-69, 171, 244-46; Lane, *I Married a Soldier,* 104.

61. Deoch Fulton (ed.), *The Journal of Lieut. Sydenham, 1889, 1890,* 16.

62. Custer, *Boots and Saddles,* 77; Carrington, *My Army Life,* 37-38.

63. King, *The Deserter and From the Ranks,* 54-137; King, *Ray's Recruit,* 38-41; Charles King, *Captain Close and Sergeant Croesus,* 223; AR 1873, p. 42.

64. George A. Forsyth, *The Story of the Soldier,* 133; Custer, *Boots and Saddles,* 82; Hein, *Memories,* 67-68; Laufe, *An Army Doctor's Wife on the Frontier,* 265.

65. Lane, *I Married a Soldier,* 72.

66. AR 1873, p. 41; Boyd, *Cavalry Life,* 54, 82; Lane, *I Married a Soldier,* 74-75.

67. *Regulations of the Army of the United States and General Orders in Force on the 17th of February, 1881,* p. 313, hereafter cited as AR 1881; *Army and Navy Journal,* April 7, 1883, p. 882.

68. Forsyth, *Story of the Soldier,* 112-13.

Notes: Chapter 2

69. Mulford, *Fighting Indians*, 52.
70. Summerhayes, *Vanished Arizona*, 71.

Chapter Three

1. *Army and Navy Journal*, January 13, 1883, p. 526.
2. Secretary of War, *Annual Report*, 1875, Vol. 1, p. 123.
3. *Army and Navy Journal*, April 29, 1882, p. 890.
4. Greene, *Ladies and Officers*, 3-4, 101-103, 133.
5. Col. James B. Fry, "Justice for the Army," *Army and Navy Journal*, August 25, 1883, p. 63.
6. King, *The Deserter and From the Ranks*, 51.
7. *Army and Navy Journal*, May 26, 1883, p. 975; July 21, 1883, p. 1150.
8. *Ibid.*, June 16, 1883, p. 1038; June 23, 1883, p. 1060; July 14, 1883, p. 1127.
9. King, *An Apache Princess*, 60; King, *The Colonel's Daughter*, 9-10; King, *Captain Blake*, 289.
10. King, *Captain Blake*, 334, 336, 337, 340; King, *Ray's Recruit*, 35.
11. King, *Two Soldiers and Dunraven Ranch*, 15.
12. *Army and Navy Journal*, May 6, 1882, p. 904.
13. King, *Marion's Faith*, 14; King, *A Trooper Galahad*, 109.
14. King, *The Deserter and From the Ranks*, 35.
15. King, *A Daughter of the Sioux*, 117.
16. Forsyth, *Story of the Soldier*, 370.
17. Boyd, *Cavalry Life*, 151-52.
18. *Army and Navy Journal*, October 9, 1886, p. 215.
19. Fougera, *With Custer's Cavalry*, 75.
20. King, *The Deserter and From the Ranks*, 297.
21. King, *Marion's Faith*, 9-12.
22. King, *The Colonel's Daughter;* King, *Marion's Faith*, 137-39; King, *Ray's Recruit.*
23. King, *The Colonel's Daughter*, 6, 9, 11, and *passim.*
24. King, *Warrior Gap*, 24.
25. *Army and Navy Journal*, May 6, 1882, p. 910; August 1, 1885, p. 7.
26. *Ibid.*, October 14, 1882, p. 237.
27. King, *Captain Blake*, 13, 290.
28. King, *Two Soldiers and Dunraven Ranch*, 136.
29. *Ibid.*

30. King, *A Soldier's Secret and An Army Portia*, 83.

31. *Ibid.*, 150.

32. King, *Under Fire*, 195.

33. King, *Ray's Recruit*, 24-29, 108-109, 172, 201.

34. Summerhayes, *Vanished Arizona*, 75, 214.

35. King, *The Deserter and From the Ranks*, 194n; Roe, *Letters*, 5.

36. Greene, *Ladies and Officers*, 149-50.

37. King, *Under Fire*, 396.

38. King, *The Way of the West*, 22.

39. King, *The Colonel's Daughter*, 26, 27, 74, 82, 86, 262, 355; King, *Two Soldiers and Dunraven Ranch*, 137; King, *Marion's Faith*, 13, 153; King, *Under Fire*, 424.

40. King, *The Colonel's Daughter*, 253-55.

41. King, *Under Fire*, 11; King, *Two Soldiers and Dunraven Ranch*, 57.

42. King, *A Soldier's Secret and An Army Portia*, 10.

43. *Ibid.*, 82.

44. *Ibid.*, 35-36.

45. King, *Campaigning with Crook*, 82-83.

46. King, *Under Fire*, 103-104.

47. *Ibid.*, 117.

48. King, *Trials of a Staff Officer*, 17-19.

49. *Army and Navy Journal*, May 5, 1883, p. 914.

50. King, *Under Fire*, 499.

51. King, *Starlight Ranch*, 210, 213, 217; King, *The Deserter and From the Ranks*, 97, 98, 134.

52. Greene, *Ladies and Officers*, 106.

53. King, *A Trooper Galahad;* King, *Starlight Ranch*, 10, 23, 28; King, *Marion's Faith.*

54. King, *The Deserter and From the Ranks*, 117; Greene, *Ladies and Officers*, 188, 192; *Army and Navy Journal*, January 31, 1881, p. 479.

55. King, *Two Soldiers and Dunraven Ranch*, 12.

56. King, *Ray's Recruit.*

57. King, *Marion's Faith*, 354-55.

58. King, *Under Fire*, 143.

59. Charles King, *A Wounded Name*, 12.

60. King, *A Soldier's Secret and An Army Portia*, 140; King, *Marion's Faith*, 137; King, *Two Soldiers*, in *Two Soldiers and Dunraven Ranch.*

61. Hein, *Memories*, 117.

62. *Army and Navy Journal*, August 12, 1882, p. 32.

63. Summerhayes, *Vanished Arizona,* 229.

64. King, *Marion's Faith,* 15.

65. King, *The Colonel's Daughter,* 81.

66. Elizabeth B. Custer, *Tenting on the Plains,* II, 420.

67. King, *The Colonel's Daughter,* 82.

68. Custer, *Tenting on the Plains,* II, 419.

69. King, *Marion's Faith,* 137.

70. King, *Ray's Recruit,* 127.

71. King, *A Trooper Galahad,* 110.

72. Roe, *Letters,* 15.

73. *Army and Navy Journal,* May 29, 1886, p. 889.

74. Henry Gaullieur, *Souvenirs D'un Voyage a Cheval dans le Desert Americaine,* quoted in review in *Army and Navy Journal,* January 20, 1883, p. 556.

75. King, *Captain Blake,* x-xviii.

76. Fougera, *With Custer's Cavalry,* 69, 145.

77. King, *The Colonel's Daughter,* 162-63; King, *Marion's Faith,* 14, 167; King, *Captain Blake,* 83, 237.

78. King, *The Colonel's Daughter,* 113; King, *A Daughter of the Sioux,* 13; King, *Marion's Faith,* 153-54.

79. King, *Trials of a Staff Officer,* 28.

80. Custer, *Following the Guidon,* 284.

81. Summerhayes, *Vanished Arizona,* 266, 268.

82. King, *The Deserter and From the Ranks,* 109-110; Charles King, *In Spite of Foes, or Ten Years Trial,* 81, hereafter cited as *In Spite of Foes.*

83. King, *The Deserter and From the Ranks,* 13.

84. Roe, *Letters,* 110.

85. King, *Marion's Faith,* 24-26.

86. *An Apache Princess, The Deserter and From the Ranks, Marion's Faith, Captain Close and Sergeant Croesus.*

87. King, *A Daughter of the Sioux,* 118; King, *Foes in Ambush,* 16; King, *Trumpeter Fred,* 48.

88. King, *Foes in Ambush,* 185.

89. King, *In Spite of Foes,* 53n; King, *Ray's Recruit,* 104, 133.

90. King, *Fort Frayne,* 41; King, *A Daughter of the Sioux,* 86; King, *Foes in Ambush,* 37.

91. King, *The Colonel's Daughter,* 90; King, *Under Fire,* 259.

92. King, *A Garrison Tangle,* 38.

93. King, *A Soldier's Secret and An Army Portia,* 152; AR 1881, p. 30; AR 1889, p. 15; General Order No. 38, Headquarters of the Army,

March 28, 1890, in *Compendium of General Orders . . . 1889 . . . 1892.*
94. King, *Campaigning with Crook,* 154-55.
95. *Army and Navy Journal,* October 16, 1886, p. 236.
96. King, *In Spite of Foes,* 50.
97. *Army and Navy Journal,* May 19, 1883, p. 956.
98. *Ibid.,* September 16, 1882, p. 151; AR 1889, p. 4.
99. King, *The Way of the West,* 117, 136.

Chapter Four

1. [Brackett], "Our Frontier Forts," *Chicago Times,* September 13, 1879.
2. Forsyth, *Story of the Soldier,* 109.
3. [Brackett], "Our Frontier Forts," *op. cit.*
4. *Ibid.*
5. Revised U. S. Army Regulations of 1861, pp. 159-60, hereafter cited as AR 1861; AR 1889, p. 116; AR 1873, p. 147.
6. Roe, *Letters,* 8; Summerhayes, *Vanished Arizona,* 25; Forsyth, *Story of the Soldier,* 105.
7. Greene, *Ladies and Officers,* 53-54; *Army and Navy Journal,* January 13, 1883, p. 528; April 28, 1883, p. 884.
8. *Army and Navy Journal,* February 5, 1887, p. 545.
9. Mattes, *Indians, Infants and Infantry,* 46; Carter, *On the Border with Mackenzie,* 44, 321; Lane, *I Married a Soldier,* 85, 134-35; Boyd, *Cavalry Life,* 50-51, 67.
10. Lane, *I Married a Soldier,* 48; Mattes, *Indians, Infants and Infantry,* 64, 142; Carrington, *My Army Life,* 104; Roe, *Letters,* 55; Boyd, *Cavalry Life,* 132, 171.
11. King, *A Garrison Tangle,* 1, 3; Baldwin, *Memoirs,* 136; Laufe, *An Army Doctor's Wife on the Frontier,* 196; Custer, *Tenting on the Plains,* II, 411-12; King, *Laramie,* 50; King, *Fort Frayne,* 99; Mattes, *Indians, Infants and Infantry,* 24, 25.
12. Biddle, *Reminiscences,* 164; King, *Laramie,* 33; *Army and Navy Journal,* March 18, 1882, p. 736.
13. King, *Captain Blake,* 116, 141, 143; Mattes, *Indians, Infants and Infantry,* 179; King, *Marion's Faith,* 175.
14. In Mattes, *Indians, Infants and Infantry,* 179, Mrs. Burt recorded in her diary that both tar paper and wallpaper had been applied by the post quartermaster to add to the warmth.
15. On the whole, the *Chicago Times* energetically covered the West and took strong editorial stands in favor of the Army and

against civilian control of Indian affairs, but King was supersensitive and had no great fondness for journalists.

16. King, *Captain Blake,* 141-45.

17. Mattes, *Indians, Infants and Infantry,* 197.

18. King, *An Apache Princess,* 42.

19. Summerhayes, *Vanished Arizona,* 216, 252.

20. Fougera, *With Custer's Cavalry,* 67, 68, 70, 224.

21. AR 1861, p. 162; AR 1881, p. 204; AR 1889, p. 113; Roe, *Letters,* 7.

22. King, *Tonio,* 24.

23. Carter, *On the Border with Mackenzie,* 34.

24. King, *Captain Blake,* 252.

25. King, *A Soldier's Secret and An Army Portia,* 190.

26. King, *The Deserter and From the Ranks,* 44.

27. Summerhayes, *Vanished Arizona,* 22.

28. Roe, *Letters,* 66-69; Boyd, *Cavalry Life,* 256-79.

29. AR 1861, p. 159; Boyd, *Cavalry Life,* 51; Roe, *Letters,* 58, 68, 103.

30. Custer, *Following the Guidon,* 227, 228; Biddle, *Reminiscences,* 88-89; King, *Marion's Faith,* 18.

31. King, *The Colonel's Daughter,* 80-81.

32. King, *Under Fire,* 220-21.

33. Fougera, *With Custer's Cavalry,* 117; Carrington, *Ab-sa-ra-ka,* 177.

34. King, *Tonio,* 12; Summerhayes, *Vanished Arizona,* 246.

35. King, *Marion's Faith,* 412, 416; King, *Trumpeter Fred,* 27-28; King, *A Garrison Tangle,* 202; King, *Captain Blake,* 285; Laufe, *An Army Doctor's Wife on the Frontier,* 218, 228-30; Carter, *On the Border with Mackenzie,* 33-34; Roe, *Letters,* 119; Baldwin, *Memoirs,* 152; Custer, *Boots and Saddles,* 53-55, 68, 162-63; Fougera, *With Custer's Cavalry,* 96, 97.

36. AR 1881, p. 312; *Army and Navy Journal,* September 16, 1882, p. 145; February 3, 1883, p. 615; King, *Captain Close and Sergeant Croesus,* 149; King, *Captain Blake,* 63, 138-39; King, *The Deserter and From the Ranks,* 124; Baldwin, *Memoirs,* 128-29; Boyd, *Cavalry Life,* 53-54, 198; Summerhayes, *Vanished Arizona;* Mattes, *Indians, Infants and Infantry,* 198.

37. King, *An Army Wife,* 195-96; King, *The Deserter and From the Ranks,* 46; Roe, *Letters,* 218; 232, 310, 311; Summerhayes, *Vanished Arizona,* 236; Laufe, *An Army Doctor's Wife on the Frontier,* 202-203, 208, 249, 253.

38. King, *A Garrison Tangle,* 218; Boyd, *Cavalry Life,* 61, 134-35; Fougera, *With Custer's Cavalry,* 71; Carrington, *My Army Life,* 105-107, 141.

39. Roe, *Letters,* 78.

40. Mattes, *Indians, Infants and Infantry,* 175; Roe, *Letters,* 232; Boyd, *Cavalry Life,* 236-37; King, *Captain Blake,* 264.

41. King, *An Apache Princess,* 42; King, *Lanier of the Cavalry,* 97; King, *Laramie,* 21.

42. King, *A Garrison Tangle,* 161.

43. *Ibid.;* King, *A Soldier's Secret and An Army Portia.*

44. *Army and Navy Journal,* September 10, 1881, p. 117.

45. Custer, *Following the Guidon,* 248, 249; Boyd, *Cavalry Life,* 174; Fougera, *With Custer's Cavalry,* 77.

46. King, *Ray's Recruit,* 103; King, *Laramie,* 15; King, *Trooper Ross and Signal Butte,* 191; King, *Under Fire,* 148;

47. King, *Ray's Recruit,* 103.

48. Mattes, *Indians, Infants and Infantry,* 102-103; Boyd, *Cavalry Life,* 146.

49. Carrington, *Ab-sa-ra-ka,* 52-53.

50. King, *Fort Frayne,* 179-80.

51. Greene, *Ladies and Officers,* 55-58.

52. King, *Campaigning with Crook,* 4.

53. Hein, *Memories,* 83-84; Summerhayes, *Vanished Arizona,* 74; Biddle, *Reminiscences,* 166.

54. Mrs. Lane made exactly the same point in *I Married a Soldier,* 84: "[Army women] never grow old in a garrison, and always receive attentions to which no woman in citizen life is accustomed when no longer young. I have seen gray-haired ladies at an army post dance at the hops with as much enjoyment as the younger ones, and they are always invited by the men, young and old, to do so as a matter of course. The hops are more like a family reunion than a gathering of strangers." After retirement, it took her a long time to adjust to the loss of such courtesies and to accept being a wallflower when she went out for an evening.

55. King, *The Colonel's Daughter,* 42-47.

56. Biddle, *Reminiscences,* 180; Roe, *Letters,* 142-43.

57. Greene, *Ladies and Officers,* 51-52.

58. *Army and Navy Journal,* September 23, 1882, p. 167.

59. *Ibid.,* February 4, 1882, p. 599 and January 9, 1886, p. 471; Biddle, *Reminiscences,* 128.

60. King makes this clear in several novels, including *Two*

Notes: Chapter 4

Soldiers and Dunraven Ranch, 51.

61. King, *Captain Blake,* 70-79.

62. *Ibid.,* 73-74.

63. Roe, *Letters,* 28; King, *Captain Blake,* 76; King, *Fort Frayne,* 301.

64. King, *Fort Frayne,* 183; Baldwin, *Memoirs,* 14; Forsyth, *Story of the Soldier,* 133; Boyd, *Cavalry Life,* 172.

65. King, *A Garrison Tangle,* 64; Carrington, *My Army Life,* 102; King, *Captain Blake,* 51; King, *A Soldier's Secret and An Army Portia,* 55; Custer, *Following the Guidon,* 256.

66. King, *An Army Wife,* 123; King, *A Soldier's Secret and An Army Portia,* 15, 221; King, *A Trooper Galahad,* 67, 79; King, *Laramie,* 50; Custer, *Tenting on the Plains,* II, 377; Baldwin, *Memoirs,* 129.

67. *Army and Navy Journal,* January 30, 1886, p. 537; Mattes, *Indians, Infants and Infantry,* 234; Greene, *Ladies and Officers,* 66-69, 84.

68. King, *The Colonel's Daughter;* King, *A Garrison Tangle,* 4; *Army and Navy Journal,* March 18, 1882, p. 736; May 5, 1883, pp. 904-905; September 11, 1886, p. 132; Custer, *Boots and Saddles,* 161; Fougera, *With Custer's Cavalry,* 13-33; Mattes, *Indians, Infants and Infantry,* 23.

69. [Brackett], "Our Frontier Forts."

70. King, *Trials of a Staff Officer,* 181.

71. King, *An Apache Princess,* 108.

72. King, *The Colonel's Daughter,* 129-30; King, *Lanier of the Cavalry,* 197; King, *The Deserter and From the Ranks,* 114, 135.

73. Fougera, *With Custer's Cavalry,* 106-13, 134, 135; Hein, *Memories,* 71; *Army and Navy Journal,* October 14, 1882, p. 237.

74. King, *Marion's Faith,* 421; King, *Tonio,* 169.

75. *Ibid.* and Fougera, *With Custer's Cavalry,* 193-96; Fulton, *The Journal of Lieut. Sydenham,* 12-13; *Army and Navy Journal,* September, 10, 1881, pp. 116-17; January 6, 1883, p. 507.

76. Summerhayes, *Vanished Arizona,* 44; Fougera, *With Custer's Cavalry,* 75, 85, 95; Mattes, *Indians, Infants and Infantry,* 178; Lane, *I Married a Soldier,* 159; Greene, *Ladies and Officers,* 88; *Army and Navy Journal,* January 16, 1885, p. 493.

77. Greene, *Ladies and Officers,* 75-77.

78. *Ibid.,* 21-22, 27, 38-39, 43-44, 75-77.

79. Roe, *Letters,* 143, 188.

80. *Army and Navy Journal,* March 4, 1882, p. 686; Fougera, *With Custer's Cavalry,* 134.

81. Custer, *Boots and Saddles,* 105.

82. Custer, *Tenting on the Plains,* I, 176.

83. Hein, *Memories,* 90-91.

84. King, *Under Fire,* 328; King, *A Trooper Galahad,* 191; King, *A Soldier's Secret and An Army Portia,* 195; King, *The Deserter and From the Ranks,* 118, 192; King, *Two Soldiers and Dunraven Ranch,* 71.

85. King, *A Garrison Tangle,* 5, 30-31; King, *Captain Blake,* 109; King, *The Colonel's Daughter,* 283.

86. King, *Two Soldiers and Dunraven Ranch,* 138.

87. King, *A Garrison Tangle,* 30-32.

88. *Ibid.,* 14-15.

89. King, *Marion's Faith,* 256; King, *Captain Blake,* 23-24.

90. King, *The Deserter and From the Ranks,* 178; King, *Under Fire, 328.*

91. Examples can be found in *Army and Navy Journal,* April 22, 1882, p. 860; February 3, 1883, p. 603; February 24, 1883, p. 676; March 10, 1883, p. 724; March 24, 1883, p. 772; June 9, 1883, p. 1012; January 5, 1884, p. 455; April 5, 1884, p. 732; and November 21, 1885, p. 327.

92. King, *Captain Blake,* 189-97.

93. Carter, *On the Border with Mackenzie,* 343-44; Colonel A. G. Brackett, "Our Cavalry on the Frontier," *Army and Navy Journal,* November 10, 1883, p. 283.

94. King, *A Soldier's Secret and An Army Portia,* 13; King, *The Colonel's Daughter,* 277; King, *Two Soldiers and Dunraven Ranch,* 160; King, *Marion's Faith,* 122; King, *Laramie,* 23-24, 25, 28, 57.

95. Hein, *Memories,* 78; Custer, *Boots and Saddles,* 117; [Brackett] "Our Frontier Forts"; AR 1881, p. 59; AR 1889, p. 35; King, *The Colonel's Daughter,* 143, 197; Baldwin, *Memoirs,* 17; King, *Captain Blake,* 25, 31; King, *Marion's Faith,* 16, 93; Greene, *Ladies and Officers,* 166-67; King, *A Daughter of the Sioux,* 11; King, *Starlight Ranch,* 25; King, *The Deserter and From the Ranks,* 43.

96. Lane, *I Married a Soldier,* 169.

97. *Army and Navy Journal,* January 6, 1883, p. 507; January 13, 1883, p. 528; Roe *Letters,* 24. For King's descriptions of Christmas preparations see *A Soldier's Secret and An Army Portia,* 31; *Ray's Recruit,* 189, 229; *Fort Frayne,* 90-91, 105.

98. King, *Under Fire,* 193; King, *A Daughter of the Sioux,* 166; Charles King, "Customs of the Service," *Army and Navy Journal,* May 5, 1883, p. 914; King, *Tonio,* 16, 256; King, *The Colonel's Daughter,* 330, 345; King, *Marion's Faith,* 31.

99. King, *Under Fire,* 17; Fougera, *With Custer's Cavalry,* 84;

Notes: Chapter 4

King, *A Soldier's Secret and An Army Portia,* 52; King, *Two Soldiers and Dunraven Ranch,* 136; King, *Captain Blake,* 60, 460, 467; King, *The Colonel's Daughter,* 51; Custer, *Boots and Saddles,* 101-102; King, *Ray's Recruit,* 147.

100. King, *The Deserter and From the Ranks,* 13.

101. Roe, *Letters,* 42; Custer, *Boots and Saddles,* 113.

102. King, *A Soldier's Secret and An Army Portia,* 39.

103. King, *Captain Blake,* 24, 110; King, *Marion's Faith,* 95; King, *The Colonel's Daughter,* 13, 17; King, *The Deserter and From the Ranks,* 42-43.

104. King, *A Garrison Tangle,* 105.

105. King, *The Colonel's Daughter,* 108-110.

106. King, *A Garrison Tangle,* 16-17, 77-80, 166-70.

107. King, *Captain Blake,* 425.

108. Milo Milton Quaife (ed.), *Army Life in Dakota: Selections from the Journal of Philippe Régis Denis de Keredern de Trobriand,* 348; Roe, *Letters,* 80.

109. King, *Captain Blake,* 426.

110. Lane, *I Married a Soldier,* 151-52.

111. Roe, *Letters,* 359.

112. AR 1881, p. 242; Henry Pickering Walker, *The Wagonmasters,* 96, 98, 227-54.

113. Mrs. Grace Bunce Paulding, "Memoir," The William and Grace Paulding Papers, Army Military History Research Collection, Carlisle Barracks, Pennsylvania, 1-14; hereafter cited as Paulding, "Memoir."

Chapter Five

1. King, *An Apache Princess,* 70-73; Roe, *Letters,* 6-7.

2. King, *The Colonel's Daughter,* 256; King, *Starlight Ranch,* 219-20; King, *Ray's Recruit,* 24; Roe, *Letters,* 6, 70-71.

3. AR 1881, p. 53; AR 1889, p. 41; General Orders No. 80, Headquarters of the Army, November 5, 1889, in *Compendium of General Orders . . . 1889 . . . 1892;* King, *Ray's Recruit,* 124; King, *Captain Blake,* 31; King, *Two Soldiers and Dunraven Ranch,* 157.

4. King, *The Colonel's Daughter,* 311.

5. King, *Trials of a Staff Officer,* 15; King, *The Deserter and From the Ranks,* 34; King, *Captain Blake,* 98; Rickey, *Forty Miles a Day on Beans and Hay,* 117.

6. King, *Under Fire,* 194.

7. King, *Trials of a Staff Officer*, 19; King, *Ray's Recruit*, 129.

8. King, *Two Soldiers and Dunraven Ranch*, 140.

9. King, *Captain Blake*, 7.

10. King, *Trials of a Staff Officer*, 16.

11. King, *A Daughter of the Sioux*, 60; King, *Lanier of the Cavalry*, 45; King, *The Deserter and From the Ranks*, 103, 227.

12. King, *Captain Blake*, 220-21.

13. King, *A Soldier's Secret and An Army Portia*, 194; King, *Captain Blake*, 219; Biddle, *Reminiscences*, 117-20.

14. King, *The Deserter and From the Ranks*, 32-33, 38.

15. King, *A Soldier's Secret and An Army Portia*, 172.

16. King, *Marion's Faith*, 387; Rickey, *Forty Miles a Day on Beans and Hay*, 117.

17. AR 1881, p. 41.

18. The composite above was formed from King, *A Soldier's Secret and An Army Portia*, 212-14, *Two Soldiers and Dunraven Ranch*, 161-62, and *The Colonel's Daughter*, 170-71.

19. King, *The Deserter and From the Ranks*, 263.

20. King, *Captain Blake*, 172; [Brackett], "Our Frontier Forts."

21. King, *Lanier of the Cavalry*, 114; [Brackett], "Our Frontier Forts."

22. King, *The Colonel's Daughter*, 209.

23. [Brackett], "Our Frontier Forts"; Fougera, *With Custer's Cavalry*, 66.

24. King, *Marion's Faith*, 176; Mattes, *Indians, Infants and Infantry*, 143.

25. King, *The Deserter and From the Ranks*, 33.

26. King, *Trials of a Staff Officer*, 5.

27. King, *Ray's Recruit*, 231.

28. King, *Under Fire*, 459.

29. AR 1881, p. 131; King, *Captain Blake*, 9; King, *The Colonel's Daughter*, 163.

30. At Fort D. A. Russell especially, the constantly strong winds usually caused the post to fly a small, tough storm flag rather than the large national standard: King, *Marion's Faith*, 89.

31. King, *A Soldier's Secret and An Army Portia*, 147-48.

32. Greene, *Ladies and Officers*, 126; Summerhayes, *Vanished Arizona*, 221, 262, 273; King, "Customs of the Service"; *Army and Navy Journal*, March 3, 1883, p. 700; May 5, 1883, p. 905.

33. King, *Marion's Faith*, 243; King, *A Soldier's Secret and An Army Portia*, 21; King, *The Deserter and From the Ranks*, 91-94, 104-105, 117,

200; King, *Two Soldiers and Dunraven Ranch;* King, *The Colonel's Daughter,* 244, 314-15, 373-75; King, *An Apache Princess.*

34. King, *Laramie,* 142; Boyd, *Cavalry Life,* 146-47, 204; Lane, *I Married a Soldier,* 47-48, 100; Summerhayes, *Vanished Arizona,* 183, 209; King, *The Colonel's Daughter,* 359-60; Baldwin, *Memoirs,* 133.

35. King, *An Apache Princess,* 55-56.

36. King, *The Colonel's Daughter,* 192.

37. King, *Tonio,* 15; King, *Under Fire,* 201; King, *Captain Blake,* 8, 11.

38. King, *Ray's Recruit,* 165; King, *A Soldier's Secret and An Army Portia,* 24; AR 1881, p. 131.

39. King, *Trials of a Staff Officer,* 12.

40. *E.g.,* King, *Ray's Recruit,* 182-88.

41. King, *Captain Blake,* 233.

42. King, *Trials of a Staff Officer,* 50.

43. Boyd, *Cavalry Life,* 176; Lane, *I Married a Soldier,* 65; Mattes, *Indians, Infants and Infantry,* 145; Baldwin, *Memoirs,* 162; Custer, *Boots and Saddles,* 97-98; King, *Marion's Faith,* 386.

44. King, *Starlight Ranch,* 65, 74; King, *The Colonel's Daughter,* 285; King, *Campaigning with Crook,* 5; King, *Trumpeter Fred,* 72; Chicago *Times,* April 16, 1877.

45. King, *Marion's Faith,* 19; King, *Trials of a Staff Officer,* 19-24.

46. Brackett, "Our Cavalry on the Frontier."

47. King, *The Colonel's Daughter,* 74; King, *Ray's Recruit,* 95; Hein, *Memories,* 95; King, *Starlight Ranch,* 83, 234; Biddle, *Reminiscences,* 166-67; King, *A Wounded Name,* 10; King, *Foes in Ambush,* 16.

48. King, *A Wounded Name,* 80.

49. *Army and Navy Journal,* October 14, 1882, p. 237.

50. King, *An Apache Princess,* 19-20.

51. King, *Tonio,* 15, 203; King, *An Apache Princess,* 57; King, *Rancho del Muerto,* 19, 39; King, *A Wounded Name,* 10; Hein, *Memories,* 80; King, *The Colonel's Daughter,* 24, 53; King, *Starlight Ranch,* 234.

52. Anson Mills, *My Story,* 147-48.

53. King, *Foes in Ambush,* 143.

54. *Army and Navy Journal,* July 22, 1882, p. 1188; August 5, 1882, p. 12; August 19, 1882, p. 58; October 14, 1882, p. 237; October 28, 1882, p. 281; May 3, 1884, p. 823; Boyd, *Cavalry Life,* 170.

55. King, *Captain Blake,* 124.

56. *Ibid.,* 284-85.

57. King, *Captain Close and Sergeant Croesus,* 152.

58. King, *Lanier of the Cavalry,* 46; Fulton, *The Journal of Lieut. Sydenham,* 7.
59. King, *Captain Blake,* 125-28.
60. *Army and Navy Journal,* May 10, 1884, p. 845.

Chapter Six

1. *Chronological List of Actions, &c., with Indians from January 1, 1866, to January, 1881,* Office Memoranda, Adjutant General's Office, n. d., 2-56.
2. King, *The Colonel's Daughter,* 264-65.
3. Boyd, *Cavalry Life,* 229.
4. Custer, *Boots and Saddles,* 71; Custer, *Tenting on the Plains,* II, 485.
5. Mattes, *Indians, Infants and Infantry,* 21.
6. Fougera, *With Custer's Cavalry,* 118-19, 159, 189.
7. King, *Fort Frayne,* 24; King, *Laramie,* 117-19; King, *Marion's Faith,* 113.
8. King, *The Colonel's Daughter;* King, *Under Fire,* 472.
9. King, *Under Fire,* 143.
10. Summerhayes, *Vanished Arizona,* 30.
11. *Army and Navy Journal,* April 29, 1882, p. 883.
12. Mattes, *Indians, Infants and Infantry,* 209, 213-14.
13. Fougera, *With Custer's Cavalry,* 189.
14. Mattes, *Indians, Infants and Infantry,* 230.
15. King, *Captain Blake,* 294-96.
16. Fougera, *With Custer's Cavalry,* 263-75.
17. Mattes, *Indians, Infants and Infantry,* 230.
18. King, *Marion's Faith,* 182.
19. Baldwin, *Memoirs,* 156, 191.
20. Laufe, *An Army Doctor's Wife on the Frontier,* 249, 259, 284, 286.
21. *Ibid.,* 260-352.
22. King, *A Daughter of the Sioux,* 70; King, *Under Fire,* 420.
23. King, *Warrior Gap,* 23-24.
24. King, *The Deserter and From the Ranks,* 5.
25. King, *The Colonel's Daughter,* 296-97; King, *Starlight Ranch,* 57; Rickey, *Forty Miles a Day on Beans and Hay,* 217; King, "George Crook," 260.
26. King, *Starlight Ranch,* 201-205.
27. John F. Finerty, *War-Path and Bivouac,* 25.

28. Brackett, "Our Cavalry on the Frontier."

29. King, *Marion's Faith,* 90-91.

30. King, *A Daughter of the Sioux,* 70-72; King, *The Colonel's Daughter,* 63.

31. King, *Marion's Faith,* 191; King, *The Colonel's Daughter,* 292.

32. Gordon Chappell, *The Search for the Well-Dressed Soldier, 1865-1890,* 21; Secretary of War, *Annual Report,* 1880, I, 72.

33. Rickey, *Forty Miles a Day on Beans and Hay,* 221; Frederic Remington, "A New Infantry Equipment," *Harper's Weekly,* Vol. 38 (September 22, 1894), 905.

34. AR 1881, p. 277; King, *The Colonel's Daughter,* 296-97; King, *Captain Blake,* 9.

35. King, *Marion's Faith,* 62-63.

36. *Ibid.,* 102.

37. King, *Under Fire,* 209-211.

38. Brackett, "Our Cavalry on the Frontier."

39. King, *An Apache Princess,* 83, 222; King, *Tonio,* 200; King, *Trooper Ross and Signal Butte,* 275; King, *Two Soldiers and Dunraven Ranch,* 88, 92; King, *Ray's Recruit,* 95.

40. King, *Warrior Gap,* 4; King, *Marion's Faith,* 219.

41. AR 1881, p. 284; General Orders No. 65, Headquarters of the Army, June 20, 1890, in *Compendium of General Orders . . . 1889 . . . 1892.*

42. King, *Ray's Recruit,* 36-37.

43. *Ibid.,* 27; Brackett, "Our Cavalry on the Frontier"; King, *Trumpeter Fred,* 107.

44. For King's better battle descriptions, see *The Colonel's Daughter,* 62, 87-91, 290; *Marion's Faith,* 189-232; *Sunset Pass; Foes in Ambush,* 186-236; *Starlight Ranch,* 113; *Under Fire,* 249-65, 374-90, 421; *Captain Close and Sergeant Croesus,* 187-213; *Fort Frayne,* 26-50; *Two Soldiers and Dunraven Ranch,* 94-107; *Trooper Ross and Signal Butte,* 18-38, 71-72, 213-64; *Warrior Gap,* 80, 222-30, 367-76; *Ray's Recruit,* 239ff; *A Garrison Tangle,* 124; *Trumpeter Fred,* 154; *A Daughter of the Sioux,* 70; *The Way of the West,* 35-106; *Tonio,* 78-82; *A Soldier's Secret and An Army Portia,* 78-80, 109-110; *An Apache Princess,* 215.

45. *Milwaukee Journal,* April 9, 1933, King Biographical File.

46. *See* pp. 148ff.

47. King, *The Deserter and From the Ranks,* 14.

48. King, *Under Fire,* 417-18.

49. King, *A Soldier's Secret and An Army Portia,* 109.

50. King, *The Way of the West,* 44.

51. King, *Starlight Ranch,* 226-33.
52. King, *Under Fire,* 425-26.
53. King, *Laramie,* 114-16.
54. King, *Warrior Gap,* 4; King, *Captain Close and Sergeant Croesus,* 139.
55. [Brackett], "Our Frontier Forts." Col. Brackett did not identify the locals of his idyll.
56. For details of the march, see Finerty, *War-Path and Bivouac,* 171, and Bourke, *On the Border with Crook,* 362ff.
57. King, *Captain Blake,* vii-viii.
58. *Ibid.,* 455.
59. *Ibid.,* 460.
60. Mattes, *Indians, Infants and Infantry,* 211. Mrs. Burt was one whose husband was gone that summer.
61. Roe, *Letters,* 216.
62. Boyd, *Cavalry Life,* 204.
63. *Ibid.,* 201.

Chapter Seven

1. Paulding, Memoir, 8; Roe, *Letters,* 333.
2. *Army and Navy Journal,* January 13, 1883, p. 526.
3. *Ibid.,* January 14, 1882, p. 525; January 13, 1883, p. 526; July 14, 1883, p. 1124.
4. "The Honor of the Soldier," 1904, King Papers.
5. King, *A Soldier's Secret and An Army Portia,* 181-82.
6. Biddle, *Reminiscences,* 108-109; *Army and Navy Journal,* March 3, 1883, p. 700: May 5, 1883, pp. 904-905; January 12, 1884, p. 475; Greene, *Ladies and Officers,* 144.
7. King, *The Colonel's Daughter,* 35.
8. King, *Marion's Faith,* 149-50.
9. King, *The Deserter and From the Ranks,* 6; *New York Herald,* October 2, 1876; Bourke Diary, XIX, 1829.
10. King, *Ray's Recruit,* 116; King, *Fort Frayne,* 66; King, *Marion's Faith,* 344; King, *An Apache Princess,* 133; King, *A Daughter of the Sioux,* 58; King, *An Army Wife,* 183; King, *A Garrison Tangle,* 263; King, *Two Soldiers and Dunraven Ranch,* 145.
11. Boyd, *Cavalry Life,* 69-70, 220; *Army and Navy Journal,* February 11, 1882, p. 612; Roe, *Letters,* 185, 202, 332.
12. King, *The Colonel's Daughter,* 59, 60, 61; King, *Under Fire;* Summerhayes, *Vanished Arizona,* 101.

13. King, *Fort Frayne,* 21.

14. *Ibid.,* 145.

15. King, *A Soldier's Secret and An Army Portia,* 29-30; Paulding, "Memoir," 9.

16. King, *An Apache Princess,* 220; King, "George Crook," 259; King, *Marion's Faith,* 200.

17. King, *Foes in Ambush;* King, *Starlight Ranch,* 20; King, *Two Soldiers and Dunraven Ranch,* 230; King, *An Army Wife,* 164; King, *A Soldier's Secret and An Army Portia,* 167-75; King, *The Colonel's Daughter,* 34.

Chapter Eight

1. R. G. Collingwood, *The Idea of History,* 282.

2. Allan Nevins, *The Gateway to History,* 43.

3. C. L. Sonnichsen, "Fiction and History," *Wilson Library Bulletin,* Vol. 43, No. 3 (November, 1968), 250-51.

4. See Henry Nash Smith, *Virgin Land,* for the confusions that resulted in Western characterizations.

Bibliography

Government Documents

Chronological List of Actions, &c., with Indians, from January 1, 1866, to January, 1881. Office Memoranda, Adjutant General's Office, n. p., n. d.

Compendium of General Orders from the Adjutant General's Office Amending Army Regulations [G. O. 43, of 1889, to G. O. 15, of 1892]. Washington, Government Printing Office, 1892.

Regulations of the Army of the United States and General Orders in Force on the 17th of February, 1881. Washington, Government Printing Office, 1881.

Regulations for the Army of the United States, 1889. Washington, Government Printing Office, 1889.

Revised United States Army Regulations of 1861. Washington, Government Printing Office, 1863.

Revised Army Regulations, House Report No. 85, 42d Congress, 3d Session, March 1, 1873. Washington, Government Printing Office, 1873.

Secretary of War. *Reports.* [For each of the years from 1866 through 1886.] Washington, Government Printing Office, 1866-86.

Manuscripts and Collections

Bourke, Lieutenant John Gregory. Diary. 127 vols. Library of the United States Military Academy, West Point, New York.

King, Charles. Biographical File. Milwaukee County Historical Society. The file consists of newspaper clippings c. 1880-1933, which are not always identified by newspaper or date.

——. Manuscript Collection. Wisconsin State Historical Society Library.

Paulding, Mrs. Grace Bunce. Memoir. In the William and Grace Paulding Papers, Archives, U. S. Army Military History Research Collection, Carlisle Barracks, Pennsylvania.

Sydenham, Lieutenant Alvin H. Manuscript Collection. New York Public Library.

Newspapers

Army and Navy Journal, 1879-91.
Chicago *Times,* 1877, 1879.
Milwaukee *Journal,* 1928-33.
New York *Herald,* 1876.
New York *Times,* 1890-1933.

Books

Baldwin, Alice Blackwood. *Memoirs of the Late Frank D. Baldwin, Major General, U. S. A.* Los Angeles, Wetzel Publishing Co., 1929.

Biddle, Ellen McGowan. *Reminiscences of a Soldier's Wife.* Philadelphia, Lippincott, 1907.

Bourke, John G. *On the Border with Crook.* Lincoln, University of Nebraska Press, 1971.

Boyd, Mrs. Orsemus. *Cavalry Life in Tent and Field.* New York, J. Selwin Tait, 1894.

Carrington, Frances C. *My Army Life and the Fort Phil. Kearney Massacre.* Philadelphia, Lippincott, 1910.

Carrington, Colonel Henry B. *Ab-sa-ra-ka, Land of Massacre: Being the Experience of an Officer's Wife on the Plains. With* an *Outline of Indian Operations and Conferences from 1865 to 1878.* [Originally published under the name of Margaret Carrington; her husband added materially to this edition.] Fourth edition. Philadelphia, Lippincott, 1878.

Carter, Captain Robert G. *On the Border with Mackenzie.* New York, Antiquarian Press, 1961. [Originally published, 1935.]

Chappell, Gordon. *The Search for the Well-Dressed Soldier, 1865-1890.* Museum Monograph No. 5. Tucson, Arizona Historical Society, 1972.

Collingwood, R. G. *The Idea of History.* New York, Oxford University Press, 1956.

Custer, Elizabeth Bacon. *"Boots and Saddles" or, Life in Dakota with General Custer.* Norman, University of Oklahoma Press, 1961.

——. *Following the Guidon.* Norman, University of Oklahoma Press, 1966.

——. *Tenting on the Plains, or General Custer in Kansas and Texas.* 3 vols. Norman, University of Oklahoma Press, 1971.

Dornbusch, C. E. *Charles King: American Army Novelist. A Bibliography from the Collection of the National Library of Australia, Canberra.* Cornwallville, New York, Hope Farm Press, 1963.

Finerty, John F. *War-Path and Bivouac.* Norman, University of Oklahoma Press, 1961.

Forsyth, Brevet Brigadier General George A. *The Story of the Soldier.* New York, Appleton, 1900.

Fougera, Katherine Gibson. *With Custer's Cavalry. From the Memoirs of the late Katherine Gibson, widow of Captain Francis M. Gibson of the Seventh Cavalry, U. S. A. (Retired).* Caldwell, Caxton, 1942.

Fulton, Deoch, ed. *The Journal of Lieut. Sydenham, 1889, 1890, and his Notes on Frederic Remington.* New York, New York Public Library, 1940.

Greene, Duane Merritt. *Ladies and Officers of the United States Army; or, American Aristocracy. A Sketch of the Social Life*

Life and Manners in the Frontier Army

and *Character of the Army.* Chicago, Central Publishing
Co., 1880.
[Hancock, Mrs. Winfield Scott]. *Reminiscences of Winfield
Scott Hancock by His Wife.* New York, Webster, 1887.
Hein, Lieutenant Colonel O. L. *Memories of Long Ago, by an
Old Army Officer.* New York, Putnam's, 1925.
King, Charles. *An Apache Princess.* New York, Grossett and
Dunlap, 1903.
———. *An Army Wife.* New York, Neely, 1896.
———. *Between the Lines; a Story of the War.* New York, Harper
and Brothers, 1888.
———. *Campaigning with Crook.* Norman, University of Okla-
homa Press, 1964.
———. *Captain Blake.* Philadelphia, Lippincott, 1891.
———. *Captain Close and Sergeant Croesus.* Philadelphia, Lip-
pincott, 1895.
———. *The Colonel's Daughter, or Winning His Spurs.* Phila-
delphia, Lippincott, 1882.
———. *A Daughter of the Sioux.* New York, Hobart, 1903.
———. *The Deserter and From the Ranks. Two Novels.* Philadel-
phia, Lippincott, 1889.
———. *Foes in Ambush.* Philadelphia, Lippincott, 1893.
———. *A Garrison Tangle.* New York, Neely, 1896.
———. *An Initial Experience and Other Stories.* Philadelphia, Lip-
pincott, 1897.
———. *In Spite of Foes, or Ten Years Trial.* Philadelphia, Lippin-
cott, 1901.
———. *Kitty's Conquest.* Philadelphia, Lippincott, 1884.
———. *"Laramie;" or, The Queen of Bedlam. A Story of the Sioux
War of 1876.* Philadelphia, Lippincott, 1891.
———. *Lanier of the Cavalry.* Philadelphia, Lippincott, 1909.
———. *Marion's Faith.* Philadelphia, Lippincott, 1889.
———. *Memories of a Busy Life.* Wisconsin State Historical
Society, n. p., n. d.
———. *Rancho del Muerto and Other Stories from Outing.* New
York, Outing, 1895.
———. *Ray's Recruit.* Philadelphia, Lippincott, 1898.

266

——. *A Soldier's Secret: A Story of the Sioux War of 1890; and An Army Portia, Two Novels.* Philadelphia, Lippincott, 1893.

——. *Starlight Ranch and Other Stories of Army Life on the Frontier.* Philadelphia, Lippincott, 1890.

——. *The Story of Fort Frayne.* New York, Neely, 1895.

——. *Sunset Pass or Running the Gauntlet Through Apache Land.* New York, Lovell, 1890.

——. *Tonio, Son of the Sierras.* New York, Dillingham, 1906.

——. *Trials of a Staff Officer.* New York, Hammersly, 1891.

——. *A Trooper Galahad.* Philadelphia, Lippincott, 1907.

——. *Trooper Ross and Signal Butte.* Philadelphia, Lippincott, 1896.

——. *The True Ulysses S. Grant.* Philadelphia, Lippincott, 1914.

——. *Trumpeter Fred: A Story of the Plains.* New York, Neely, 1896.

——. *Two Soldiers and Dunraven Ranch, Two Novels.* Philadelphia, Lippincott, 1892.

——. *Under Fire.* Philadelphia, Lippincott, 1895.

——. *Warrior Gap. A Story of the Sioux Outbreak of '68.* New York, Hobart, 1901.

——. *The Way of the West.* New York, Rand McNally, 1902.

——. *A Wounded Name.* New York, Hobart, 1901.

Lane, Lydia Spencer. *I Married a Soldier or Old Days in the Old Army.* Albuquerque, Horn & Wallace, 1964. [First published, 1893.]

Laufe, Abe, ed. *An Army Doctor's Wife on the Frontier: Letters from Alaska and the Far West, 1874-1878.* Pittsburgh, University of Pittsburgh Press, 1962. These are the edited letters of Mrs. Dr. Jenkins A. FitzGerald.

Mattes, Merrill J., ed. *Indians, Infants and Infantry: Andrew and Elizabeth Burt on the Frontier.* Denver, Old West Publishing Co., 1960. Edited selections from the diary of Mrs. Burt.

Mulford, Ami Frank. *Fighting Indians in the 7th United States Cavalry, Custer's Favorite Regiment.* 2d ed. Corning, New York, Paul Lindsley Mulford, 1879.

Nevins, Allan. *The Gateway to History.* Revised edition. New York, Anchor Books, Doubleday, 1962.

Price, George F. *Across the Continent with the Fifth Cavalry.* New York, Antiquarian Press, 1959.

Quaife, Milo Milton, ed. *Army Life in Dakota: Selections from the Journal of Philippe Régis Denis de Keredern de Trobriand.* Chicago, Donnelly, 1941.

Rickey, Don, Jr. *Forty Miles a Day on Beans and Hay. The Enlisted Soldier Fighting the Indian Wars.* Norman, University of Oklahoma Press, 1963.

Roe, Frances M. A. *Army Letters from an Officer's Wife, 1871-1888.* New York, Appleton, 1909.

Schmitt, Martin F. *General George Crook: His Autobiography.* Norman, University of Oklahoma Press, 1960.

Schott, Joseph L. *Above and Beyond.* New York, Putnam's, 1963.

Smith, Henry Nash. *Virgin Land.* Boston, Harvard University Press, 1970.

Summerhayes, Martha. *Vanished Arizona: Recollections of the Army Life of a New England Woman.* 2d ed. Salem, Mass., Salem Press Co., 1911. This second edition contains some important additions to the first edition published by Lippincott in 1908, as well as a change in the subtitle.

Van Doren, Carl. *The American Novel.* New York, Macmillan, 1940.

Walker, Henry Pickering. *The Wagonmasters.* Norman, University of Oklahoma Press, 1966.

Articles

Anon. "Brig. Gen. Charles King, the Soldier Novelist." *Current Literature.* Vol. 27 (January, 1900), 20-21.

——. "General Gossip of Authors and Writers." *Current Literature.* Vol. 29 (August, 1900), 150.

——. "General King." *The Publishers Weekly.* Vol. 123 (March 25, 1933), 1063.

——. Review of *Campaigning with Crook. The Dial.* Vol. 11 (January, 1891), 293.

Bibliography

———. Review of *Campaigning with Crook. Harper's New Monthly Magazine.* Vol. 82 (January, 1891), 316-18.

———. Review of *Foes in Ambush. The Athenaeum.* Vol. 103, No. 3462 (March 3, 1894), 276.

———. Review of *The Story of Fort Frayne. Bookman.* Vol. 20 (October, 1895), 147-48.

———. Review of *Under Fire. The Athenaeum.* Vol. 105, No. 3526 (May 25, 1895), 670.

[Brackett, Colonel A. G.]. "Our Frontier Forts." Chicago *Times,* September 13, 1879, p. 14. Brackett was identified as the author by the *Army and Navy Journal,* October 18, 1879, 198.

Brackett, Colonel A. G. "Our Cavalry on the Frontier." *Army and Navy Journal,* November 10, 1883, 283-84.

Filipiak, Jack D. "A Biographical Sketch of General Charles King." *The Denver Westerners Monthly Roundup.* Vol. 22, No. 6 (June, 1966).

Fry, Colonel James B. "Justice for the Army," *Army and Navy Journal,* August 25, 1883, 63.

King, Charles. "George Crook." *War Papers Read Before the Commandery of the State of Wisconsin, Military Order of the Loyal Legion of the United States.* Milwaukee, Burdick, Armitage & Allen, 1891. Vol. 1, 251-69.

———. "Customs of the Service." *Army and Navy Journal,* May 5, 1883, 914.

———. "Thirty Years of Pencraft." *Lippincott's Magazine.* Vol. 86, No. 514 (October, 1910), 469-75; Vol. 86, No. 515 (November, 1910), 576-82.

Reade, Lt. Philip. "Captain Charles King." *Lippincott's Magazine.* Vol. 42 (December, 1888), 856-62.

Remington, Frederic. "A New Infantry Equipment." *Harper's Weekly.* Vol. 38, No. 1970 (September 22, 1894), 905.

Sonnichsen, C. L. "Fiction and History." *Wilson Library Bulletin.* Vol. 43, No. 3 (November, 1968), 248-55.

Index

Bullis, Lt. John L.: 81
Burt, Lt. Andrew: 115
Burt, Elizabeth Reynolds (Mrs. Andrew): 58, 60, 188-89, 192

Camp Date Creek: 115
Camp followers: 42
Camp Halleck: 58, 64, 69, 114, 124, 227
Camp Verde: 14, 36, 81, 134, 196; as "Camp Sandy," 36, 47-48, 50, 179-80
Campaigns: Arizona and Plains contrasted, 178-79, 203-204; march order, 194-95; beards protect faces, 198; encampment, 203, 205-207; march distance, 205; rations, 215; return from, 217-18; *see also* Indian-fighting; Patrols
Carr, Lt. Col. Eugene: 28
Carrington, Frances Grummond (Mrs. Henry B.): 67, 240 n.
Carrington, Col. Henry B.: 46, 240 n.
Carrington, Margaret (Mrs. Henry B.): 58, 240 n.
Carter, Lt. Robert G.: 114, 122
Carter, Mrs. Robert: 47
Casey, John Joseph: 31-32
Caste: 150
"Catch the weasel" (game): 139
Cattle boom: 81
"Cattle Upon a Thousand Hills, The": 59
Cavalry: mustache, 82, 87; traditions, 96; proficiency criticized, 184-85; marches, 205; dislike of fences, 227; *see also* Officers, cavalry; Horsemanship; Indian-fighting; *regi-*

ments by designation
Cedar Springs (Ariz.): 204
Chaffee, Capt. Adna R.: 181
Chaplains: 171, 172
Chenati Mountains (Tex.): 81
Cheyenne (Wyo.): 24, 29, 129, 190, 227
Cheyenne Indians: 229
Cheyenne *Leader*: 25
Chicago *Times*: 59, 177, 250 n.
Children: 6, 44, 56, 60, 63, 64, 66, 69, 111, 150, 155, 173, 218
Chinese: 128-29, 224
Christmas, in garrison: 155-56
Church services: 171-72
Civilians: 57, 189-90, 220-30 *passim*; as Army employees, 7, 29, 236; aid, cheat deserters, 23, 224-25; frontier, 227, 236
Cleveland, President Grover: 103
Cliques: 43, 54-55, 102
Clothing: 64-65, 126, 127, 141-42
Cody, Buffalo Bill: 13, 15, 30, 207, 236
Collingwood, R. G.: 232, 233
Conduct, code of: *see* Officers, code of conduct
Copper Canyon (Ariz.): 81
Courts-martial: 26, 31-32, 35, 72, 73, 93, 128, 170, 234
Courtship in garrison: 139, 140
Crazy Horse: 15, 177, 190
Crenneville, Count de: 13
Crime: burglaries, 22, 33, 130-31; embezzlement, 22, 26, 73, 93; theft, 22, 23, 31-32, 129, 175-76; horse-theft, 24, 224, 226; robbery, 25, 179, 224; violent, 66, 128, 224; misuse of government property, 73; wife-

Index

Indian campaigns, 57, 69, 173, 188-94, 217-19; regimental pride of, 59, 60; and complexion, hair, 62-63; response to frontier, 63-65, 66; fears of, 65-67; with troops in field, 101, 144; relationships among, 111, 129, 131; as harassers of quartermaster, 124-26; and homemaking, 126; as widows, 160; and appreciation of winter, 170
Orderly trumpeter: 174
Ours: 59

Parades: 167-68
Parker, Charles: 25
Parties: 138
Patrols: 187, 204-205
Payday: 225-26
Perry, Mrs. David: 193, 194
Phillips, Portugee: 30
Physicians: *see* Surgeons, Army
Porter, Col. Andrew: 115
Porter, Mrs. Andrew: 115
Porter, Caroline Wilkins (Mrs. Charles): 53
Porter, Capt. Charles: 53
Post, daily routine of: 164f.
Post commanders: *see* Officers, commanding
Post headquarters: 173-74
Post trader: 6, 33, 129, 154, 195
Promotion: 80, 102-103, 157, 170
Punishment: 68; 73-74, 92, 93; *see also* Courts-martial
Purgatoire River: 225

Quartermaster, post: 44, 121, 124-26
Quartermaster's Department: 103

Quarters, officers': variety of, described; 3, 112-20, 250n.; tents as, 45, 114, 122; allowances by rank, 112; left unlocked, 130; bachelor, 122; "ranking out," 123-24

Racial prejudice: *see* Anti-Semitism; Mexicans; Negroes
Randall, Maj. George M.: 204
Rations: *see* Campaigns, rations; Enlisted men, rations; Food
Rawlins (Wyo.): 33, 203
Rawolle, Capt. W. C.: 75
Reade, Lt. Philip: 12
Reading material: 58-59
Recruits: 107, 108
Remington, Frederic: 38, 200
Retreat: 167-68
Reveille: 163
Rhoades, Lucille: 19
Rhodes, Eugene Manlove: 34, 237
Rice, Col. Edmund: 200
Ricketts, Mrs. James B.: 51
Riding: 63, 97-98, 157; *see also* Horsemanship
River crossings: 65-66
Road ranches: 180
Robertson, Thomas William: 59, 150
Roe, Lt. Fayette: 64, 103, 112
Roe, Frances (Mrs. Fayette): 55, 63-64, 84, 97, 115, 123, 124, 128-29, 144, 155-56; 157, 160-61
Roll calls: 163
Romances: 139
Rosenlecher, Capt. George: 13
Royall, Lt. Col. W. B.: 88

St. John's Military Academy: 16

Index